REFORMATION THOUGHT

KT-416-167

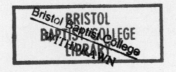

REFORMATION THOUGHT

An Introduction

Alister E. McGrath

Basil Blackwell

First published 1988

Basil Blackwell Ltd
108 Cowley Road, Oxford, OX4 1JF, UK

Basil Blackwell Inc.
432 Park Avenue South, Suite 1503
New York, NY 10016, USA

British Library Cataloguing in Publication Data

McGrath, Alister E.
    Reformation thought : an introduction
    1. Reformation
    I. Title
    270.6   BR305.2

    ISBN 0-631-15802-2
    ISBN 0-631-15803-0 Pbk

Typeset in 12/14pt Bembo
by System 4 Associates, Farnham Common, Buckinghamshire
Printed in Great Britain by Page Bros (Norwich) Ltd

Contents

Preface

The European Reformation of the sixteenth century is one of the most fascinating areas of study available to the historian. It also continues to be of central importance to anyone interested in the history of the Christian church or its religious ideas. The Reformation embraced a number of areas – the reform of both the morals and structures of church and society, the renewal of Christian spirituality, and the reform of Christian doctrine. It was a movement based upon a more or less coherent set of ideas, which it believed were capable of functioning as the foundation of its programme of reform.

But what were those ideas? And how may their origins be accounted for? And how were they modified by the social conditions of the period? One serious difficulty – indeed, perhaps the most serious difficulty – facing the historian of the Reformation is the *strangeness* of the ideas underlying it. For example, the great reforming slogan 'justification by faith alone' seems incomprehensible to many today, as do the intricacies of the debates over the eucharist. Why should these apparently obscure questions have caused such a storm at the time? There is an obvious temptation for the student of the Reformation to avoid engaging with the ideas of the Reformation, and treat it as a purely social phenomenon. This book is written in the conviction that there are many who will not be prepared to rest content with this superficial engagement with the Reformation, and wish to deal with it seriously – but who are discouraged from doing so by the formidable difficulties encountered in trying to understand its ideas.

A further difficulty placed in the path of such a student is the remarkable advances made within the last twenty years and more concerning our understanding of both the Reformation itself, and its background in the late Renaissance, particularly in relation to late medieval scholasticism. Much of this work has yet to filter through to the student, and there is an urgent need for a work which will explain the findings of recent scholarship, and indicate its importance for our understanding of the Reformation.

The present work aims to introduce the student to the Reformation world of ideas and their backdrop in the late Renaissance in the light of the most recent scholarship. It will be assumed that the student knows little about Christian theology, and every effort will be made to explain the theological ideas of the Reformers and their contemporary relevance to both the individual and society. The religious ideas of the Reformers will be identified, analysed and explained, and related to their intellectual and social context. A number of appendixes will deal with some of the more common difficulties experienced by students unfamiliar with the Reformation period and its associated literature. It will also be assumed that the student speaks no language other than English, and all Latin quotations or slogans will be translated and explained. A bibliography of works available in English is provided for such a reader, although a more comprehensive bibliography is also included. It is thus hoped that this work may make the Reformation more intelligible to the reader.

This book arose from a number of years' experience of teaching the field of Reformation studies to students at Oxford University, and I wish to acknowledge my complete indebtedness to those students. It is they who have taught me just how much about the Reformation, so often taken for granted, actually needs to be *explained*. It is they who have identified the points of particular difficulty which need special discussion. It is they who have identified the need for precisely this work – and if the reader finds it helpful, it is those students who must be thanked. I am also grateful to my colleagues from the Oxford University faculties of theology and history for many helpful discussions concerning the difficulties encountered in teaching Reformation thought in the modern period.

How to Use this Book

Three words sum up the aim of this book: introduce; explain; contextualize. The book aims to *introduce* the leading ideas of the European Reformation in the period 1500–45. It is like a sketch map, which indicates the main features of the intellectual landscape: notes and suggestions for further reading will allow the reader to add finer detail later. Second, the book aims to *explain* these ideas. It assumes that the reader knows nothing about the Christian faith underlying the Reformation, and explains exactly what terms such as 'justification by faith' mean, and why they are of religious and social relevance. Third, it aims to *contextualize*, by setting these ideas in their proper intellectual, social and political context. That context includes such great intellectual movements as humanism and scholasticism, the alternative religious ideologies of the radical Reformation and Roman Catholicism, and the political and social realities of the imperial cities of the early sixteenth centuries. All these factors affected the thought of the Reformers – and this work aims to explain what that influence was, and what its effects were.

A series of seven appendices then deal with difficulties which experience suggests most students encounter as they read works relating to the Reformation. What do these abbreviations mean? How can I make sense of those references to primary and secondary sources? What does 'Pelagian' mean? Where should I go to find out more about the Reformation? These questions and others are dealt with at length, making this book unique. Two bibliographies, in addition to suggestions for further reading, will ensure that the student can develop his or her studies to whatever level seems appropriate.

1

Introduction

Many students approach the Reformation in much the same way as medieval travellers approached the vast dark forests of southern Germany – with a sense of hesitation and anxiety, lest what lies ahead should prove impenetrable, or at best something in which it is exceptionally easy to get lost. They may be like explorers venturing into new terrain, unsure what there is to find, at times feeling lost in an unmapped wilderness, at others exhilarated by unexpected vistas and valleys. Like Dante, they find themselves longing for a guide who will be a Virgil to them – guiding them through the intricacies of what otherwise is virtually incomprehensible, and certainly confusing. It is tempting for such students to ignore the *ideas* of the Reformation altogether, in order to concentrate upon its social aspects. The price of making the Reformation easier to handle in this way, however, is both to fail to capture its essence as an historical phenomenon and to understand why it remains an essential reference point for much contemporary debate in the religious world and far beyond.

To gain even the slightest insight into the Reformation involves wrestling with the ideas which underlay and motivated it. The social and political dimension of the Reformation is linked with the religious ideas of that movement – and whoever wrestles with the former will inevitably have to come to terms with the latter. This book has been written for those who will not rest content with a purely superficial engagement with the Reformation, but who want to try to understand the ideas which lay behind and beyond its social structures.

It is understandably difficult for a student sympathetic to the secularism of modern western culture to come to terms with a movement motivated by religious ideas. It is tempting to marginalize these ideas, and approach the sixteenth century with the world-view of the modern period. Like any historical phenomenon, however, the Reformation demands that its interpreters attempt to enter into *its* world-view. We must learn to empathize with its concerns and outlook, in order to understand how these affected the great flux of history. Unlike the English Reformation, which was fundamentally political in character,[1] the Reformation in Switzerland and Germany was directly based upon religious ideas which demand and deserve consideration. The present work is written on the assumption that its readers know nothing about Christian theology, and aims to *explain* exactly what the religious ideas underlying the Reformation actually were, and how they affected those who entertained them.

The present chapter aims to deal with some preliminary matters, in order to prepare the ground for discussion of the thought of the Reformation in later chapters.

The Cry for Reform

The term 'Reformation' immediately suggests that something – in this case, western European Christianity – was being reformed. Like many other terms used by historians to designate eras in human history – such as 'Renaissance' or 'Enlightenment' – it is open to criticism. For example, the twelfth century witnessed a comparable attempt to reform the church in western Europe – but the term 'Reformation' is not used to designate this earlier movement. Other terms might be thought by some to be more appropriate to refer to the sixteenth-century phenomenon under consideration. Nevertheless, the fact remains that the term 'Reformation' *is* generally accepted as the proper designation for this movement, partly on account of the fact that the movement was linked with the recognition of the need for drastic overhaul of the institutions, practices and ideas of the western church. The term helpfully indicates that there were both social and intellectual dimensions to the movement which it designates.

By the beginning of the sixteenth century it was obvious that the church in western Europe was once more in urgent need of reform. The cry for 'reform in head and members' summed up both the nature of the crisis and its perceived solution. It seemed that the life-blood of the church had ceased to flow through its veins. The church legal system was badly in need of overhaul, and ecclesiastical bureaucracy had become notoriously inefficient and corrupt. The morals of the clergy were often lax, and a source of scandal to their congregations. Clergy, even at the highest level, were frequently absent from their parishes. In Germany, it is reported than only one parish in every fourteen had their pastor in residence. The Frenchman Antoine du Prat, Archbishop of Sens, turned up for only one service at his cathedral: his presence at and role within this service was somewhat passive, as it was his funeral. Most higher ecclesiastical posts were secured through dubious means, generally relying upon the political or financial status of the candidates, rather than their spiritual qualities. Thus Pope Alexander VI, a member of the Borgia family (famous for its lethal dinner parties), secured his election to the papacy in 1492 despite his several mistresses and seven children, largely because he bought the papacy outright over the heads of his nearest rivals.

Machiavelli put the loose morals of late Renaissance Italy down to the poor example set by the church and its clergy. For many, the cry for reform was a plea for the administrative, moral and legal reformation of the church. Abuses and immorality must be eliminated, the pope must become less preoccupied with worldly affairs, the clergy must be properly educated, and the administration of the church must be simplified and purged of abuses. For others, the most pressing need concerned the spirituality of the church. There was an urgent – even a vital – need to recapture the vitality and freshness of the Christian faith. Many looked over their shoulders and down the centuries, envying the simplicity and excitement of apostolic Christianity. Could not this Golden Age of the Christian faith be regained, perhaps by returning to ponder anew the New Testament documents? This was the pro-gramme of reform which was the pipe-dream of intellectuals throughout half of Europe. Yet the Renaissance popes seemed more interested in secular than in spiritual matters, and managed between them to achieve a hitherto unprecedented level of avarice, venality, immorality and spec-tacularly unsuccessful power politics. The words of Gianfresco Pico della Mirandola (often confused with his uncle, Giovanni), spoken in March 1517, sum up succinctly the thoughts which preyed on many educated minds at the time: 'If we are to win back the enemy and the apostate

apostate to our faith, it is more important to restore fallen morality to its ancient rule of virtue than that we should sweep the Euxine sea with our fleet.'

There were, however, others who added another demand to this list – the demand for a reformation of Christian doctrine, of theology, of religious ideas. For men such as Luther at Wittenberg and Calvin at Geneva, the church had lost sight of its intellectual heritage. It was time to reclaim the ideas of the 'Golden Age' of the Christian church, during its first five hundred years. The sad state of that church in the early sixteenth century was simply a symptom of a more radical disease – a deviation from the distinctive *ideas* of the Christian faith, a loss of intellectual identity, a failure to grasp what Christianity really was. Christianity could not be reformed without an understanding of what Christianity was actually meant to be. For these men, the obvious failings of the late Renaissance church was the latest stage in a gradual process which had been going on since about the thirteenth century – the corruption of Christian doctrine and ethics. The distinctive ideas which men such as Luther and Calvin held to underlie Christian faith and practice had been obscured, if not totally perverted, through a series of developments in the Middle Ages. It was, according to these thinkers, time to reverse these changes, to undo the work of the Middle Ages in order to return to a purer and fresher version of Christianity which beckoned to them across the centuries. The Reformers echoed the cry of the humanists: 'back to the sources (*ad fontes*)', back to the Golden Age of the church, in order to reclaim its freshness, purity and vitality in the midst of a period of staleness and corruption.

Contemporary writings unquestionably paint a picture of growing ecclesiastical corruption and inefficiency, indicating how much the late medieval church was in need of reform. It is, however, necessary to enter a note of caution on the manner in which these sources are to be interpreted. It is quite possible that these sources document growing levels of expectation within the late medieval church as much as declining levels of performance. The growth of an educated laity – one of the more significant elements in the intellectual history of late medieval Europe – led to increasing criticism of the church on account of the obvious disparity between what the church *was* and what it *might be*. The growing level of criticism may well reflect the fact that more people were, through increasing educational opportunities, in a position to criticize the church – rather than any further decline in the ecclesiastical standards of the day.

But who could reform the church? By the first decade of the sixteenth century, a fundamental shift in power within Europe was essentially complete. The power of the pope had diminished, as the power of secular European governments increased. In 1478 the Spanish Inquisition was established, with power over clergy and religious orders (and eventually also over bishops) – and the control of this system of courts resting not with the pope, but with the Spanish king. The Concordat of Bologna (1516) gave the King of France the right to appoint all the senior clergy of the French church, effectively giving him direct control of that church and its finances. Across Europe, the ability of the pope to impose a reformation upon his church was steadily diminishing: even had the will to reform been there in the later Renaissance popes (and there are few indications that it was), the ability to reform was gradually slipping away.

It is therefore important to notice the manner in which Protestant Reformers allied themselves with regional or civic powers in order to effect their programme of reform. Luther appealed to the German nobility and Zwingli to the Zurich city council for reform, pointing out the benefits which would result to both as a consequence. The English Reformation is not typical of the European movement as a whole: where the English monarch Henry VIII virtually imposed a reformation upon his church as a naked act of state, the European movement proceeded by a symbiotic alliance of Reformer and state or civic authority, each believing that the resulting Reformation was to their mutual benefit. The Reformers were not unduly concerned that they gave added authority to their secular rulers by their theories of the role of the state or the 'godly prince': the important thing was that the secular rulers supported the cause of the Reformation, even if their reasons for doing so might not be entirely praiseworthy. The mainstream Reformers were pragmatists, men who were prepared to allow secular rulers their pound of flesh provided that the cause of the Reformation was advanced. In much the same way, of course, the opponents of the Reformation had little hesitation in calling upon the support of secular authorities which felt that their interests were best served by a maintenance of the religious *status quo*. No study of the

Reformation can overlook its political and social dimensions, as secular authorities in northern Europe saw their chance to seize power from the church, even at the cost of committing themselves to a new religious order by doing so. Nevertheless, the fact remains that certain distinctive religious ideas achieved widespread circulation and influence within western European society in the sixteenth century. These ideas cannot be ignored or marginalized by anyone concerned with the study of the Reformation. It is hoped that the present work will introduce, explain and contextualize those ideas.

The Concept of 'Reformation'

The term 'Reformation' is used in a number of senses, and it is helpful to distinguish them. Four elements may be involved in its definition, and each will be discussed briefly below: Lutheranism, the Reformed church, the 'radical Reformation', often still referred to as 'Anabaptism', and the 'Counter Reformation' or 'Catholic Reformation'. In its broadest sense, the term 'Reformation' is used to refer to all four movements. The term is also used in a somewhat more restricted sense, meaning 'the Protestant Reformation', excluding the Catholic Reformation. In this sense, it refers to the three Protestant movements noted above. In many scholarly works, however, the term 'Reformation' is used to refer to what is sometimes known as the 'magisterial Reformation', or the 'mainstream Reformation' – in other words, the Lutheran and Reformed churches. Each of these three senses of the term 'Reformation' is defensible, and you are likely to encounter all three in the course of your reading. The term 'magisterial Reformation' is increasingly used to refer to the first two senses of the term, taken together, and the term 'radical Reformation' to refer to the third. The present work is primarily concerned with the ideas of the magisterial Reformation.

The term 'Protestant' requires comment. It derives from the aftermath of the Diet of Speyer (February 1529), which voted to end the toleration of Lutheranism in Germany. In April of the same year, six German princes and fourteen cities protested against this oppressive measure, defending freedom of conscience and the rights of religious minorities.

The term 'Protestant' derives from this protest. It is therefore not strictly correct to apply the term 'Protestant' to individuals prior to April 1529, or to speak of events prior to that date as constituting 'the Protestant Reformation'. The term 'evangelical' is often used in the literature to refer to the reforming factions at Wittenberg and elsewhere (e.g., in France and Switzerland) prior to this date. Although the word 'Protestant' is often used to refer to this earlier period, this use is, strictly speaking, an anachronism.

The Lutheran Reformation

The Lutheran Reformation is particularly associated with the German territories and the pervasive personal influence of one charismatic individual – Martin Luther. Luther was particularly concerned with the doctrine of justification, which formed the central point of his religious thought. The Lutheran Reformation was initially an academic movement, concerned primarily with reforming the teaching of theology at the University of Wittenberg. Wittenberg was an unimportant university, and the reforms introduced by Luther and his colleagues within the theology faculty attracted little attention. It was Luther's personal activities – such as his posting of the famous Ninety-Five Theses (31 October 1517) and the Leipzig Disputation (June–July 1519) – which attracted considerable interest, and brought the ideas in circulation at Wittenberg to the attention of a wider audience.

Strictly speaking, the Lutheran Reformation only began in 1522, when Luther returned to Wittenberg from his enforced isolation in the Wartburg. At this point, Luther's programme of academic reform changed into a programme of reform of church and society. No longer was Luther's forum of activity the university world of ideas – he now found himself regarded as the leader of a religious, social and political reforming movement which seemed to some contemporary observers to open the way to a new social and religious order in Europe. In fact, Luther's programme of reform was much more conservative than that associated with his Reformed colleagues, such as Zwingli. Furthermore, it met with considerably less success than might have been expected. The movement remained obstinately tied to the German territories, and – Scandinavia apart – never gained the foreign powerbases it might have expected. Luther's understanding of the role of the 'godly prince' (which effectively ensured that the monarch had control of the church) does not seem to have had the attraction it might have been expected to, particularly in the light of the generally republican sentiments of Reformed thinkers. The case of England is particularly illuminating: here, as in Holland, the Protestant theology which gained the ascendancy was Reformed rather than Lutheran.

The Reformed Church

The origins of the Reformed church lie with developments within the Swiss Confederation. Whereas the Lutheran Reformation had its origins in an academic context, the Reformed church owed its origins to a series of attempts to reform the doctrine, morals and worship of the church according to a more biblical pattern. Although most of the early Reformed theologians – such as Zwingli – had an academic background, their reforming programmes were not academic in nature. They were directed towards the church, as they found it in the Swiss cities, such as Zurich, Berne and Basle. Whereas Luther was convinced that the doctrine of justification was of central significance to his programme of social and religious reform, the early Reformed thinkers had relatively little interest in doctrine, let alone one specific doctrine. Their reforming programme was institutional, social and ethical, in many ways similar to the demands for reform emanating from the humanist movement. It is therefore important to appreciate that the all the major early Reformed theologians had strongly humanist inclinations – inclinations which were not shared by Luther, who regarded the humanist movement with some suspicion.

The consolidation of the Reformed church is generally thought to reflect the emergence of Geneva as its power base, and John Calvin as its leading spokesman. The gradual shift in power within the Reformed church (initially from Zurich to Berne, and subsequently from Berne to Geneva) took place over the period 1520–60, eventually establishing both the city of Geneva, its political system (republicanism) and its religious thinkers (initially John Calvin, and after his death Theodore Beza) as predominant within the Reformed church. This development was consolidated through the establishment of the Genevan Academy (at which Reformed pastors were trained).

The term 'Calvinism' is often used to refer to the religious ideas of the Reformed church. This practice is now generally discouraged, as it is becoming increasingly clear that later sixteenth-century Reformed theology represents a development of the ideas of Calvin himself. To refer to later sixteenth- and seventeenth-century Reformed thought as 'Calvinist' implies that it is essentially the thought of Calvin – and it is now generally agreed that Calvin's ideas were modified subtly by his successors. The term 'Reformed' is preferred, whether to refer to those churches (in Switzerland, Holland and Germany) or religious thinkers (such as Theodore Beza, William Perkins or John Owen) which based themselves upon Calvin's celebrated religious textbook, *The Institutes of the Christian Religion*, or church documents (such as the famous *Heidelberg Catechism*) based upon it.

An additional factor should be noted in connection with the term 'Calvinist'. The origin of the term dates from the 1560s, when a significant alteration in the political situation in the German territories took place. Germany had been seriously destabilized in the 1540s and early 1550s by conflicts between Lutherans and Roman Catholics, and it was widely recognized that such conflicts were damaging to the Empire. The Peace of Augsburg (September 1555) settled the religious question in Germany by allocating certain areas of Germany to Lutheranism, and the remainder to Roman Catholicism – the famous principle often referred to as *cuius regio, eius religio* ('your region determines your religion'). No provision was made for the Reformed faith, which was effectively declared to be 'non-existent' in Germany. In February 1563, however, the *Heidelberg Catechism* was published, indicating that the Reformed theology had gained a foothold in the Palatinate. This catechism was immediately attacked by Lutherans as being 'Calvinist' – in other words, foreign. The term 'Calvinist' was used by German Lutherans to attempt to discredit this new and increasingly influential document, by implying that it was unpatriotic. Given the original polemical associations of the term, it would seem appropriate for the historian to abandon it in favour of a more neutral term – and the term 'Reformed' unquestionably serves this function.

Of the three constituents of the Protestant Reformation, it is the Reformed wing which is of particular importance to the English-speaking world. Puritanism, which figures so prominently in seventeenth-century

English history and is of such fundamental importance to the religious and political views of New England in the seventeenth century and beyond, is a form of Reformed theology. To understand the religious and political history of New England, for example, it is necessary to come to terms with at least some of the theological insights of Puritanism, which underlie their social and political attitudes. It is hoped that this work will help with this process of familiarization.

The Radical Reformation [Anabaptism]

The term 'Anabaptist' owes its origins to Zwingli (the word literally means 'rebaptizers'). Initially, the movement arose in Germany and Switzerland, although it subsequently became influential in Holland. The movement produced relatively few theologians (the three most significant are generally agreed to be Balthasar Hubmaier, Pilgram Marbeck and Menno Simons). This failure reflects the fact that the movement did not have any substantial theological basis. A number of common elements can be discerned within the various strands of the movement: a general distrust of external authority, the rejection of infant baptism in favour of the baptism of adult believers, the common ownership of property, and an emphasis upon pacifism and non-resistance. It is for this reason that 'Anabaptism' is often referred to as the 'left wing of the Reformation' (Roland H. Bainton) or the 'radical Reformation' (George Hunston Williams). For Williams, the 'radical Reformation' was to be contrasted with the 'magisterial Reformation', which he broadly identified with the Lutheran and Reformed movements. These terms are increasingly being accepted within Reformation scholarship, and the reader is likely to encounter them in his reading of more recent studies of the movement.

The Catholic Reformation

This term is often used to refer to the revival within Roman Catholicism in the period following the opening of the Council of Trent (1545). In older scholarly works, the movement is often designated the 'Counter Reformation': as the term suggests, the Roman Catholic church developed means of combating the Protestant Reformation, in order to limit its influence. It is, however, becoming increasingly clear that the Roman Catholic church countered the Reformation partly by reforming itself from within, in order to remove the grounds of Protestant criticism. In this sense, the movement was a reformation of the Roman Catholic church, as much as it was a reaction against the Protestant Reformation. The same concerns underlying the Protestant Reformation in northern Europe were channelled into the renewal of the catholic church, particularly in Spain and Italy. The Council of Trent introduced much needed reforms in relation to the conduct of the clergy, ecclesiastical discipline, religious education and missionary activity. The movement was greatly stimulated by the reformation of many of the older religious orders, and the establishment of new orders (such as the Jesuits).

As a result of the Catholic Reformation, many of the abuses which originally lay behind the demands for reform – whether these came from humanists or Protestants – were removed. By this stage, however, the Protestant Reformation had reached a point at which the mere removal of malpractices and abuses was no longer sufficient to reverse the situation: the demand for the reformation of the doctrine, of the religious ideology, of the church was now regarded as an essential aspect of the Protestant–Roman Catholic controversies. This point highlights the need to consider the religious ideas lying behind the 'magisterial Reformation', which became of increasing importance to the Protestant–Roman Catholic debate as the sixteenth century progressed.

The Importance of Printing

Recent technological developments in the field of data processing and transfer have revolutionized many aspects of modern life. It is important to realize that one technological development destined to have an enormous influence over western Europe was developed on the eve of the Reformation. This development is, of course, printing. It is impossible to underestimate the impact of this development on the Reformation.

Although originally developed centuries earlier by the Chinese, the first European printed documents which can be dated reliably originate from the press of Johann Gutenberg at Mainz around 1454. In 1456, the same press produced a printed Latin bible. This was followed in 1457 by the so-called 'Mainz Psalter', which established the custom of identifying the printer, the location of the press, and the date of publication on the title-page of the work. From Germany, the technology was taken to Italy, presses being established at Subiaco (1464) and Venice (1469). Caxton set up his printing shop at Westminster, London, in 1476. The famous Aldine press was established at Venice in 1495 by Aldus Manutius Romanus. This press was responsible for two important developments: 'lower case' letters (so-called because they were kept in the lower of two cases containing type), and the sloping 'italic' type (so-called in English-language works, on account of Venice being located in Italy. Aldus called the type 'Chancery').

Why would printing have such a major impact upon the Reformation? The following major factors identify its importance.

First, printing meant that the propaganda of the Reformation could be produced quickly and cheaply. The tedious process of copying manuscripts by hand was no longer necessary. Anyone who could read and who could afford to pay for books was in a position to learn of the sensational new ideas coming out of Wittenberg or Geneva. Thus the English upper classes were those who knew most about Lutheranism in the third decade of the sixteenth century – Lutheran books were smuggled in through the Hanseatic trade route to Cambridge via Antwerp and Ipswich. There was no need for Luther to visit England to gain a hearing for his ideas – they were spread by the printed word.

This point is of interest in relation to the sociology of the early Reformation. In both England and France, for example, the first Protestants were often drawn from the upper strata of society, precisely because these strata possessed the ability to read and the money to pay for books (which, as they often had to be smuggled in from abroad, were generally rather expensive). Similarly, the greater influence of Protestantism at Cambridge than at Oxford partly reflects the former's proximity to the continental ports from which Protestant books were being (illicitly) imported.

Second, the Reformation was based upon certain specific sources – as we shall see, the Bible and the Christian theologians of the first five centuries (often referred to as 'the fathers', or 'the patristic writers').

The invention of printing had two immediate effects upon these sources, of considerable importance to the origins of the Reformation. First, it was possible to produce more accurate editions of these works. Copying errors could be eliminated, for example. By comparing the printed text of a work with manuscript sources, the best possible text could be established and used as the basis of theological reflection. In the late fifteenth and early sixteenth centuries, humanist scholars rummaged through the libraries of Europe in search of patristic manuscripts which they could edit and publish. Second, these sources were made much more widely available than had ever been possible before. Almost anyone could gain access to a reliable edition of the New Testament, or the writings of Augustine of Hippo (a patristic writer particularly favoured by the Reformers).

Two examples will illustrate these points. The eleven volumes of the collected works of Augustine were published at Basle by the Amerbach brothers, after an editorial process lasting from 1490 to 1506. Although only 200 copies of each volume seem to have been published, they were widely used to gain access to the most reliable text of this important writer. Second, Erasmus of Rotterdam produced the first published Greek New Testament in 1516. Although the work does not show Erasmus' editorial skills at their best, it was widely used as a source. For the Reformers – especially Luther and his colleagues at Wittenberg – the religious ideas of the Reformation were based upon 'the Bible and Augustine'. The advent of printing meant that accurate and reliable texts of these sources were widely available, thus facilitating both the initial development and the subsequent spread of these ideas.

This is not, however, to say that the Reformation was wholly dependent upon a technological innovation! The evidence available points to printing as an agent of change in the intellectual climate, whereas the cities were generally converted to the cause of the Reformation through the impact of specific religious preachers and personalities. We must remember that the pulpit was of decisive importance in influencing what was a largely illiterate public – and much of the output of the printing houses took the form of collections of sermons.

The Social Context of the Reformation

The German and Swiss reformations were based largely upon the cities, and it is becoming increasingly clear that the success or failure of the Reformation in these cities was dependent in part upon political and social factors. By the late fifteenth and early sixteenth century, the city councils of the 65 so-called 'Imperial Cities' had managed to gain a substantial degree of independence. In effect, each city seems to have regarded itself as a miniature state, with the city council functioning as a government, and the remainder of the inhabitants as subjects.

The growth in the size and importance of the cities of Germany is one of the more significant elements in late fourteenth- and fifteenth-century history. An extended food crisis, linked with the ravages of the Black Death, led to an agrarian crisis. Wheat prices dropped alarmingly in the period 1450–1520, leading to rural depopulation as agrarian workers migrated to the cities. Denied access both to the trade guilds and to the city councils, discontent grew within the new urban proletariat.

The early sixteenth century thus witnessed growing social unrest in many cities, as demands for broader-based and more representative government gained momentum. In many cases, the Reformation came to be linked with these demands for social change, so that religious and social change went together, hand in hand. We must not think that religious concerns swamped all other mental activities – they simply provided a focal point for them. Economic, social and political factors help explain why the Reformation succeeded, for example, in Nuremberg and Strasbourg, yet failed in Erfurt.

An important difference may be noted at this point between Lutheran and Reformed thought. Luther was the product of a small Saxon town under the thumb of the local prince, but the great Reformed thinkers Zwingli and Bucer were the product of the great free cities of Zurich and Strasbourg. For these latter, the Reformation involved the identification of 'citizen' and 'Christian', with a great emphasis upon the political dimension of life quite absent from Luther's thought. Thus Zwingli lays great emphasis upon the need to reform and redeem a *community*, whereas Luther tended to concentrate upon the need to reform and redeem *the individual*. Luther, through his doctrine of the

'Two Kingdoms', effectively separated religious ideas from secular life, whereas Zwingli insists upon their mutual integration. It is therefore significant that Reformed church gained its most secure power bases in the cities of southern Germany and Switzerland, which were more advanced socially, culturally and economically than the northern cities destined to become Lutheran strongholds.

The social context of the Reformation is a fascinating subject in itself, but is noted here primarily on account of its obvious influence upon at least some of the religious ideas of the Reformers. For example, there are excellent reasons for suggesting that many of Zwingli's ideas (especially his ideas concerning the sacraments) were directly conditioned by the political, economic and social circumstances of Zurich. We shall consider this question at a number of points in the course of this work.

The Religious Ideas of the Reformers

It is appropriate to introduce the religious ideas of the Reformers at this point. These ideas will be amplified and developed throughout this study, and the present section is intended to give the reader a preliminary overview. Just as a sketch map provides a broad survey of an area, in order that fine detail may be mapped in later, so the present section is intended to give the reader an idea of the ideas to be encountered as this work progresses.

The fundamental belief motivating the magisterial Reformers was that Christianity could best be reformed and renewed by returning to the beliefs and practices of the early church. The first five centuries – often designated 'the patristic period' – tended to be regarded as the 'Golden Age of Christianity'. The great vision of many sixteenth-century Reformers was summed up in the Latin slogan *Christianismus renascens* – 'Christianity being born again'. How could this rebirth take place? The Reformers pointed to the vitality of Christianity in the apostolic period, as witnessed by the New Testament, and argued that it was both possible and necessary to recapture the spirit and the form of this pivotal period in the history of the Christian church. It was necessary to go back to the New Testament and its earliest interpreters, in order to learn from them. These were the title-deeds of Christendom, the fountainhead of Christian belief and practice.

Standing in the great tradition of the Old Testament prophets, the Reformers laid down a challenge to the religious leaders of their day. They were guilty of condoning additions to and distortions of the Christian faith – additions and distortions which reflected the interests of ecclesiastical fund-raisers and popular superstition. The doctrines of purgatory and indulgences were singled out as representing sub-Christian cults, which exploited the hopes and fears of the ordinary people. It was time to eliminate such additions and corruptions through the consistent appeal to the beliefs and practices of the early church.

This great emphasis upon early Christianity as a norm or point of reference for the sixteenth-century vision of *Christianismus renascens* allows us to understand why the Reformers placed such great emphasis upon the New Testament and the early Christian writers usually known as 'the fathers' or 'the patristic writers'. It was in these writings that a blueprint for the reformation and renewal of the church was to be found. Here could be found the original ideals of Christianity. Thus the production of the first Greek New Testament and the first edition of the works of Augustine (regarded by most reformers as *the* patristic writer) were milestones in the sixteenth-century programme of reform. Here were the sources upon the basis of which the church might be remolded and renewed – and, through the courtesy of the printing presses and humanist editors, they were now widely available throughout Europe. For Martin Luther, the programme of reform could be summed up in a simple phrase: 'the Bible and St Augustine'. What the New Testament and the fathers practised and believed was the norm by which the Reformers judged the practices and beliefs of the church in their own day and age.

The rise of Renaissance humanism was widely regarded as providential, in that the great advances made in Hebrew and Greek studies in western Europe paved the way for the direct engagement with the scriptural text, in place of the unreliable Latin translation of the Vulgate. The new textual and philological techniques pioneered by the humanists were regarded as holding the key to the world of the New Testament, and hence authentic Christianity. As the sixteenth century entered its second decade, there were many who felt that a new era was dawning, in which the voice of authentic Christianity, silent for so long, would be heard once more.

Simple though this programme of reform might seem, it was accompanied by formidable difficulties, which we shall be exploring in the course of this work. But the vision of a resurgent Christianity which had regained the vitality of its youth captivated the minds of many as the sixteenth century dawned. The agenda for the Reformation had been set, and the tools by which it might be achieved were being prepared. We must now plunge into the heady waters of fifteenth- and early sixteenth-century thought, if we are to understand the backdrop to this drama in human history.

For further reading

For general reading on the background to the Reformation, see:
Brenda Bolton, *The Medieval Reformation* (London/Baltimore, 1983).
John Bossy, *Christianity in the West 1400-1700* (Oxford/New York, 1987).
Owen Chadwick, *The Reformation* (Pelican History of the Church 3: London, 1972).
Hans J. Hillerbrand, *The Protestant Reformation* (New York, 1968)
Alister E. McGrath, 'Reformation to Enlightenment', in *The History of Christian Theology I: The Science of Theology*, ed. Paul Avis (Grand Rapids/Basingstoke, 1986), pp. 105–229, especially pp. 105–49.
Francis Oakley, 'Religious and Ecclesiastical Life on the Eve of the Reformation', in *Reformation Europe: A Guide to Research*, ed. Steven Ozment (St Louis, 1982), pp. 5–32.
Steven Ozment, *The Age of Reform 1250-1550: An Intellectual and Religious History of Late Medieval and Reformation Europe* (New Haven, 1973).

For an excellent account of the various ways in which the Reformation has been interpreted as an historical phenomenon, from the sixteenth century to the present day, see:

A. G. Dickens and John M. Tonkin, *The Reformation in Historical Perspective* (Cambridge, Mass., 1985).

On the social context of the Reformation, see:

Hans Baron, 'Religion and Politics in the German Imperial Cities during the Reformation', *English Historical Review* 52 (1937), pp. 405–27; 614-33.
Basil Hall, 'The Reformation City', *Bulletin of the John Rylands Library* 54 (1971), pp. 103–48.
Berndt Moeller, *Imperial Cities and the Reformation: Three Essays* (Philadelphia, 1972).
Steven Ozment, *The Reformation in the Cities: The Appeal of Protestantism to Sixteenth-Century Germany and Switzerland* (New Haven/London, 1975).

On the impact of printing, see:

M. U. Chrisman, *Lay Culture, Learned Culture: Books and Social Change in Strasbourg, 1480-1599* (New Haven/London, 1982).

Elizabeth L. Eisenstein, *The Printing Press as an Agent of Change: Communications and Cultural Transformations in Early Modern Europe* (2 vols: New York, 1979).

2

Late Medieval Religion

The backdrop to the Reformation is the late medieval period. In recent scholarship, there has been a growing emphasis upon the need to place the Reformation movement in its late medieval context, and to bring together the insights of late medieval, Renaissance and Reformation studies. The separation of these fields – for example, through each having their own chairs, journals and learned societies – has greatly hindered this process of synthesis and consolidation, essential to the correct understanding of the ideas of the Reformation. In the two chapters which follow, we shall examine in some detail the two most important intellectual forces in late medieval Europe: humanism and scholastic theology. The present chapter deals with some preliminary points about late medieval religion.

The Growth of Popular Religion

Older studies of the background to the Reformation tended to portray the later Middle Ages as a period in which religion was in decline. In part, this reflected the uncritical attitude adopted by these studies towards the literature of the fifteenth century which was critical of the church. Modern studies, using more reliable criteria, have indicated that precisely the reverse is true. Between 1450 and 1520, Germany saw a considerable increase in popular religious piety. This point was brought out with particular clarity by Bernd Moeller in an article entitled 'Piety in Germany around 1500'.[1]

Moeller drew upon a range of studies, which demonstrated that just about every objective criterion conceivable pointed to a remarkable growth in popular religion in Germany on the eve of the Reformation. Between 1450 and 1490, the number of masses endowed by upper

Austrian gentry increased steadily, reaching a peak in the period 1490–1517. The fashion grew for forming religious brotherhoods for the purpose of providing masses for their members when they died. These fraternities were basically poor men's chantries, ensuring that funeral masses were said for their members after their deaths. Their very existence was linked with a cluster of beliefs concerning death and eternity – ideas such as purgatory and the intercession of the saints. In Hamburg alone there were 99 such brotherhoods on the eve of the Reformation, most of which had been established after 1450. Church building programmes flourished in the later fifteenth century, as did pilgrimages and the vogue for collecting relics of one sort or another. The fifteenth century has been referred to as 'the inflation-period of mystic literature', reflecting the growing popular interest in religion. And it is this popular interest in religion which led to criticism of the institutional church where it was felt to be falling short of its obligations. This criticism – treated by older studies as evidence of religious *decline* – thus actually points to religious *growth*. Interestingly, this growth in piety appears to be largely restricted to the laity: the clergy of the day show little, if any, sign of spiritual renewal. The scene was set for the rise of anticlericalism, in that the clergy came to be seen as exploiting the new interest in religion, without contributing to it.

An important part of fifteenth-century German religion is the phenomenon of antipapalism and anticlericalism. This phenomenon is not, of course, restricted to Germany – the Lollard movement in England displayed the same characteristics, for example. Hostility to the pope was perhaps greatest among the educated and ruling classes, who resented his interference in local ecclesiastical and political matters; hostility to the clergy was greatest among the ordinary people, especially in the towns, who resented their privileges (such as exemption from taxation, and the oppressive role often played by the clergy as landlords to the German peasants).[2] Studies of this tradition of anticlerical and antipapal feeling have pointed to the existence of what might be called an 'ecclesiastical grievance literature'.[3] The papal and clerical abuses which Luther listed in his famous reforming treatise of 1520, *Appeal to the German Nobility*, parallel similar lists in circulation in the fifteenth century. Luther appears to have been tapping a tradition of longstanding complaints against the church, in order to gain support for his programme of reform. In the popular mind, Luther and men such as Ulrich von Hutten were identified as common liberators from an oppressive church. Furthermore, there is evidence which strongly suggests that German nationalism, fanned by antipapal and anti-Italian sentiment, reached a peak in the years 1517–21. A popular mythology had developed which saw in Germany a nation chosen by God to fulfil his purposes. Although these legends were systematically discredited by humanists in the period 1530–60, it seems that many regarded the German Reformation under Luther as divinely guided and inspired.

One final point must be made concerning the growth of popular religion in the later Middle Ages. In part, popular religion represented an attempt to convert the abstract ideas of theologians into something more tangible – such as social practices. Baptism, marriage and death became events surrounded by popular beliefs and practices which, although ultimately based upon the textbooks of the theologians, often came to bear little relation to them. Folk-religion became incorporated with Christian ideas. The concept of purgatory – a sort of intermediate clearing-house for the dead as they await the final judgement – held a particular popular fascination, as the later growth of the indulgence trade demonstrated.

As the rift between popular belief and theology grew wider, so reform became an increasingly faint possibility. To reform popular belief by bringing it back into line with an 'official' theology presupposed agreement upon what that theology was – and, as we shall see in the following sections, the growth of doctrinal pluralism and confusion effectively negated this option. In the end, the Reformers cut this Gordian knot by attacking both the popular beliefs and practices *and* the theology upon which they were ultimately, if tenuously, based, and undertaking a massive educational programme. However, the problems facing those wishing to reform popular religion in the later Middle Ages are brought into sharp focus through the relative failure of these massive programmes of the Reformation period: folk-religion and popular superstition proved virtually impossible to eradicate.[4]

The Rise of Doctrinal Pluralism

One of the most significant aspects of medieval religious thought is the growth of 'schools' of theology. Just as the twentieth century has witnessed the growth of the 'Freudian' and 'Adlerian' schools in psychoanalysis, and the 'Barthian' school of theology, so the Middle Ages saw a number of quite well-defined theological schools of thought establishing themselves. For example, there was the school of thought based upon the writings of Thomas Aquinas (usually referred to as 'Thomism'), and that based upon the rather different ideas found in the writings of John Duns Scotus ('Scotism'). The Middle Ages was a period of expansion in the universities and schools of Europe, as new universities were founded and older ones expanded. An inevitable result of this expansion was intellectual diversification. In other words, the more academics you have, the more opinions you find in circulation as a result. By the beginning of the sixteenth century, as many as nine such schools had established themselves within the western European church.

Now each of these schools of thought had rather different understandings of a number of major questions. For example, the doctrine of justification (to which we shall return in chapter 5) saw the schools of thought split on a number of important questions – such as what the individual had to do if he was to be justified. Similar divisions existed over a whole range of questions of direct importance to both personal religion and ecclesiastical politics. But which of these schools of thought was *right*? Which corresponded most closely to the teaching of the church? In a period which witnessed unprecedented expansion in intellectual activities in religious houses and universities, it was clearly essential that some way of *evaluating* the reliability of the new doctrines should be brought into play. For reasons which we shall explore shortly, no such evaluation was undertaken. To use the appropriate terms, what was merely 'theological opinion', and what was 'catholic dogma'? The papacy was reluctant to define, and apparently incapable of enforcing, 'true doctrine'. The result was inevitable: confusion. Nobody could be quite sure exactly what the teaching of the church on certain matters was. As one of those matters was the doctrine of justification, it is perhaps not surprising that this doctrine should have been at the centre of one major Reformation movement – that associated with Martin Luther.

We can speak of a *spectrum* of thought within the late Middle Ages. A remarkably wide range of doctrines was in circulation, as we shall demonstrate presently in the case of the doctrine of justification. It is all too easy for twentieth-century writers, with the benefit of hindsight, to recognize the potential seriousness of the ideas being developed by the first Reformers – but *at the time* these ideas were not recognized as having any pivotal importance. The Reformers initially appear to have developed ideas which were not exceptional within the late medieval church. So great was the diversity of opinion within the church that the ideas initially associated with the Reformers attracted little attention. The boundary lines between what was orthodox and what was not were so hopelessly confused that it was virtually impossible to treat individuals such as Luther as heretical – and by the time this move had to be made, the Reformation had gained such momentum that it proved difficult to obstruct it.

Doctrinal diversity is thus an essential element of the intellectual backdrop to the Reformation. The pluralism within late medieval religious thought meant that the Reformers were at liberty to explore their religious ideas, without being identified as potential threats to the church. By the time that such identification was made, Reformers such as Luther had gained too great a following to be stopped dead in their tracks. The scene for a future religious confrontation was set by the doctrinal pluralism of the late medieval church.

A Crisis of Authority

A development in the later medieval period which is of central importance to a study of the Reformation is the growing crisis in authority, evident from the fourteenth century onwards. To whom, or to what, should someone look for an authoritative pronouncement concerning doctrine? Who was in a position to state unequivocally that 'the position of the catholic church on *this* matter is *that*'? In a period which witnessed a remarkable growth in theological debate, it was essential that someone laid down what was just theological speculation and what was actually catholic doctrine. There was a widespread recognition within the church that theological speculation was acceptable – after all, academics had to do something with their spare time, and the church was sufficiently confident in the truth of its teachings to allow them to be subjected to close scrutiny. It will also be obvious that there needed to be some way of enforcing orthodoxy (assuming, of course that 'orthodoxy' could be defined!). The papacy required the means of coercing those with unorthodox views to abandon them, or at least stop teaching them.

Two major developments within the late medieval church combined to make the definition and enforcement of orthodoxy virtually impossible in the late fifteenth and early sixteenth centuries. First, the authority of the pope was called into question through the Great Schism and its aftermath. The Great Schism (1378–1417) led to the division of western Christendom on the death of Gregory XI. An Italian faction was led by Urban VI, and a French faction by Clement VII. This situation continued until 1417, when the Council of Constance elected Martin V as pope. For a brief period around 1409, there were three claimants to the papacy.

The crucial question was this: how could the dispute concerning who was *really* pope be resolved? It was widely accepted that the final arbiter in all doctrinal disputes within the church was the pope – but *which* pope could settle this dispute? Eventually it was agreed that a Council should meet with authority to settle the dispute. The Council of Constance (1414–17) was convoked to choose between the three rival candidates for the papacy (Gregory XII, Benedict XIII and John XXIII). The Council conveniently resolved the matter by passing over all three, and choosing their own candidate (Martin V). It seemed that an important general principal had been established: councils have authority over the pope. Martin V thought otherwise.

The scene was thus set for the development of two rival theories of authority within the church: those who held that supreme doctrinal authority resided in a General Council (the 'conciliarist' position), and those who argued that it resided in the person of the pope (the 'curialist' position). As the recognition of the need for reform of the church grew in the fifteenth century, the conciliarist party argued that the only hope for such reform lay in calling a reforming general council. Martin Luther reflects such a position in his 1520 *Appeal to the German Nobility*, in which he argued that the German princes had the right to convoke such a council. The failure of the conciliarist movement is generally regarded as a central cause of the Reformation, for two reasons. First, it led to hopes being raised that the church might be reformed from within – and when such hopes were dashed, many began to look for means of *imposing* reform upon the church, perhaps through an appeal to the secular authorities. Second, it posed a challenge to the doctrinal authority of the pope, thus contributing to the theological confusion of the later medieval period. As it was not clear who held ultimate doctrinal authority, many theologians developed their theological opinions without asking too many questions concerning their authenticity.

The second major factor concerns the rise of the power of the secular rulers of Europe, who increasingly came to regard the pope's problems as having somewhat limited relevance. The popes seem to have been reluctant to make use of the channels already available for enforcing doctrinal orthodoxy. For example, the German diocesan and provincial synods had the power to suppress heresy – but these synods were not convened when required in the early sixteenth century. The attention of many European rulers was focused initially upon the Franco-Italian war, and subsequently on the Hapsburg–Valois conflict, at the time when the Reformation *could* have been forcibly suppressed, had the political will been present.

There was thus a twofold crisis of authority in the later medieval church. There was obvious confusion concerning the nature, location and manner of exercise of *theological* authority, just as there was either a reluctance or an inability to exercise the *political* authority required to suppress the new ideas of the Reformation. And in the midst of this impotent confusion, the Reformation proceeded with increasing pace, until its local suppression was no longer a realistic possibility.

For further reading

For an excellent overview of western European religious life in the later Middle Ages, and how it was affected by the Reformation, see:

John Bossy, *Christianity in the West 1400-1700* (Oxford, 1987).

For useful overviews of late medieval religious thought, see:

Heiko A. Oberman, 'Fourteenth Century Religious Thought: A Premature Profile', in *The Dawn of the Reformation: Essays in Late Medieval and Early Reformation Thought* (Edinburgh, 1986), pp. 1–17.
——, 'The Shape of Late Medieval Thought', in *The Dawn of the Reformation*, pp. 18–38.

For the importance of doctrinal diversity in the later Middle Ages, see:

Alister E. McGrath, *The Intellectual Origins of the European Reformation* (Oxford, 1987), pp. 9–31.
Jaroslav Pelikan, *The Christian Tradition: A History of the Development of Doctrine. 4. Reformation of Church and Dogma (1300-1700)* (Chicago/London, 1984), pp. 10–22.

3

Humanism and the Reformation

Of the many tributaries which contributed to the flux of the Reformation, by far the most important was Renaissance humanism. Although the Reformation may have begun in the cities of Germany and Switzerland, there are excellent reasons for suggesting that it may well have been the inevitable outcome of developments in fourteenth-century Italy as the movement we now know as the 'Italian Renaissance' gained momentum. The present chapter will survey the methods and ideas of Renaissance humanism, in order that their relevance to the Reformation may be understood.

When the word 'humanism' is used by a twentieth-century writer, we are usually meant to understand an anti-religious philosophy which affirms the dignity of humanity without any reference to God. 'Humanism' has acquired very strongly secularist, perhaps even atheist, overtones. It is perhaps inevitable that many students approach the theme 'Humanism and the Reformation' on the basis of this twentieth-century understanding of the word 'humanist'. The scene seems set for the confrontation of religion and atheism. Yet that confrontation never materializes. As we shall see, however, remarkably few – if any – humanists of the fourteenth, fifteenth or sixteenth centuries correspond to our modern understanding of 'humanism'. Indeed, they were remarkably religious, if anything concerned with the *renewal* rather than the *abolition* of the Christian church. The word 'humanist' had a meaning in the sixteenth century which is quite different from the twentieth-century meaning of the word, as we shall see shortly. To anticipate a little, it is now clear that humanism was generally theologically neutral in the Renaissance. The reader is asked to set aside the modern sense of the word 'humanism', as we prepare to meet this phenomenon in its late Renaissance setting.

One important terminological point must also be made before we begin our discussion of humanism and the Renaissance, as they relate to the Reformation. The reader is likely to encounter reference, even in English language works, to the Italian terms *Trecènto*, *Quattrocènto* and *Cinquecènto* (often with the accent omitted). These refer, respectively, to the 1300s, the 1400s and the 1500s – in other words, to the *fourteenth*, *fifteenth* and *sixteenth* centuries. Similarly, a *quattrocentista* is a fifteenth-century, and a *cinquecentista* a sixteenth-century, figure. Many English-speaking readers wrongly assume that the *Quattrocento* is the *fourteenth* century, and find themselves hopelessly confused as a result.

The Concept of 'Renaissance'

Although the French term 'Renaissance' is now universally used to designate the literary and artistic revival in fourteenth- and fifteenth-century Italy, contemporary writers tended to refer to the movement using other terms: 'restoration', 'revival', 'awakening' and 're-flowering'.[1] ('Italy', of course, here designates a geographical rather than a political entity.) In 1546 Paolo Giovio referred to the fourteenth century as 'that happy century in which Latin letters are conceived to have been reborn (*renatae*)', anticipating this development. Certain historians, most notably Jacob Burckhardt, argued that the Renaissance gave birth to the modern era. It was in this era, Burckhardt argued, that human beings first began to think of themselves as *individuals*. The communal consciousness of the medieval period gave way to the individual consciousness of the Renaissance.[2] Florence became the new Athens, the intellectual capital of a brave new world, with the river Arno separating the old and the new worlds.

It is not entirely clear why Italy in general, or Florence in particular, became the cradle of this brilliant new movement in the history of ideas. A number of factors have been identified as having some bearing on the question.

1 Scholastic theology – the major intellectual force of the medieval period – was never particularly influential in Italy. Although many Italians achieved fame as theologians (such Thomas Aquinas and Gregory of Rimini), they operated in northern Europe. There was thus an intellectual vacuum in Italy during the fourteenth century.

Vacuums tend to be filled – and Renaissance humanism filled this particular gap.

2 The political stability of Florence depended upon the maintenance of her republican government. It was thus natural to turn to the study of the Roman Republic, including its literature and culture, as a model for Florence.

3 The economic prosperity of Florence created leisure, and hence a demand for literature and the arts. Patronage of culture and the arts was seen as a suitable use for surplus wealth.[3]

4 As Byzantium began to crumble, there was an exodus of Greek-speaking intellectuals westward. Italy happened to be conveniently close to Constantinople, with the result that many such emigrés settled in her cities. A revival of the Greek language was thus inevitable, and with it a revival of interest in the Greek classics.

The Concept of 'Humanism'

The term 'humanism' was first used in 1808, to refer to a form of education which placed emphasis upon the Greek and Latin classics. The term was not used at the time of the Renaissance itself, although we find frequent use of the Italian word *umanista*. This word refers to a university teacher of *studia humanitatis* – 'human studies', or 'liberal arts', such as poetry, grammar and rhetoric.[4] Although some early studies suggested that humanism originated outside a university context, the evidence available unquestionably points to a close link between humanism and the universities of northern Italy.

This present section is chiefly concerned with the problem of defining humanism. The term is still used widely in Renaissance and Reformation studies, often with an irritating degree of fluidity. What is meant by the term 'humanism'? In the recent past, two major lines of interpretation of the movement were predominant. First, humanism was viewed as a movement devoted to classical scholarship and philology. Second, humanism was the new philosophy of the Renaissance. As will become clear, both these interpretations of humanism have serious shortcomings.

Classical Scholarship and Philology

It is beyond doubt that the Renaissance witnessed the rise of classical scholarship. The Greek and Latin classics were widely studied in their original languages. It might therefore seem that humanism was essentially a scholarly movement devoted to the study of the classical period. This is to overlook, however, the question of *why* the humanists wished to study the classics in the first place. The evidence available unquestionably indicates that such study was regarded as *a means to an end*, rather than *an end in itself*. That end was the promotion of contemporary written and spoken eloquence.[5] In other words, the humanists studied the classics as models of written eloquence, in order to gain inspiration and instruction. Classical learning and philological competence were simply the tools used to exploit the resources of antiquity. As has often been pointed out, the writings of the humanists devoted to the promotion of eloquence, written or spoken, far exceed those devoted to classical scholarship or philology.

The New Philosophy of the Renaissance

According to several recent interpreters of humanism, the movement embodied the new philosophy of the Renaissance, which arose as a reaction to scholasticism. Thus it was argued that the Renaissance was an age of Platonism, whereas scholasticism was a period of Aristotelianism. Others argued that the Renaissance was essentially an anti-religious phenomenon, foreshadowing the secularism of the eighteenth-century Enlightenment. Hans Baron argued that humanism was basically a republican movement, which studied Cicero in order to benefit from his political ideas.[6]

Two major difficulties confronted this rather ambitious interpretation of humanism. First, humanists appear to have been primarily concerned with the promotion of eloquence – for example, by promoting classical scholarship, through the study of Greek and Latin, or through patronage of artists and sculptors. While it is not true to say that humanists made no significant contribution to philosophy, the fact remains that they were primarily men of letters. Thus in comparison with those devoted to the 'pursuit of eloquence', there are remarkably few humanist writings devoted to philosophy – and these are generally somewhat amateurish. Baron's theory concerning the humanist use of Cicero was weakened through the observation that most humanists read Cicero to benefit from his style of writing, rather than from his political ideas.[7]

Second, intensive study of humanist writings uncovered the disquieting fact that 'humanism' was remarkably heterogeneous. For example, many humanist writers did indeed favour Platonism – but others favoured Aristotelianism. The stubborn persistence of Aristotelianism (for example, at the University of Padua) throughout the Renaissance is a serious obstacle to those who regard humanism as philosophically homogeneous. Some Italian humanists did indeed display what seem to be anti-religious attitudes – but other Italian humanists were profoundly pious. Some humanists were indeed republicans – but others adopted different political attitudes. Recent studies have also drawn attention to a less attractive side of humanism – the obsession of some humanists with magic and superstition – which is difficult to harmonize with the conventional view of the movement. In short, it became increasingly clear that 'humanism' seemed to lack any coherent philosophy. No single philosophical or political idea dominated or characterized the movement. It seemed to many that the term 'humanism' would have to be dropped from the vocabulary of historians, because it had no meaningful content. Designating a writer as a 'humanist' conveys no essential information concerning his philosophical, political or religious views.

In fact, it is clear that the Italian Renaissance is so multi-faceted that just about every generalization concerning its 'characteristic ideas' tends to distort the phenomenon. It is for this reason that the view of humanism developed by Paul Oskar Kristeller is of decisive importance. Kristeller's view of humanism has gained wide acceptance within North American and European scholarship, and has yet to be discredited.

Kristeller's View of Humanism

Kristeller envisages humanism as a cultural and educational movement, primarily concerned with the promotion of eloquence in its various forms. Its concerns with matters of morals, philosophy and politics are of secondary importance. To be a humanist is to be concerned with eloquence first and foremost, and with other matters incidentally.

Humanism was essentially a cultural programme, laying emphasis upon the promotion of eloquence, which appealed to classical antiquity as a model of that eloquence. In art and architecture, as in the written and spoken word, antiquity was seen as a cultural resource, which could be appropriated by the Renaissance. Petrarch referred to Cicero as his father, and Virgil as his brother. The architects of the *Quattrocento* studiously ignored the Gothic style of northern Europe, in order to return to the classical styles of antiquity. Cicero was studied as an orator, rather than as a political or moral writer.

In short: humanism was concerned with *how ideas were obtained and expressed*, rather than with *the actual substance of those ideas*. A humanist might be a Platonist or an Aristotelian – but in both cases, the ideas involved derived from antiquity. A humanist might be a sceptic or a believer – but both attitudes could be defended from antiquity. The enormous attractiveness of Kristeller's view of humanism derives from the fact that it accounts brilliantly for the remarkable diversity of the Renaissance. Where Baron identifies one set of ideas as central, and Burckhardt another, Kristeller points to the way in which ideas are generated and handled as being central. The diversity of *ideas* which is so characteristic of Renaissance humanism is based upon a general consensus concerning *how to derive and express those ideas*.

It will be obvious that any discussion of the relation of humanism and the Reformation will be totally dependent upon the definition of humanism employed. Kristeller's definition of humanism allows the most reliable assessment of the relation of these two movements now available.

Ad fontes – Back to the Sources

The literary and cultural programme of humanism can be summarized in the slogan *ad fontes* – back to the original sources. The squalor of the medieval period is bypassed, in order to recover the intellectual and artistic glories of the classical period. The 'filter' of medieval commentaries – whether on legal texts or on the Bible – is abandoned, in order to engage directly with the original texts. Applied to the Christian church, the slogan *ad fontes* meant a direct return to the title-deeds of Christianity – to the patristic writers, and supremely to the Bible.

The slogan, however, does more than specify the sources to be used in the rebirth of civilization. It also specifies the attitude to be adopted towards these sources. It is necessary to remember that the Renaissance was an era of discovery, both geographical and scientific. The discovery of the Americas fired the imagination of the late Renaissance, as did new insights into the functioning of the human body and the natural world. And so classical sources were read with a view to rediscovering the experiences they reflected. In his *Aeneid*, Virgil described the discovery of new and strange lands – and so late Renaissance readers approached Virgil with a sense of expectation, for they too were in the process of discovering *terrae incognitae*. Galen was read in a new light: he described the gaining of physiological insights to a generation who were repeating that experience in their own day and age. And so it was also with scripture. The New Testament described the encounter of believers with the risen Christ – and late Renaissance readers approached the text of scripture with the expectation that they too could meet the risen Christ, a meeting which seemed to be denied to them by the church of their day.

This point is often overlooked, but holds the key to the humanist reverence for ancient texts. For the humanists, classical texts mediated an experience to posterity – an experience which could be regained by handling the text in the right way. The new philological and literary methods developed by the thinkers of the Renaissance were thus seen as a way of recapturing the vitality of the classical period. For the Christian church, this opened up a new, exciting and challenging possibility – that the experience of the first Christians, described in the New Testament, could be regained, and transferred to a much later point in history. It is this factor, perhaps more than any other, which helps explain the remarkably high regard in which humanists were held in reforming circles throughout Europe. It seemed to many that the sterile form of Christianity associated with the Middle Ages could be replaced with a new vital and dynamic form, through the study of scripture. *Ad fontes* was more than a slogan – it was a lifeline to those who despaired of the state of the late medieval church. The Apostolic Age, the Golden Age of the church, could once more become a present reality.

It is perhaps difficult for some modern readers to empathize with this sense of excitement and anticipation. Yet to enter into the thought-world of Europe on the eve of the Reformation, we must try to recapture this sense of expectation. To many individuals and groups throughout Europe, it seemed that a new day in the history of the church was about to dawn, in which the risen Christ would be restored to the church. It seemed to many, such as Luther, that God in his providence had given the church the key (in the new humanist textual and philological tools) by which the New Testament experience of Christ could be unlocked and made available.

Northern European Humanism

At this point, we must pause to clarify one important point. The 'humanism' which affected the Reformation is primarily *northern European humanism*, rather than *Italian* humanism. We must therefore consider what form this northern European movement took.

The Northern European Reception of the Italian Renaissance

It is becoming increasingly clear that northern European humanism was decisively influenced by Italian humanism at every stage of its development. If there were indigenous humanist movements in northern Europe which originated independently of their Italian counterpart (which, it has to be stressed, is very much open to doubt), the evidence unambiguously points to those movements having subsequently been decisively influenced by Italian humanism. Three main channels for the northern European diffusion of the methods and ideals of the Italian Renaissance have been identified.

1　Through northern European scholars moving south to Italy, perhaps to study at an Italian university or as part of a diplomatic mission. On returning to their homeland, they brought the spirit of the Renaissance back with them.

2　Through the foreign correspondence of the Italian humanists. Humanism was concerned with the promotion of written eloquence, and the writing of letters was seen as a means of embodying and spreading the ideals of the Renaissance. The full extent of the foreign correspondence of Italian humanists was considerable, extending to most parts of northern Europe.

3 Through printed books, originating from sources such as the Aldine Press in Venice. These works were often reprinted by northern European presses, particularly those at Basle in Switzerland. Italian humanists often dedicated their works to northern European patrons, thus ensuring that they were taken notice of in the right quarters.

The Ideals of Northern European Humanism

Three main themes dominate northern European humanism. First, we find the same concern for *bonae litterae* – written and spoken eloquence, after the fashion of the classical period – as in the Italian Reformation. Second, we find a religious programme directed towards the corporate revival of the Christian church. The Latin slogan *Christianismus renascens*, 'Christianity being born again', summarizes the aims of this programme, and indicates its relation with the 'rebirth' of letters associated with the Renaissance. Although Burckhardt is unquestionably right to state that the Renaissance led to a new emphasis upon the subjective consciousness of the individual, northern European humanists supplemented this new emphasis upon the individual with a recognition of the need to reform the communities (both church and state) to which the individual belonged. It is worth noting at this point that the Renaissance emphasis upon the subjective consciousness of the individual is particularly linked with the doctrine of justification by faith, to which we shall return in chapter 5. Third, northern European humanism was strongly pacifist during the early sixteenth century, largely in reaction to the tragedy of the Franco-Italian war. The quest for international peace and mutual understanding was espoused by most humanists at the time, particularly in Switzerland, which was caught up in the disastrous Franco-Italian war. Distaste for papal political manoeuvring was an important element in the background to the Swiss Reformation.

Erasmus of Rotterdam

One figure stands head and shoulders above other northern European humanists, not least in terms of his influence upon both the German and Swiss reformations – Erasmus of Rotterdam.[8] Although the direct influence of Erasmus upon Luther and Calvin is less than might be expected, many other Reformers (such as Zwingli and Bucer) were heavily influenced by him. It is therefore essential that his considerable contribution to the thought of the Reformation be considered in some detail.

Before we do this, one point should be noted. Erasmus is often presented as reflecting northern European humanism at its best. While there is much that could be said in support of this suggestion, certain tensions within northern European humanism must be recognized. Two are of particular interest.

1   The question of national languages. Erasmus regarded himself as a 'citizen of the world', and Ciceronian Latin as the language of that world. National languages were an obstacle to his vision of a cosmopolitan Europe united by the Latin language. To other humanists, especially in Germany and Switzerland, national languages were to be encouraged as promoting a sense of national identity. Erasmus, however, regarded any sense of national identity as an obstacle to a culturally united Europe – which explains his negative attitude to national boundaries.

2   The question of national boundaries. For Erasmus, the vision of a cosmopolitan Europe was threatened by nationalism. The adoption of Latin as the cosmopolitan language would remove outdated concepts such as a 'sense of national identity', and associated ideas such as national boundaries. Other humanists, however, saw themselves as engaged in a struggle to *promote* national identity. Thus the Swiss humanists Glarean, Myconius and Xylotectus saw themselves as having a sacred duty to defend Swiss national identity and culture by literary means – where Erasmus would much have preferred to concentrate upon *eliminating* such nationalist ideas.

This tension between the 'cosmopolitan' and 'nationalist' humanist visions, between *abolishing* and *consolidating* national identities, indicates both the variety of views current within humanism: it also demonstrates that Erasmus cannot be regarded as a totally representative spokesman for humanism, as some scholars appear to suggest.

The most influential humanist writing to circulate in Europe during the first decades of the sixteenth century was Erasmus' *Enchiridion Militis Christiani*, 'Handbook of the Christian Soldier'.[9] Although the work was first published in 1503, and then reprinted in 1509, the real impact of the work dates from its third printing in 1515. From that moment onwards, it became a cult work, apparently going through twenty-three editions in the next six years. Its appeal was to educated lay men and women, whom Erasmus regarded as the true treasure of the church. Its amazing popularity in the years after 1515 may allow us to suggest that a radical alteration in lay self-perception took place as a result – and it can hardly be overlooked that the reforming rumbles at Zurich and Wittenberg date from so soon after the *Enchiridion* became a bestseller. Erasmus' success also highlighted the importance of printing as a means of disseminating radical new ideas – a point which neither Zwingli nor Luther overlooked, when their turns came to propagate such ideas.

The *Enchiridion* developed the attractive thesis that the church of the day could be reformed by a collective return to the writings of the fathers and scripture. The reading of scripture on a regular basis is put forward as the key to a new lay piety, on the basis of which the church may be renewed and reformed. Erasmus conceived his work as a lay person's guide to scripture, providing a simple yet learned exposition of the 'philosophy of Christ'. This 'philosophy' is really a form of morality: the New Testament concerns the knowledge of good and evil, in order that its readers may eschew the latter and love the former. The New Testament is the *lex Christi*, 'the law of Christ', which Christians are called to obey. Christ is the example whom Christians are called to imitate. Yet Erasmus does not understand Christian faith to be a mere external observance of some kind of morality. His characteristically humanist emphasis upon inner religion leads him to suggest that reading of scripture *transforms* its reader, giving him a new motivation to love God and his neighbour.

A number of points are of particular importance. First, Erasmus understands the future vitality of Christianity to lie with the laity, not the clergy. The clergy are seen as educators, whose function is to allow the laity to achieve the same level of understanding as themselves. There is no room for any superstitions which give the clergy a permanent status superior to their lay charges. Second, Erasmus' strong emphasis upon the 'inner religion' results in an understanding of Christianity which makes no reference to the church – its rites, priests or institutions. Why bother confessing sin to another human, asks Erasmus, just because he's a priest, when you can confess them directly to God himself? Religion is a matter of the individual's heart and mind: it is an inward state. Erasmus pointedly avoids any reference to the sacraments, for example. Similarly, he discounts the view that the 'religious life' (in other words, being a monk or a nun) is the highest form of the Christian life: the lay person who reads scripture is just as faithful to his calling as the pious monk.

The revolutionary character of Erasmus' *Enchiridion* lies in its daring new suggestion that the recognition of the Christian vocation of the lay person holds the key to the revival of the church. Clerical and ecclesiastical authority is discounted. Scripture should and must be made available to all, in order than all may return *ad fontes*, to drink of the fresh and living waters of the Christian faith, rather than the murky and stagnant ponds of late medieval religion.

Erasmus, however, came to recognize that there were serious obstacles in the path of the course he proposed, and was responsible for a number of major developments to relieve them. First, there was a need to be able to study the New Testament in its original language, rather than in the inaccurate Vulgate translation. This necessitated two tools, neither of which was then available: access to the Greek text, and the necessary philological competence to handle the text.

The second difficulty began to be relieved through Erasmus' discovery of Lorenzo Valla's fifteenth-century notes on the Greek text of the New Testament, which Erasmus published in 1505. The first was resolved through the publication by Erasmus of the first printed Greek New Testament, the *Novum Instrumentum omne*, which rolled off Froben's presses at Basle in 1516. Although a superior version of the same text had been set up in type at Alcalá in Spain two years earlier, publication of this version (the so-called Complutensian Polyglot) was delayed until 1520. Erasmus' text was not as reliable as it ought to have been: Erasmus had access to a mere four manuscripts for most of the New Testament, and only one for its final part, the Book of Revelation. As it happened, that manuscript left out five verses, which Erasmus had to translate into Greek from Latin! Nevertheless, it proved to be a literary milestone. For the first time, theologians had the opportunity of comparing the original Greek text of the New Testament with the later Vulgate translation into Latin. As we shall see in the following section, one result of this comparison was a general loss of confidence in the reliability of the Vulgate, the 'official' Latin translation of the Bible.[10] No longer could 'scripture' and 'the Vulgate text' be regarded as one and the same thing.

Erasmus also demonstrated that the Vulgate was seriously inaccurate at many points in its translation of the Greek text of the New Testament. Drawing on work carried out earlier by Lorenzo Valla, Erasmus showed that the Vulgate translation of a number of major New Testament texts could not be justified. As a number of medieval church practices and beliefs were based upon these texts, Erasmus' allegations were viewed with consternation by many conservative catholics (who wanted to retain these practices and beliefs) and with equally great delight by the Reformers (who wanted to eliminate them). Some examples will indicate the relevance of Erasmus' biblical scholarship.

The Christian church has always attached particular importance to certain rites or forms of worship, which are referred to as *sacraments*. Two such sacraments were recognized by the early church as 'dominical' (in other words, as going back to Jesus Christ himself). These were baptism, and the sacrament now known by a variety of names, such as 'the Mass', 'the Lord's supper', the 'breaking of the bread', or 'the eucharist'. By the end of the twelfth century, however, this number had increased to seven. The additions to the list now included matrimony and penance. The development and consolidation of the sacramental system of the church is one of the most important aspects of medieval theology.

Erasmus' new translation of the New Testament seemed to many to call this entire system into question. For example, the inclusion of matrimony in the list of sacraments was justified on the basis of a New Testament text – as translated by the Vulgate – which spoke of marriage being a *sacramentum* (Ephesians 5:31–2). Erasmus followed Valla in pointing out that the Greek simply meant 'mystery'. There was no reference whatsoever to marriage being a 'sacrament'. One of the classic proof texts used by medieval theologians to justify the inclusion of matrimony in the list of sacraments was thus rendered virtually useless.

Similarly, the Vulgate translated the opening words of Jesus' ministry (Matthew 4:17) as '*do penance*, for the Kingdom of heaven is at hand', with a clear reference to the sacrament of penance. Erasmus, again following Valla, pointed out that the Greek should be translated as '*repent*, for the Kingdom of heaven is at hand'. In other words, where the Vulgate seemed to refer to the sacrament of penance, Erasmus insisted that the reference was to a psychological attitude – that of 'being repentant'. Once more, an important justification of the sacramental system of the church was challenged.

Another area of theology which medieval theologians had developed far beyond the modest views of the early church relates to Mary, the mother of Jesus. For many later medieval theologians, Mary was to be treated rather like a reservoir of grace, which could be tapped when needed. In part, this view rested upon the Vulgate translation of Gabriel's words to Mary (Luke 1:28). According to the Vulgate, Gabriel greeted Mary as 'the one who is full of grace (*gratia plena*)', thus suggesting the image of a reservoir. But, as Erasmus and Valla both pointed out, the Greek simply meant 'favoured one', or 'one who has found favour'. Once more, an important development in medieval theology seemed to be contradicted by humanist New Testament scholarship.

For the Reformers, however, these developments were nothing less than providential. As we have seen, the Reformers wanted to return to the beliefs and practices of the early church – and if Erasmus' new translation of the New Testament helped demolish medieval additions to those beliefs and practices, then so much the better. Humanist biblical scholarship was therefore regarded as an ally in the struggle for the return to the apostolic simplicity of the early church.[11]

Erasmus' programme of reform also required ready access to the writings of the fathers. This necessitated the production of reliable editions of the writings of theologians such as Ambrose, Augustine and Jerome (Erasmus' favourite patristic writer). Erasmus was responsible for a remarkable feat of editorial work, producing a series of patristic editions which were the marvel of the age. Although Erasmus' edition of the writings of Augustine compares unfavourably with the great eleven-volume Amerbach edition of 1506, his edition of the works of Jerome was widely regarded as an intellectual wonder of the world.

The importance of these editions is too easily overlooked. Medieval theologians cited the fathers, especially Augustine, extensively. Why should so much importance be attached to these new editions of works which everybody already knew about? Two answers may be given. First, medieval writers tended to quote very short extracts, usually referred to as 'sentences', from the fathers. These sentences were quoted without reference to context. As the full versions of the works from which they were quoted were to be found in a few manuscripts locked away in monastic libraries, it was virtually impossible to check that a father's viewpoint was being accurately presented. Augustine in particular was often misunderstood through being quoted out of context. The production of printed editions of these works allowed the context of these sentences to be studied, so that it was possible to gain an understanding of the fathers at a depth denied to the earlier medieval writers.

Second, a large number of works ascribed to Augustine in circulation in the Middle Ages were actually written by somebody else. These 'pseudo-Augustinian' works frequently developed views opposed to those of Augustine, making it remarkably difficult for readers to make sense of his apparently contradictory statements. The arrival of the textual-critical methods of humanist scholarship led to these 'pseudo-Augustinian' works generally being recognized for what they were, and hence being excluded from the definitive editions of Augustine's writings.[12] The way was thus opened to more reliable interpretation of the fathers, by eliminating spurious 'patristic' writings. The scholarly techniques for identifying spurious writings had been developed by Lorenzo Valla in the fifteenth century, and used to demonstrate the inauthenticity of the famous *Donation of Constantine* (a document allegedly drawn up by the emperor Constantine giving certain privileges to the western church).

Humanism and the Reformation – An Evaluation

What impact did humanism have upon the Reformation? In order to give a reliable answer to this perennial question, it is necessary to draw a distinction between two wings of the Reformation: the Reformation as it developed at Wittenberg, under Martin Luther; and the Reformation as it developed at Zurich, under Huldrych Zwingli. These two wings of the Reformation had very different characters, and generalizations about 'the Reformation' tend to confuse them. As we emphasized earlier, the Wittenberg and Swiss reformations – which ultimately led to the establishment of the Lutheran and Reformed churches – were very different in character. Even though they appealed to much the same theological sources (scripture and the fathers) as the basis of their reforming programmes, they did so using very different methods and with correspondingly different results. One of the most striking differences between these wings of the Reformation concerns their very different relation to humanism. We shall consider them individually, before returning to some more general points.

Humanism and the Swiss Reformation

The origins of the Swiss Reformation may be traced back to the rise of humanist groups (usually known as 'sodalities') at the universities of Vienna and Basle in the early 1500s.[13] Swiss students, who in the fifteenth century had tended to study at universities noted for their links with scholastic theology, now demonstrated a marked preference for universities with strongly humanist associations. Switzerland was geographically close to Italy, and appears to have become a clearing-house for the northern European dissemination of the ideas of the Renaissance by the beginning of the sixteenth century. Many of the leading printing houses of Europe – for example, Froschauer in Zurich, and Froben and Cratander in Basle – were Swiss. At a time when Swiss national identity appeared to be threatened by the Franco-Italian war, many Swiss humanists appear to have been inspired by the vision of establishing the literary and cultural identity of Switzerland.

The overall impression gained of early sixteenth-century Swiss intellectual life is that of groups of intellectuals based in the Swiss university cities, beginning to develop the vision of *Christianismus renascens*. The turning point for this movement came when one member of a humanist sodality, Huldrych Zwingli, was called to Zurich as a preacher in January 1519. Exploiting his position, Zwingli initiated a programme of reform based on broadly humanist principles, especially the vision of the corporate renewal of church and society on the basis of scripture and the fathers.

Zwingli had earlier studied at the humanist universities of Vienna (1498–1502) and Basle (1502–6), and his early works reflect the particular concerns of Swiss humanism. Zwingli had met Erasmus, however, while the latter was at Basle in 1516, seeing his Greek New Testament through Froben's presses, and was deeply influenced by his ideas and methods. The following points illustrate Erasmus' influence upon Zwingli:

1 Religion is seen as something spiritual and internal; external matters (e.g., the precise ordering of church services, or the form of church government adopted) are of no fundamental importance.
2 Considerable emphasis is placed upon moral and ethical regeneration and reform. To many scholars, the early Swiss Reformation appears to be primarily a *moral* reformation, with emphasis upon the need to regenerate both individual and society.
3 The relevance of Jesus Christ to the Christian is primarily as a moral example. Erasmus developed the idea of Christian faith as an *imitatio Christi*, an 'imitation of Christ', and Zwingli follows him in this respect.
4 Certain of the early church fathers are singled out as being of particular importance. For both Erasmus and Zwingli, Jerome and Origen are to be particularly valued. Although Zwingli would later begin to recognize the importance of Augustine, this development dates from the 1520s: the *origins* of Zwingli's reforming programme seem to owe nothing to Augustine.
5 Reformation concerns primarily the life and morals of the church, rather than its doctrine. For most humanists, 'philosophy' was about the process of living, rather than a set of philosophical doctrines (see, for example, Erasmus' concept of the *philosophia Christi*, the 'philosophy of Christ', which is essentially a code of life). Initially, Zwingli does not seem to have regarded reformation of the church as extending to its doctrine – merely to its life. Thus Zwingli's initial reforming actions concerned the practices of the Zurich church – such as the way in which services were ordered, or the manner in which churches were decorated.
6 Reformation is viewed as a pedagogical or educational process. It is an essentially human process, based upon the insights contained in the New Testament and the early church fathers. It was only in the early 1520s that we find Zwingli breaking away from this idea, to embrace the idea of Reformation as a divine action over-ruling human weakness.

To summarize, then: the Swiss Reformation was dominated by humanism, which was the only intellectual force of any significance in the region at the time. Zwingli's early programme of reform is thoroughly humanist, drawing both on the characteristic insights of

Swiss humanism, and on those of Erasmus. The influence of humanism upon the Swiss Reformation was nothing less than decisive. This makes the contrast with the Reformation at Wittenberg, to which we now turn, all the more obvious.

Humanism and the Wittenberg Reformation

Although humanism was a fairly important intellectual force in Germany by the early 1500s, its impact upon Martin Luther appears to have been limited.[14] Luther was an academic theologian, whose world was dominated by the thought-patterns of scholastic theology. Through a careful reading of the writings of Augustine, Luther became convinced that the form of scholastic theology he was familiar with was wrong. It failed to do justice to the grace of God, and tended to suggest that the individual could earn his or her own salvation. His task now was to oppose this theology. Where Zwingli regarded the *morals* of the church as requiring reform, Luther saw that it was her theology which was in need of reform. Luther's reforming theology is thus set in an academic context (the University of Wittenberg), and aimed at an academic target (the theology of 'nominalism', or the *via moderna*, which we shall consider in more detail in the following chapter). Furthermore, Luther's controversy with scholastic theology concerned the doctrine of justification – a concern which finds no echo in the Swiss Reformation.

Equally, Luther's concern with *doctrine* as such finds no echo in either humanism or the early Swiss Reformation. As we noted above, humanism saw reformation as concerning the *life and morals* of the church – but not doctrine. Indeed, most humanists seem to have regarded an interest in doctrine as equivalent to an obsession with scholastic theology! With Luther, however, we find a determination to inquire into the teaching of the church, with a view to reforming it in the light of scripture. This interest in doctrine in general distinguishes Luther sharply from humanism in general, and the early Swiss Reformation in particular. It is, of course, true that the later Swiss Reformation – especially under the leadership of Bullinger and Calvin – would become much more concerned with matters of doctrine. But at this early stage, under Zwingli's leadership, doctrine was marginalized.

In order to combat scholasticism, Luther drew heavily upon scripture and the fathers, supremely Augustine. In doing so, of course, he used the new editions of the Greek New Testament and the writings of Augustine which had been prepared by humanist editors. Luther regarded it as nothing less than providential that these new sources were available to support his programme of reform. There is, however, no real evidence that Luther had any interest in humanism as such – he simply exploited its products for his own ends. Both Luther and the humanists were strongly opposed to scholasticism (although for different reasons, as we shall see below) – and many humanists seem to have thought that Luther's strongly antischolastic attitude at the Leipzig Disputation (1519) demonstrated that he was one of their number. The Leipzig Disputation might have remained an obscure academic debate, had not humanists taken up Luther's cause with enthusiasm.

The overall impression which emerges of the relation between the Wittenberg Reformation and humanism is that Luther exploited the resources of humanism for his own ends. The origins of Luther's reforming theology owe nothing to humanism, except indirectly through its providing him with the tools he needed to carry out his programme of reform. His knowledge of Hebrew; his editions of Augustine; his Greek text of the New Testament – all were provided by humanist editors and educationalists. In many ways, the theological programme developed by Luther and Karlstadt at Wittenberg, which can be summed up in the slogan 'back to the Bible and Augustine!', could be seen as humanist. Yet the superficial similarities between the two programmes mask profound differences. Luther and his colleagues used only the textual and philological skills of humanism, while remaining hostile to humanist attitudes. In the final section of this chapter, we shall develop this point further.

Tensions between Reformation and Humanism

It will be obvious that humanism had a decisive contribution to make to the Reformation. Humanist and Reformer alike rejected scholastic theology, in favour of a more simple theology based upon scripture and the fathers. We have already seen how humanism made decisive contributions to the development of the Reformation, through making available reliable editions of the New Testament and the fathers. Yet tensions remained between humanism and both wings of the Reformation. Five areas may be singled out for comment.

1   *Their attitude to scholastic theology*. The humanists, the Swiss Reformers and the Wittenberg Reformers had no hesitation in rejecting scholasticism. In this respect, there is a strong degree of affinity between the three movements. The humanists, however, rejected scholasticism because of its unintelligibility and inelegance of expression: a simpler and more eloquent theology was required. Similar attitudes are evident within the Swiss Reformation, indicating strong affinity with humanism at this point. The Wittenberg Reformers however (especially Luther and Karlstadt), had no difficulty in understanding scholastic theology: their rejection of scholasticism was based on their conviction that its theology was fundamentally wrong. Where the humanists and Zwingli dismissed scholasticism as an irrelevance, the Wittenberg Reformers regarded it as the most important obstacle in the path of a reforming theology.

2   *Their attitude to scripture*. All three groups held that scripture held the key to reform of the church, in that it bore witness to Christian belief and practice in its original form. For the humanists, the authority of scripture rested in its eloquence, simplicity and antiquity. The Swiss and Wittenberg Reformers, however, grounded the authority of scripture in the concept of the 'word of God'. Scripture was seen as embodying the commands and promises of God, thus giving it a status over and above any purely human document. The phrase *sola scriptura*, 'by scripture alone', expresses the basic Reformation belief that no source other than scripture need be consulted in matters of Christian faith and practice. A further tension exists between the Swiss and Wittenberg Reformers: the former regarded scripture primarily as a source of moral guidance, whereas the latter regarded it primarily as a record of God's gracious promises of salvation to those who believed.

3   *Their attitudes to the fathers*. For the humanists the writers of the patristic period represented a simple and comprehensible form of Christianity, lent authority by their antiquity and eloquence. In general, humanists appear to have regarded the fathers as being of more or less equal value, in that all dated from roughly the same period of antiquity. Erasmus, however, regarded certain fathers as being of particular importance: in the early 1500s, he singled out Origen (a Greek father from the third century, noted as much for the unorthodoxy as for the elegance of his writings) for special mention, while by 1515 he had decided to opt for Jerome. His new preference for Jerome is to be explained on

the basis of Erasmus' textual studies in the New Testament, leading to the publication of the Greek edition of the New Testament in 1516. Jerome had earlier undertaken extensive work on the scriptural texts, and Erasmus appears to have regarded Jerome with new interest for this reason. This Erasmian attitude towards the fathers is also evident within the Swiss Reformation.

The Wittenberg Reformers Luther and Karlstadt, however, regarded Augustine as pre-eminent among the fathers. The humanists employed two criteria in evaluating the fathers: antiquity and eloquence. Thus Erasmus' preference for both Origen and Jerome is justified by the elegance of their writings, in addition to their antiquity, in common with the other patristic writings. The Wittenberg Reformers, however, used an explicitly *theological* criterion in evaluating the fathers: how reliable were they as interpreters of the New Testament? On the basis of this criterion, Augustine was to be preferred, and Origen to be treated with some suspicion. The humanists were not prepared to use such an explicitly theological criterion in evaluating the relative merits of the fathers, thus heightening the tension between these two movements.

4 *Their attitudes to education.* In that the Reformation witnessed the birth of a series of new religious ideas (or, at least, ideas which were new to most people in the sixteenth century), it was essential to both the Wittenberg and Swiss reformations that a major programme of religious education be undertaken. Humanism was essentially an educational and cultural movement based upon reform of the liberal arts, with the result that most early sixteenth-century humanists were professional educators. It is therefore interesting to note that most northern European humanists joined the cause of the Reformation, not necessarily because they approved of its *religious* ideas, but because they were attracted strongly by its *educational* ideals. The tension is obvious: the Reformers were concerned with the religious ideas being taught, viewing the educational methods as the means to that end – whereas the professional humanist educators were primarily concerned with the development of educational techniques, rather than the ideas being taught.

5 *Their attitude to rhetoric.* As we have seen, humanism was concerned with eloquence, both written and spoken. Rhetoric was thus studied as a means to this end. The Reformers, in both Germany and Switzerland, were concerned with the promotion of their religious ideas through

the written word (e.g., as in Calvin's famous *Institutes of the Christian Religion*) and the spoken word in sermons (Luther and Calvin both being, by all accounts, superb preachers). Rhetoric was therefore the means to the end of the propagation of the ideas of the Reformation. Recent studies, for example, have emphasized how Calvin's style is heavily influenced by rhetoric. Both humanist and Reformer, therefore, regarded rhetoric highly – but for different reasons. For the humanists, rhetoric promoted eloquence; for the Reformers, it promoted the Reformation. Once more, we encounter superficial similarities between the two groups, which mask profound differences.

On the basis of our discussion so far, it will be clear that the Swiss wing of the Reformation was influenced to a far greater extent by humanism than its counterpart at Wittenberg. Even at Wittenberg, however, the new programme of study of the Bible and Augustine appeared to many to be thoroughly humanist in inspiration. With the benefit of hindsight, it is very easy for us to distinguish Luther and Karlstadt from the humanists – yet *at the time*, this distinction was virtually impossible to make. To most observers, Luther and Erasmus were engaged in precisely the same struggle. We have one very famous illustration of this misunderstanding of Luther by humanists. In 1518 Luther delivered the famous Heidelberg Disputation, in which he developed a radically antihumanist and antischolastic theology. One of his audience was the young humanist Martin Bucer, later to become a leading Reformer in the city of Strasbourg. Bucer wrote with enthusiasm to his humanist correspondent Beatus Rhenanus, declaring that Luther merely stated Erasmus' views, but did so more forcefully. As a close examination of that letter indicates, Bucer seems to have misunderstood Luther on virtually every point!

The full extent of the tension between humanism and the Reformation only became fully apparent in 1525. In this year, both Zwingli and Luther composed attacks on Erasmus, both concentrating their attention on the concept of the 'freedom of the will'. For both Reformers, Erasmus' teaching of the total freedom of the human will led to a grossly overoptimistic conception of human nature. With the publication of Zwingli's *Commentary on True and False Religion* and Luther's *On the Bondage of the Will*, the tensions that had always been in existence between humanism and the Reformation were made obvious to all.

For further reading

Paul O. Kristeller, *Renaissance Thought and Its Sources* (New York, 1979).

——, 'The European Diffusion of Italian Humanism', in *Renaissance Thought II: Humanism and the Arts* (New York, 1965), pp. 69–88.

Alister E. McGrath, *The Intellectual Origins of the European Reformation* (Oxford, 1987), pp. 32–68.

James D. Tracey, 'Humanism and the Reformation', in *Reformation Europe: A Guide to Research*, ed. Steven E. Ozment (St Louis, 1982), pp. 33–57.

On northern European humanism, see:

Albert Hyma, *The Brethren of the Common Life* (Grand Rapids, 1950).

R. R. Post, *The Modern Devotion: Confrontation with Reformation and Humanism* (Leiden, 1968).

Lewis W. Spitz, *The Religious Renaissance of the German Humanists* (Cambridge, Mass., 1963).

On Erasmus, see:

Roland H. Bainton, *Erasmus of Christendom* (New York, 1969).

Margaret M. Philipps, *Erasmus and the Northern Renaissance* (London, 1949).

James D. Tracy, *The Politics of Erasmus: A Pacifist Intellectual and His Political Milieu* (Toronto, 1978).

On the educational methods of the Reformers, see:

Gerald Strauss, *Luther's House of Learning: Indoctrination of the Young in the German Reformation* (Baltimore, 1978).

4

Scholasticism and the Reformation

Scholasticism is probably one of the most despised intellectual movements in human history. Thus the English word 'dunce' (fool) derives from the name of one of the greatest scholastic writers, Duns Scotus. Scholastic thinkers – the 'schoolmen' – are often represented as debating earnestly, if pointlessly, over how many angels could dance on the head of a pin. Although this particular debate never actually took place, intriguing though its outcome would unquestionably have been, it summarizes precisely the way in which scholasticism was regarded by most people, especially the humanists, at the beginning of the sixteenth century: it was pointless, arid intellectual speculation over trivia. Erasmus, who had the misfortune to spend a few semesters towards the end of the fifteenth century at the scholasticism-dominated University of Paris, wrote of the learned debates which vexed the schoolmen: could God have become a cucumber instead of a man?

Most textbooks dealing with the Reformation therefore feel justified in dismissing scholasticism, without actually explaining what it is, and why it is of fundamental importance to the Wittenberg Reformation. This chapter explains exactly what scholasticism was, and why it is of such importance as background to the Reformation. We begin by attempting to give a definition of the word 'scholasticism'.

'Scholasticism' Defined

Scholasticism is best regarded as the medieval movement, flourishing in the period 1250–1500, which placed great emphasis upon the rational justification of religious belief. When the Dark Ages finally lifted from over western Europe, the scene was set for revival in every field of academic work. The restoration of some degree of political stability in France in the late eleventh century encouraged the re-emergence of the University of Paris, which rapidly became recognized as the intellectual centre of Europe. A number of theological 'schools' were established on the Left Bank of the Seine, and on the Île de la Cité, in the shadow of the newly-built cathedral of Notre Dame de Paris. Two themes began to dominate theological debate: the need to *systematize* and *expand* Christian theology; and the need to *demonstrate the inherent reasonableness* of that theology. Although most early medieval theology was little more than a replay of the views of St Augustine, there was growing pressure to systematize Augustine's ideas, and take them further. But how could this be done? A 'theory of method' was urgently needed. And on the basis of what philosophical system could the rationality of Christian theology be demonstrated?

The answer to these problems came through the rediscovery of Aristotle, in the late twelfth and early thirteenth centuries.[1] By about 1270, Aristotle had become established as 'the Philosopher'. His ideas came to dominate theological thinking, despite fierce opposition from more conservative quarters. Through the influence of writers such as Thomas Aquinas and Duns Scotus, Aristotle's ideas became established as the best means of establishing and developing Christian theology. The ideas of Christian theology were thus arranged and correlated systematically, on the basis of Aristotelian presuppositions. Equally, the rationality of Christian faith was demonstrated on the basis of Aristotelian ideas. Thus some of Thomas Aquinas' famous 'proofs' for the existence of God actually rely on principles of Aristotelian physics, rather than Christian theology![2]

This, then, is the essence of scholasticism: the demonstration of the inherent rationality of Christian theology by an appeal to philosophy, and the demonstration of the complete harmony of that theology by the minute examination of the relationship of its various elements. Scholastic writings tended to be long and argumentative, frequently relying upon closely-argued distinctions. Thus Duns Scotus, generally known as the 'subtle doctor', is obliged to distinguish as many as fifteen senses of the Latin word *ratio*, 'reason' in order to justify his views on its role in theology.

The noted medieval historian Etienne Gilson has aptly described the great scholastic systems as 'cathedrals of the mind'. Each scholastic system tried to embrace reality in its totality, dealing with matters of logic, metaphysics and theology. Everything was shown to have its logical place in a totally comprehensive intellectual system. In what follows, we shall look briefly at the main types of scholasticism encountered in the Middle Ages.

Scholasticism and the Universities

For obvious reasons, the influence of scholasticism was at its greatest in the medieval universities. Unlike *Quattrocento* humanism, which both flourished in the universities and enjoyed enormous influence in society, scholasticism had a very limited sphere of influence. Humanism made its appeal to the world of education, art and culture, where scholasticism could at best make a limited appeal (in bad Latin) to those who enjoyed dialectics. In an age in which rhetoric and dialectic were seen as mutually incompatible, the superior appeal of the former virtually guaranteed the decline of the latter. In the late fifteenth century, a confrontation between humanism and scholasticism developed in many universities.[3] The University of Vienna, of fundamental importance to the development of the Swiss Reformation, witnessed precisely such a humanist revolt against scholasticism in the final decade of the fifteenth century. In the early sixteenth century, many students seem to have begun avoiding universities traditionally dominated by scholasticism, in favour of those with humanist educational programmes. Thus the influence of scholasticism was gradually being eroded even in its academic strongholds as the sixteenth century dawned.

Although on the wane as an academic force, however, the fact remains that Martin Luther's theological development took place in reaction against scholastic theology. Whereas scholasticism was a negligible intellectual force in Switzerland, it was still of major importance in Germany, particularly at the University of Erfurt, at which Luther was educated. Luther's early work as a theological reformer was carried out in a university context, fighting against an academic opponent. In marked contrast the Swiss Reformers were, as we have seen, humanists, bent on reforming the life and morals of the church of their day, who had no need to pay any attention to scholasticism – whereas Luther was forced to enter into dialogue with the major force on his intellectual horizon, scholasticism. The Swiss Reformers could afford to ridicule scholasticism, for it posed no threat to them – but Luther had to engage with it directly.

This serves to emphasize the differences between the Swiss and Wittenberg reformations, whose totally different contexts are too often overlooked. Zwingli began by reforming a city (Zurich); Luther began by reforming a university faculty of theology (Wittenberg). Zwingli began by opposing the life and morals of the pre-Reformation Zurich church; Luther began by opposing a particular form of scholastic theology. Initially Zwingli had no need to propose a reformation of the doctrine of the church, whereas for Luther, a doctrinal reformation was the essential platform of his programme of reform. In a later chapter, we shall consider Luther's reaction against scholastic theology. Our attention now turns to the types of scholasticism encountered in the later Middle Ages.

Types of Scholasticism

The reader must accept an apology before proceeding any further. It has proved impossible to simplify any further the material which follows. The sense of utter tedium which will probably grip the reader as he proceeds goes some considerable way towards explaining why humanism proved so attractive at the time of the Reformation. To understand Luther's theological development, however, it is necessary to try to grasp at least the basics of two major movements in late medieval scholasticism.

Realism versus Nominalism

In order to understand the complexities of medieval scholasticism, it is unfortunately necessary to understand the distinction between 'realism' and 'nominalism'. The early part of the scholastic period (c.1200–c.1350) was dominated by realism, whereas the later part (c.1350–c.1500) was dominated by nominalism. The difference between the two systems may be summarized as follows.[4] Consider two white stones. Realism affirms that there is a universal concept of 'whiteness' which these two stones embody. These particular white stones possess the universal characteristic of 'whiteness'. While the white stones exist in time and space, the universal of 'whiteness' does not. Nominalism, however, asserts that the universal concept of 'whiteness' is unnecessary, and instead argues that we should concentrate on particulars. There are these two white stones – and there is no need to start talking about 'a universal concept of whiteness'.

This debate may strike many readers as typical of scholasticism: pointless and pedantic. Nevertheless, it is important for the reader to appreciate that the term 'nominalism' refers to a debate concerning universals. *It has no direct theological relevance, and defines no specific theological opinion.* We shall return to this point shortly.

Two major scholastic 'schools' influenced by realism dominate the earlier medieval period. These are *Thomism* and *Scotism*, derived from the writings of Thomas Aquinas and Duns Scotus respectively. Neither of these schools had any major influence upon the Reformation, and need not, therefore, be discussed any further.[5] Two later forms of scholasticism, however, appear to have had a major influence upon the Reformation, and thus merit careful attention. These are the *via moderna* and *schola Augustiniana moderna*.

Many textbooks dealing with the Reformation refer to a confrontation between 'Nominalism' and 'Augustinianism' on the eve of the Reformation, and interpret the Reformation as the victory of the latter over the former. In recent years, however, considerable progress has been made in understanding the nature of late medieval scholasticism, leading to a rewriting of the intellectual history of the early Reformation. In what follows, we shall indicate the situation as established by most recent scholarship.

An earlier generation of scholars, writing in the period 1920–65, regarded 'nominalism' as a religious school of thought which captured most northern European university faculties of theology in the later Middle Ages. It proved remarkably difficult, however, to identify the exact features of this theology. Some 'nominalist' theologians (such as William of Ockham and Gabriel Biel) seemed to be very optimistic about human abilities, suggesting that it was possible for a human being to do everything that was necessary to enter into a relationship with God. Other 'nominalist' theologians (such as Gregory of Rimini and Hugolino of Orvieto) appeared to be profoundly pessimistic about those same abilities, suggesting that without the grace of God, humanity was totally unable to enter into such a relationship. In desperation, scholars began to speak of 'nominalistic diversity'. Eventually, however, the real solution to the problem emerged: there were actually *two* different schools of thought, whose sole common feature was antirealism. Both schools adopted a nominalist position in matters of logic and the theory of knowledge – but their theological positions differed radically. Earlier, we noted that the term 'nominalism' strictly referred to the question of universals, and did not designate any particular theological position. In other words, both schools rejected the necessity of universals – but thereafter could agree on virtually nothing. One was profoundly optimistic concerning human abilities, the other considerably more pessimistic. These two schools are now generally known as the *via moderna*, 'the modern way', and the *schola Augustiniana moderna*, 'the modern Augustinian school'. We shall consider these two schools presently. Our attention is first claimed by the terms 'Pelagian' and 'Augustinian', which are invariably encountered in any discussion of late medieval scholasticism. In what follows, we shall explain what is meant by these terms.

'Pelagianism' and 'Augustinianism'

The doctrine of justification, which assumed particular importance within the Lutheran Reformation, concerns the question of how an individual enters into a relationship with God. How can a sinner be accepted by a righteous God? What must the individual do, in order to be acceptable to God? This question was debated with some intensity in the early fifth century during the controversy between Augustine and Pelagius. This controversy is known as the 'Pelagian controversy', and Augustine's writings concerning the doctrines of grace and justification which arose out of this controversy are known as the 'antiPelagian writings'.[6] In many ways, this controversy was replayed in the fourteenth and fifteenth centuries, with the *via moderna* tending towards the position of Pelagius, and the *schola Augustiniana moderna* towards that of Augustine. In what follows, we shall give a brief outline of each position.

For Augustine, humanity was trapped in its situation, and could not redeem itself. Left to its own devices and resources, it was impossible for humanity ever to enter into a relationship with God. Nothing that a man or woman could do was sufficient to break the stranglehold of of sin. To use an image which Augustine was fortunate enough never to have encountered, it is like a narcotic addict trying to break free from the grip of heroin or cocaine. The situation cannot be transformed from within – and so, if transformation is to take place, it must come from outside the human situation. According to Augustine, God intervenes in the human dilemma. He need not have done so, but out of his love for fallen humanity, he enters into the human situation in the person of Jesus Christ in order to redeem it.

Augustine lays such emphasis upon 'grace' that he is often designated *doctor gratiae*, 'the doctor of grace'. 'Grace' is the unmerited or undeserved gift of God, by which God voluntarily breaks the hold of sin upon humanity. Redemption is possible only as a divine gift. It is not something which we can achieve ourselves, but is something which has to be done for us. Augustine thus emphasizes that the resources of salvation are located outside of humanity, in God himself. It is God who initiates the process of salvation, not men or women.

For Pelagius, however, the situation looked very different. Pelagius taught that the resources of salvation are located within humanity. Individual human beings have the capacity to save themselves. They are not trapped by sin, but have the ability to do all that is necessary to be saved. Salvation is something which is earned through good works, which place God under an obligation to humanity. Pelagius marginalizes the idea of grace, understanding it in terms of demands made of humanity in order that salvation may be achieved – such as the Ten Commandments. The ethos of Pelagianism could be summed up as 'salvation by merit', whereas Augustine taught 'salvation by grace'.

It will be obvious that the two different theologies have very different understandings of human nature. For Augustine, human nature is weak, fallen and impotent; for Pelagius, it is autonomous and self-sufficient. For Augustine, it is necessary to depend upon God for salvation; for Pelagius, God merely indicates what has to be done if salvation is to be attained, and then leaves men and women to meet the conditions unaided. For Augustine, salvation is an unmerited gift; for Pelagius, salvation is a justly-earned reward.

One aspect of Augustine's understanding of grace needs further comment. As human beings were incapable of saving themselves, and as God gave his gift of grace to some (but not all), it followed that God had 'preselected' those who would be saved. Developing hints of this idea to be found in the New Testament, Augustine developed a doctrine of predestination. The term 'predestination' refers to God's original or eternal decision to save some, and not others. It was this aspect of Augustine's thought which many of his contemporaries, not to mention his successors, found unacceptable. It need hardly be said that there is no equivalent in Pelagius' thought.[7]

In the ensuing controversy within the western church, Augustine's position was recognized as authentically Christian, and Pelagius' views were censured as heretical. Two important councils established Augustine's views as normative: the Council of Carthage (418), and the Second Council of Orange (529). Interestingly, Augustine's views on predestination were diluted somewhat, even though the remainder of his system was enthusiastically endorsed. The term 'Pelagian' hence came to be pejorative as well as descriptive, meaning 'placing excessive reliance upon human abilities, and insufficient trust in the grace of God'. At the time of the Reformation, Luther was convinced that most of the western church had lost sight of the idea of the 'grace of God', and had come to rely upon human self-sufficiency. He therefore regarded it as his duty to recall the church to the views of Augustine, as we shall see in chapter 5.

We must now consider the fourteenth- and fifteenth-century replay of this controversy between the *via moderna* and *schola Augustiniana oderna*, the former assuming broadly the role of Pelagius and the latter that of Augustine.

Via Moderna, *alias 'Nominalism'*

The term *via moderna* is now becoming generally accepted as the best way of referring to the movement once known as 'nominalism', including among its adherents such fourteenth- and fifteenth-century thinkers as William of Ockham, Pierre d'Ailly, Robert Holcot and Gabriel Biel. During the fifteenth century, the *via moderna* began to make significant inroads into many northern European universities – for example, at Paris, Heidelberg and Erfurt. In addition to its philosophical nominalism, the movement adopted a doctrine of justification which many of its critics branded as 'Pelagian'. In view of the importance of this form of scholasticism to Luther's theological breakthrough, we shall explain its understanding of justification in some detail.[8]

The central feature of the soteriology, or doctrine of salvation, of the *via moderna* is a covenant between God and humanity. The later Middle Ages saw the development of political and economic theories which were based upon the concept of a covenant (for example, between a king and his people), and the theologians of the *via moderna* were quick to realize the theological potential of this idea. A *political* covenant between a king and his people defined the obligations of king to people, and people to king; a *religious* covenant between God and his people defined God's obligations to his people, and their obligation to God.[9] This covenant was not negotiated, of course, but was unilaterally imposed by God. As the concept of a 'covenant' between God and humanity was an important theme in the Old Testament, the theologians of the *via moderna* were able to develop this theme using ideas borrowed from their own political and economic world.

According to the theologians of the *via moderna*, the covenant between God and man laid down the conditions necessary for justification. God has ordained that he will justify an individual, on condition that this individual first fulfils certain demands. These demands were summarized using the Latin tag *facere quod in se est*, literally 'doing what lies within you', or 'doing your best'. When the individual met this precondition, God was obliged, by the terms of the covenant, to justify him. A Latin maxim was often used to express this point: *facienti quod in se est Deus non denegat gratiam*, 'God will not deny his grace to whoever does what lies within him'. The noted late medieval theologian Gabriel Biel, who is known to have influenced Luther through his writings, explained that 'doing your best' meant rejecting evil and trying to do good.

At this point, the parallels between the *via moderna* and Pelagius become obvious. Both assert that men and women are justified through their own efforts. Justification is by good works, and not by grace. Both assert that human works place God under an obligation to reward them. It would seem that the *via moderna* is simply reproducing the ideas of Pelagius, using a more sophisticated covenantal framework. At this point, however, the theologians of the *via moderna* drew upon contemporary economic theory to argue that they were doing nothing of the sort. Their use of late medieval economic theory is fascinating, in that it illustrates the extent to which medieval theologians were prepared to exploit ideas drawn from their social context. We shall consider their argument in some detail.

The classic example invariably cited by these theologians to illustrate the relation between good works and justification is the king and the small lead coin.[10] Most medieval coinage systems used gold and silver coins. This had the advantage of guaranteeing the value of the coins, even if it also encouraged the practice of 'clipping' precious metal from the coin's sides. The introduction of milled edges to coins represented an attempt to prevent removal of gold or silver in this way. Occasionally, however, kings found themselves in a financial crisis, through war for example. A standard way of meeting this was to recall gold and silver coins, and melt them down. The gold and silver thus retrieved could be used to finance a war.

In the meantime, however, currency of some sort was still required. To meet this need, small leaden coins were issued, which bore the same face value as the gold and silver coins. Although their *inherent* value was negligible, their *ascribed* or *imposed* value was considerable. The king would promise to replace the lead coins with their gold or silver equivalents once the financial crisis was past. The value of the lead coins thus resided in the king's promise to redeem them at their full ascribed value at a later date. The value of a gold coin derives from the gold – but the value of a lead coin derives from the royal covenant to treat that coin *as if it were gold*. A similar situation, of course, exists in most modern economies. For example, paper money is of negligible inherent value. Its value derives from the promise of the issuing back to honour bank notes to their full face value.

The theologians of the *via moderna* used this economic analogy to counter the charge of Pelagianism. To the suggestion that they were exaggerating the value of human works (in that they seemed to be making them capable of meriting salvation), they replied that they were doing nothing of the sort. Human works were like lead coins, they argued – of little inherent value. But God had ordained, through the covenant, to treat them as if they were of much greater value, in just the same way as a king could treat a lead coin as if it were gold. Pelagius, they argued, certainly treated human works as if they were gold, capable of purchasing salvation. But they were arguing that human works were like lead: the only reason they were of any value was that God had graciously undertaken to treat them as if they were much more valuable. The theological exploitation of the difference between the inherent and imposed value of coins thus served to get the theologians of the

via moderna out of a potentially awkward situation, even it if would
not satisfy their more severe critics, such as Martin Luther.

It is this 'covenantal' understanding of justification which underlies
Martin Luther's theological breakthrough, to which we shall return
in the following chapter. Our attention now turns to the late medieval
scholastic theology which re-embraced the ideas of Augustine, in
deliberate opposition to the *via moderna*.

Schola Augustiniana Moderna, *alias 'Augustinianism'*

One of the strongholds of the *via moderna* in the early fourteenth century
was the University of Oxford.[11] A group of thinkers, largely based
upon Merton College, developed the ideas on justification noted above,
characteristic of the *via moderna*. And it was at Oxford that the first
backlash against the *via moderna* occurred.[12] The individual responsible
for this backlash was Thomas Bradwardine, later to become Archbishop
of Canterbury. Bradwardine wrote a furious attack on the ideas of the
Oxford *via moderna*, entitled *De causa Dei contra Pelagium*, 'The case
of God against Pelagius'. In this book, he charged his Merton colleagues
with being 'modern Pelagians', and developed a theory of justification
which represents a return to the views of Augustine, as they are found
in the antiPelagian writings.

Important though Oxford was as a theological centre, the Hundred
Years War led to it becoming increasingly isolated from the continent
of Europe. Although Bradwardine's ideas would be developed in England
by John Wycliffe, they were taken up by Gregory of Rimini at the
University of Paris. Gregory had one particularly significant advantage
over Bradwardine: he was a member of a religious order (the Order
of the Hermits of St Augustine, generally referred to as the 'Augustinian Order'). And just as the Dominicans propagated the views of
Thomas Aquinas and the Franciscans those of Duns Scotus, so the
Augustinians would promote the ideas of Gregory of Rimini. It is this
transmission of an Augustinian tradition, deriving from Gregory of
Rimini, within the Augustinian Order which is increasingly referred
to as the *schola Augustiniana moderna*, 'the modern Augustinian school'.
What were these views?

First, Gregory adopted a nominalist view on the question of universals.
Like many thinkers of his time, he had little time for the realism of

Thomas Aquinas or Duns Scotus. In this respect, he has much in common with thinkers of the *via moderna*, such as Robert Holcot or Gabriel Biel. Second, Gregory developed a soteriology, or doctrine of salvation, which reflects the influence of Augustine. We find an emphasis upon the need for grace, upon the fallenness and sinfulness of humanity, upon the divine initiative in justification, and upon divine predestination. Salvation is understood to be *totally* a work of God, from its beginning to its end. Where the *via moderna* held that humans could initiate their justification by 'doing their best', Gregory insisted that only God could initiate justification. Where the *via moderna* held that all necessary soteriological resources were located *within* human nature, Gregory of Rimini argued that these resources were located exclusively *outside* human nature. It is obvious that these are two totally different ways of understanding the human and divine roles in justification.

It is this academic Augustinianism which appears to have been propagated at a number of centres throughout Europe. Although the movement was particularly associated with the Augustinian Order, not every Augustinian monastery or university school seems to have adopted its ideas. Nevertheless, it seems that a school of thought which was strongly Augustinian in cast was in existence in the late Middle Ages on the eve of the Reformation. In many ways, the Wittenberg Reformers, with their particular emphasis upon the antiPelagian writings of Augustine, may be regarded as the heirs of this tradition. As the views of the Reformers parallel those of this academic Augustinianism, the question has often been asked: were the Reformers influenced, directly or indirectly, by this Augustinian tradition? Two important hypotheses relating to this question have been put forward in recent decades: Heiko A. Oberman's hypothesis concerning Luther, and Karl Reuter's hypothesis concerning Calvin. We shall consider these in the following section.

Medieval Scholasticism and the Reformation: Two Hypotheses

It is beyond doubt that the two leading lights of the Reformation are Martin Luther and John Calvin. In what follows, we shall consider two major scholarly hypotheses suggesting that both these thinkers were decisively influenced by medieval scholasticism.

Oberman's Hypothesis:
Augustinianism and the Young Luther

In the fall of 1508 Martin Luther went to teach philosophical ethics at the newly-founded University of Wittenberg. Earlier that year important changes had been introduced in the university statutes, especially those relating to the faculty of arts. Up to that point, members of that faculty were permitted to teach only according to the *via Thomae* and *via Scoti* – in other words, Thomist and Scotist ideas were allowed, but not those of the *via moderna*. According to the new statutes, they were now also permitted to teach according to the *via Gregorii*. But what is this hitherto unknown *via*? Earlier scholars had regarded it as simply another way of referring to the *via moderna*, thus bringing Wittenberg into line with other German universities of the period. But in an important essay published in 1974, Heiko A. Oberman argued that a very different interpretation was to be placed upon the phrase.[13]

According to Oberman, the *via Gregorii* referred to the *schola Augustiniana moderna*, deriving from Gregory of Rimini (the 'Gregorius' of the *via Gregorii*). Noting a number of ways in which the ideas of this school could have been transmitted to the young Luther, Oberman concludes:

> Taking stock of this cumulative, admittedly circumstantial evidence, we can point to the *schola Augustiniana moderna*, initiated by Gregory of Rimini, reflected by Hugolin of Orvieto, apparently spiritually alive in the Erfurt Augustinian monastery, and transformed into a pastoral reform theology by Staupitz, as the *occasio proxima* – not *causa*! – for the inception of the *theologia vera* at Wittenberg.[14]

If Oberman is right, Luther and his 'true theology' stand at the end of a long medieval Augustinian tradition, suggesting that the Lutheran Reformation may represent the triumph of this tradition in the sixteenth century.

Important though Oberman's suggestion unquestionably is, a number of serious difficulties lie in its path. The following may be noted briefly.[15]

1 Luther does not seem to have come across anything written by Gregory of Rimini until 1519 – yet Oberman's hypothesis requires that the Reformer should have encountered him by 1508.

2 Johannes von Staupitz, referred to by Oberman as a channel of transmission of this tradition, and who is known to have exercised some influence over Luther's development, cannot be regarded as a representative of the *schola Augustiniana moderna*.

3 Gregory of Rimini is specifically identified by the statutes of the University of Paris as a leading representative, along with William of Ockham, of the *via moderna*, suggesting that the *via Gregorii* is indeed nothing more than an alternative way of referring to the *via moderna*.

4 Luther's early theology (1509–14) shows no trace of the radical Augustinianism associated with Gregory of Rimini and the *schola Augustiniana moderna*. How can this be explained, if Luther was as familiar with this theology as Oberman suggests? The consensus among most recent studies appears to be that Oberman's hypothesis, although a valuable stimulus to research on Luther's relation to late medieval thought, is untenable.

Reuter's Hypothesis: Scholasticism and the Young Calvin

Calvin began his academic career at the University of Paris in the 1520s. In 1963 Karl Reuter published a work on Calvin's thought in which he developed a major hypothesis of Calvin research, which he further developed in 1981:[16] that Calvin was decisively influenced by the leading Scottish scholastic theologian John Major (or Mair), then teaching at Paris. Reuter argued that Major introduced Calvin to 'a new conception of antiPelagian and Scotist theology, and a renewed Augustinianism' at Paris. It was through the influence of Major, according to Reuter, that Calvin encountered the ideas of writers such as Augustine, Thomas Bradwardine and Gregory of Rimini.

Reuter's hypothesis was subjected to considerable criticism. Most criticism centred upon the circumstantial nature of the evidence Reuter offered. For example, there is no evidence that Calvin was taught by Major, whatever similarities there may be between their ideas. Equally, Calvin's earlier writings (for example, the 1536 edition of the *Institutes*) make no reference to Major. Nevertheless, it is evident that Calvin does show remarkable affinities with the ideas of the *schola Augustiniana moderna*, and it is possible that Calvin reflects the influence of this tradition, rather than that of one specific individual.[17] Even if Reuter's hypothesis as originally stated is untenable, it seems that there are excellent reasons for suggesting that Calvin may well reflect the influence of a late medieval Augustinian tradition, such as that associated with the *schola Augustiniana moderna*.

The Social Context of Scholasticism

In assessing the significance of any intellectual movement, it is essential to determine the sections of society in which its ideas were transmitted and developed. For example, we have already seen that humanism was primarily a cultural and educational movement, whose ideas achieved a wide circulation at the time of the Renaissance in the upper strata of Italian (and, to a lesser extent, northern European) society, in liberal arts faculties, and in educationalist circles. Humanist ideas are also known to have been adopted by many members of religious orders.[18] The impression gained is that of an intellectual movement whose ideas were received and transmitted across a number of important sociological boundaries.

In the case of scholasticism, however, we are faced with a very different situation. The main scholastic schools were specifically linked with religious orders. Thus the Dominicans tended to propagate Thomism and the Franciscans Scotism, although the ideas of the *via moderna* were well established within both orders by the fifteenth century. A scholastic would generally be a member of a religious order. The University of Padua represents a relatively rare instance of a scholasticism which is not specifically linked with a religious order. It will therefore be clear that the impact of scholasticism was severely limited in society. The social mobility of humanism is strikingly absent, in that scholasticism was widely seen in the early sixteenth century as the exclusive preserve of the religious orders, and restricted to certain universities. Equally, it will be obvious that scholasticism was subject to geographical restrictions: thus, for example, scholasticism was a significant intellectual force in early sixteenth-century Germany, but not Switzerland. Thus while it was virtually impossible for an educated person to avoid being influenced by humanism in the early sixteenth century, scholasticism was then an intellectual force on the wane, increasingly confined to certain strongholds in northern Europe.

Two points of relevance to the Reformation will be obvious. First, the background of the Reformers prior to the genesis of their reforming vocation is of major importance in determining the extent to which they are influenced by, or feel obliged to enter into argument with, scholasticism. Luther, it may be noted, is the only major Reformer whose origins point to such an encounter with scholasticism: he was a member of a religious order engaged in university teaching, whereas Zwingli was simply a parish priest. Similarly, Luther was German, and Zwingli Swiss. Second, the social mobility associated with humanist ideals enables us to understand how Luther's somewhat scholastic ideas of 1517–19 achieved such wide circulation. Luther's theology at this stage is still remarkably scholastic in form. However, as Berndt Moeller helpfully puts it, Luther's scholastic ideas were generally 'productively misunderstood' by the humanist sodalities as embodying *humanist* values, thus giving those ideas the mobility normally only associated with humanism. The main carrier of the ideals of the Reformation, whether in Germany or Switzerland, was the humanist movement: the essential difference between the two Reformations is that Zwingli's ideas *were* initially humanist, whereas Luther's *were misunderstood* as being humanist.

In the present chapter we have considered the phenomenon of medieval scholasticism, and indicated its potential relevance to the Reformation. In the following chapter, we shall explore how humanism and scholasticism converged in the theological breakthrough of Martin Luther.

For further reading

An excellent introduction to the phenomenon of 'scholasticism' is

Josef Pieper, *Scholasticism: Personalities and Problems of Medieval Philosophy* (London, 1960).

On the via moderna, *see:*

W. J. Courtenay, 'Nominalism and Late Medieval Religion', in *The Pursuit of Holiness in Late Medieval Religion*, ed. C. Trinkaus and H. A. Oberman (Leiden, 1974), pp. 26–59.

——, 'Late Medieval Nominalism Revisited: 1972–1982', *Journal of the History of Ideas* 44 (1983), pp. 159–64.

Alister E. McGrath, *The Intellectual Origins of the European Reformation* (Oxford, 1987), pp. 70–85.

On the schola Augustiniana moderna, *see:*

McGrath, *Intellectual Origins of the European Reformation*, pp. 86-93.

Heiko A. Oberman, *Masters of the Reformation: The Emergence of a New Intellectual Climate in Europe* (Cambridge, 1981), pp. 64–110.

David C. Steinmetz, *Luther and Staupitz: An Essay in the Intellectual Origins of the Protestant Reformation* (Durham, NC, 1980), pp. 13–27.

5

The Doctrine of Grace

The first major theme of Reformation thought to be considered is the doctrine of grace. As used by Christian theologians, the word 'grace' basically means 'the undeserved and unmerited divine favour towards humanity'. Within the New Testament, the idea of grace is especially associated with the writings of St Paul. Within the history of the Christian church, the writer who developed and defended the concept of the grace of God most powerfully was Augustine of Hippo. Indeed, such was his emphasis upon this concept that he became generally known as *doctor gratiae*, 'the doctor of grace'. As the late Renaissance and Reformation periods witnessed a renewal of interest in the writings of both Paul and Augustine, it is understandable that there should have been renewed interest in the concept of grace.

It is this concept which underlies the doctrine of justification by faith, which is generally and rightly regarded as underlying the origins of the Lutheran Reformation in Germany. A similar concern for the concept of grace underlies the Swiss Reformation, although this concern was expressed in a very different manner. Zwingli and Calvin laid considerable emphasis upon the related idea of divine sovereignty, particularly associated with the doctrine of predestination. We begin by considering Luther's discovery of the doctrine of justification by faith alone.

Martin Luther's Theological Breakthrough

Martin Luther is widely regarded as the most significant personality of the European Reformation. He looms large, not merely in the history of the Christian church, but in the intellectual, political and social history of Europe, and especially Germany. In many ways, he appears as a tragic figure, with magnificent strengths and serious flaws. His stand against the Emperor at the Diet of Worms demonstrates his considerable personal courage, even if it is unlikely he actually used the famous words attributed to him, 'Here I stand; I can no other.' Yet within a matter of years, his condemnation of the German peasants for revolting against their oppression seemed to many to indicate his political naivety.

Luther stepped on to the stage of human history on account of an idea. That idea convinced him that the church of his day had misunderstood the gospel, the essence of Christianity. It was necessary to recall it to fidelity, to reform initially its ideology, and subsequently its practices. This idea is summarized in the phrase 'justification by faith alone', and it is necessary to explain precisely what this idea is, and why it is of such importance. Luther's theological breakthrough, often referred to as the *Turmerlebnis* ('Tower Experience'), concerned the question of how it was possible for a sinner to enter into a relationship with a righteous God. In view of the enormous importance of this question to the development of the German Reformation, we propose to consider it in some detail.

The Doctrine of Justification

At the heart of the Christian faith lies the idea that human beings, finite and frail though they are, can enter into a relationship with the living God. This idea is articulated in a number of metaphors or images, both in the New Testament and in later Christian theology.[1] For example, the ideas of 'salvation' and 'redemption' both refer to this process. By the late Middle Ages, one image had come to be seen as especially significant: that of justification. The term 'justification' and the verb 'to justify' came to signify 'entering into a right relationship with God', or perhaps 'being made righteous in the sight of God'. The doctrine of justification came to be seen as dealing with the question of what an individual had to do in order to be saved. As contemporary sources indicate, this question came to be asked with increasing frequency as the sixteenth century dawned. We have already seen (p. 35) how the rise of humanism brought with it a new emphasis upon individual consciousness, and a new awareness of human individuality. In the wake of this dawn of the individual consciousness came a new interest in the doctrine of justification – the question of how human beings, *as individuals*, could enter into a relationship with God. A new interest developed in the writings of both Paul and Augustine, reflecting their concern with individual subjectivity.[2] This interest is particularly evident in the writings of Petrarch (1304–74), 'the first modern man'.

But what was the church's answer to the crucial question, 'What must I do to be saved?' Earlier, (pp. 21–3) we drew attention to the doctrinal confusion of the later Middle Ages. It seems that this confusion was perhaps at its greatest in relation to the doctrine of justification. A number of factors contributed to this confusion. First, there had been no authoritative pronouncement from the church on the matter for over a thousand years. In 418, the Council of Carthage discussed the question, and more detailed proposals were set forth by the Second Council of Orange in 529. But for reasons which defy explanation, this latter council and its decisions were unknown to the theologians of the Middle Ages! The council appears to have been 'rediscovered' in 1546 – by which time the Reformation had been under way for a generation. Second, the doctrine of justification appears to have been a favourite topic of debate among later medieval theologians, with the result that a disproportionately large number of opinions on the question passed into circulation. But which of these opinions were *right*? The reluctance or inability of the church to evaluate these opinions ensured that an already difficult question became even further confused.

The practical result of this confusion can be illustrated from events in northern Italy in the year 1510. For some time, a group of young aristocratic humanists, all educated at the University of Padua, had been meeting to discuss how they might ensure their personal salvation. What were they to do? Unable to find any convincing answers amidst the theological incoherence of the period, the group split into two parts: those who entered a local monastery, convinced that this was their only hope of salvation; and those who felt that salvation could be had in the everyday world. Before Luther began to agonize over much the same question, others in Italy and Spain had also found themselves bewildered by it. The central question forced upon the church by the rise of humanism – what must I, *as an individual*, do to be saved? – could not be answered with any degree of confidence. Humanism forced a question upon a church which, as events would demonstrate, was unable to answer it. The scene was set for a tragedy, and Luther happened to wander on to the stage as its chief actor.

Luther's Early Views on Justification

Luther was educated at the University of Erfurt (1501–5), then dominated by the *via moderna*. After an unfortunate incident during a thunderstorm, bearing certain curious parallels to Moses' experience at the Burning Bush, Luther entered the local Augustinian monastery, where he undertook the study of theology under the influence of teachers committed to the *via moderna*. In 1508, he was invited to lecture for a year on moral philosophy at the newly-founded University of Wittenberg, which tended to draw upon the Augustinian Order for many of its teachers. Oberman's suggestion (see pp. 62–3) that the *schola Augustiniana moderna* was established at Wittenberg by this time is to be rejected. After a period in which he performed various functions for his Order, Luther was appointed to the chair of biblical studies at Wittenberg in 1511. In accordance with his job specification, he lectured on various books of the Bible: the Psalms (1513–15), Romans (1515–16), Galatians (1516–17) and Hebrews (1517–18), before he returned to lecture on the Psalms for a second time (1519–21). We possess the text of Luther's lectures (in various forms) in every case, allowing us to follow the development of his ideas over the period leading up to the Ninety-Five Theses (1517) and the famous Leipzig Disputation (1519).

Our interest especially concerns the first course of lectures on the Psalms, universally known as the *Dictata super Psalterium*. For two or three hours every week over a period of two years, Luther explained the meaning of each Psalm, as he understood it, to an audience who, by all accounts, were entranced by his style. Luther frequently discusses the doctrine of justification in the course of these lectures, allowing us to determine precisely what his early views on this matter were. It turns out that Luther is initially a remarkably faithful follower of the views of the *via moderna* (see pp. 57–60).[3] God has established a covenant (*pactum*) with humanity, by which he is obliged to justify anyone who meets a certain minimum precondition (*quod in se est*). In effect, Luther teaches that God gives his grace to the humble, so that whoever humbles himself before God can expect to be justified as a matter of course. The sinner humbles himself before God, and thus obliges God to reward him with justification. Two quotations will illustrate this principle:

It is for this reason that we are saved: God has made a testament and a covenant with us, so that whoever believes and is baptized will be saved. In this covenant God is truthful and faithful, and is bound by what he has promised.

'Ask and you will receive; seek and you will find; knock and it shall be opened to you. For everyone who asks, receives, etc.' (Matthew 7:7-8) Hence the doctors of theology rightly say that God gives grace without fail to whoever does what lies within him (*quod in se est*).[4]

The sinner thus recognizes his need for grace, and calls upon God to bestow it – which places God under an obligation to do this, thus justifying the sinner. In other words, the sinner takes the initiative, by calling upon God: the sinner is able to do something which ensures that God responds by justifying him. As we saw in the previous chapter (pp. 58–60), the covenant between God and humanity established a framework within which a relatively small human effort results in a disproportionately large divine reward. Nevertheless, a definite human effort is required to place God under an obligation to reward the sinner with grace.

As we shall see in the following section, Luther found himself faced with impossible difficulties over the idea of *iustitia Dei*, the 'righteousness of God'. The idea of the 'righteousness of God' is prominent in both the Psalms and the letter to the Romans, upon which Luther was lecturing in the period 1513–16. We thus find him occasionally dealing with this idea at length in his lectures. At this stage in his development, he understood the 'righteousness of God' to refer to an impartial divine attribute. God judges individuals with complete impartiality. If the individual has met the basic precondition for justification, he or she is justified; if he has not, he or she is condemned. God shows neither leniency nor favouritism: he judges solely on the basis of merit. God is both equitable and just, in that he gives each individual exactly what he or she merits – nothing more, and nothing less.[5]

Luther's Discovery of the 'Righteousness of God'

The difficulty of this theory appears to have become increasingly clear to Luther in late 1514 or early 1515. What happens if the sinner is incapable of meeting this basic precondition? What happens if the sinner is so crippled and trapped by sin that he cannot fulfil the demand which is made of him? Pelagius and Gabriel Biel, both of whom work with this idea of the 'righteousness of God',[6] assumed that humans were capable of meeting this precondition without any undue difficulty – but Luther seems to have begun to appropriate the insights of Augustine at this point, arguing that humanity was so trapped in its sinfulness that it could not extricate itself except through special divine intervention.

Luther's own comments on his dilemma are enlightening. He relates how he tried with all his abilities to do what was necessary to achieve salvation, but found himself more and more convinced that he could not be saved.

> I was a good monk, and kept my order so strictly that I could say that if ever a monk could get to heaven through monastic discipline, I was that monk. All my companions in the monastery would confirm this...And yet my conscience would not give me certainty, but I always doubted and said, 'You didn't do that right. You weren't contrite enough. You left that out of your confession.' The more I tried to remedy an uncertain, weak and troubled conscience with human traditions, the more I daily found it more uncertain, weaker and more troubled.

It seemed to Luther that he simply could not meet the preconditions of salvation. He did not have the resources needed to be saved. There was no way that God could justly reward him with salvation – only condemnation.

The idea of the 'righteousness of God' thus became a threat to Luther. To the sinner, it meant only condemnation. God, in his justice, would punish the sinner. The promise of justification was real enough – but the precondition attached to the promise made its fulfilment impossible. It was as if God was promising a blind man a million dollars, provided that he could see. The idea of the 'righteousness of God' was simply not gospel, not good news, for sinners, in that it spelled nothing but condemnation. Luther's growing pessimism concerning the abilities of sinful humanity led him to despair of his own salvation, which increasingly seemed an impossibility. 'How can I find a gracious God (*Wie kriege ich einen gnädigen Gott*)?' By the end of 1514, it seems that Luther had failed to find an answer to this question.

Yet this was no mere theological problem, of purely academic interest. Luther felt that his salvation was at stake. Luther's growing anxiety with this problem shows a strongly existentialist dimension. It concerned him, personally – it was no mere textbook difficulty. For Luther, as for so many others, the crucial question of human existence concerned how to clinch one's salvation. Some modern readers may understandably find it difficult to empathize with this concern. However, to enter into Luther's personal situation, and hence to appreciate the importance of his 'theological breakthrough', it is necessary to appreciate how crucial this question seemed to him. It was *the* central question on his personal agenda.

And then something happened. We shall probably never know exactly what it was, or when it occurred. We do not even know where it happened: many scholars like to refer to the discovery as the *Turmerlebnis*, 'the tower experience', on account of a later (and somewhat confused) personal recollection of Luther. But whatever it was, and whenever and wherever it happened, it changed Luther's outlook on life completely, and ultimately propelled him into the forefront of the Reformation struggle. In the year before he died, Luther contributed a preface to the first volume of the complete edition of his Latin writings, in which he described how he came to break with the church of his day. In this 'autobiographical fragment' (as it is usually known), he deals with his personal difficulties with the problem of the 'righteousness of God':

I had certainly wanted to understand Paul in his letter to the Romans. But what prevented me from doing so was not so much cold feet as that one phrase in the first chapter: 'the righteousness of God is revealed in it' (Romans 1:17). For I hated that phrase, 'the righteousness of God', which I had been taught to understand as the righteousness by which God is righteous, and punishes unrighteous sinners.

Although I lived a blameless life as a monk, I felt that I was a sinner with an uneasy conscience before God. I also could not believe that I had pleased him with my works. Far from loving that righteous God who punished sinners, I actually hated him...I was in desperation to know what Paul meant in this passage.

At last, as I meditated day and night on the relation of the words 'the righteousness of God is revealed in it, as it is written, the righteous person shall live by faith', I began to understand that 'righteousness of God' as that by which the righteous person lives by the gift of God (faith); and this sentence, 'the righteousness of God is revealed', to refer to a passive righteousness, by which the merciful God justifies us by faith, as it is written, 'the righteous person lives by faith'. This immediately made me feel as though I had been born again, and as though I had entered through open gates into paradise itself. From that moment, I saw the whole face of scripture in a new light...And now, where I had once hated the phrase, 'the righteousness of God', I began to love and extol it as the sweetest of phrases, so that this passage in Paul became the very gate of paradise to me.[7]

What is Luther talking about in this famous passage, which vibrates with the excitement of discovery? It is obvious that his understanding of the phrase 'the righteousness of God' has changed radically. But what is the nature of this change, and when did it take place?

The basic change is fundamental. Originally Luther regarded the precondition for justification as a human work, something which the sinner had to do, to perform, before he or she could be justified. Increasingly convinced, through his reading of Augustine, that this was an impossibility, Luther could only interpret the 'righteousness of God' as a *punishing* righteousness. But in this passage, he narrates how he discovered a 'new' meaning of the phrase – a righteousness which God *gives* to the sinner. In other words, God himself meets the precondition. God graciously gives the sinner what he requires if he is to be justified. An analogy (not used by Luther) may help bring out the difference between these two approaches.

Let us suppose that you are in prison, and are offered your freedom on condition that you pay a heavy fine. The promise is real – so long as you can meet the precondition, the promise will be fulfilled. Pelagius and Gabriel Biel work on the presupposition, initially shared by Luther, that you have the necessary money stacked away somewhere. As your freedom is worth far more, you are being offered a bargain. So you pay the fine. This presents no difficulties, so long as you have the necessary resources. Luther increasingly came to share the view of Augustine – that sinful humanity just doesn't have the resources needed to meet this precondition. To go back to our analogy, Augustine and Luther work on the assumption that, as you don't have the money, the promise of freedom has little relevance to your situation. For both Augustine and Luther, therefore, the good news of the gospel is that you have been *given* the necessary money with which to buy your freedom. In other words, the precondition has been met for you by someone else. What you don't have has been provided by someone else.

Luther's insight, which he describes in this passage, is that God graciously assists the sinner to gain his or her justification. The God of the gospel is not a harsh judge who rewards individuals according to their merits, but a merciful and gracious God who gives sinners something which they could never attain through their own unaided efforts. Earlier (pp. 55–7), we noted the distinction between the 'Augustinian' and 'Pelagian' views on justification. We could say that in his earlier phase Luther adopted something like a Pelagian position, which gave way to more of an Augustinian position. It is for this reason that Luther scholars tend to put quotation marks round the words 'new' or 'discovery': Luther's ideas may have been new to him, but they were hardly a new discovery for Christianity! Luther's 'discovery' is really a '*re*discovery' or a 'reappropriation' of the insights of Augustine. This is not to say that Luther simply reproduces exactly what Augustine teaches – he introduces elements which would have horrified Augustine (for example, his insistence that divine righteousness contradicts human ideas of righteousness: for Augustine, the two were complementary). The contrast with Karlstadt here is important: Karlstadt merely repeats Augustine's views, as stated in the antiPelagian writings, where Luther 'creatively reinterprets' them on occasion. Nevertheless, the basic *framework* within which Luther now works is unquestionably Augustinian. True repentance is to be seen as the result, rather than the precondition, of grace.

When did this change take place? On the basis of the evidence of the *Dictata super Psalterium* (1513–15) and the Romans lectures (1515-16), it seems that the basic change Luther described in 1545 took place at some point in 1515. Inevitably, there are doubts and uncertainties about this, for a number of reasons. For example, it is possible that Luther's 1545 recollection of events in the 1510s may have been slightly confused. It is also not entirely clear how some parts of the 1545 autobiographical fragment are to be interpreted. Nevertheless, the general consensus among Luther scholars is that his theology of justification underwent a decisive alteration at some point in 1515.[8] The Luther who posted the Ninety-Five Theses in October 1517 was already in possession of the insights on which he would base his programme of reform.

Central to these insights was the doctrine of 'justification by faith alone', and it is important to appreciate what is meant by this term. The idea of 'justification' is already familiar – it refers to the restoration or establishment of a relationship between a sinner and God, taking in ideas such as 'forgiveness' and 'reconciliation'. But what about the phrase 'by faith alone'? This doesn't mean that the sinner is justified because he or she believes, on account of that faith – that is what Luther certainly believed in his earlier period, as we saw. This view regards faith as a human action or work – the precondition for justification. Luther's breakthrough, however, involves the recognition that God provides everything necessary for justification, so that all that the sinner needs to do is to receive it. God is active, and humans are passive, in justification. The phrase 'justification *by* grace *through* faith' brings out the meaning of the doctrine more clearly: the justification of the sinner is based upon the grace of God, and is received through faith. Or perhaps we could cite the somewhat rambling title of Heinrich Bullinger's 1554 work on this subject as a comprehensive, if not particularly eloquent, statement of Luther's ideas: *The grace of God that justifies us for the sake of Christ through faith alone, without good works, while faith meanwhile abounds in good works*. God offers and gives; men and women receive and rejoice. The doctrine of justification by faith alone is an affirmation that God does everything necessary for salvation. Even faith itself is a gift of God, rather than a human action. God himself meets the precondition for justification. Thus, as we saw, the 'righteousness of God' is not a righteousness which judges whether or not we have met the precondition for justification, but the righteousness which is given to us so that we may meet that precondition.[9]

This view was regarded by many of Luther's critics as outrageous. It seemed to suggest that God despised morality, having no time for good works. Luther was branded as an 'antinomian' – in other words, someone who has no place for the law (Greek: *nomos*) in the religious life. Perhaps we could use the word 'anarchist' to convey much the same idea. In fact, Luther was simply stating that good works are not the *cause* of justification, but are its *result*, a point captured somewhat laboriously in the title of Bullinger's book, noted above. In other words, Luther treats good works as the *natural result of having been justified*, rather than the *cause of that justification*. Far from destroying morality, Luther simply saw himself as setting it in its proper context. The believer performed good works as an act of thankfulness to God for having forgiven him, rather than in an attempt to get God to forgive him in the first place.

Let us pause briefly to consider how both humanism and scholasticism were implicated in Luther's theological breakthrough. The role of humanism will be obvious. The editions of Augustine, which gave Luther access to the ideas of this great writer, were prepared by humanists. Luther appears to have used the Amerbach edition of Augustine, widely regarded as representing humanist scholarship at its best in the first decade of the sixteenth century (before Erasmus began his editorial work in the 1510s, that is). Similarly, Luther is able to make use of his knowledge of Hebrew as he expounded the Psalms – and both his knowledge of the language and his Hebrew text of some of the Psalms were provided by the humanist Reuchlin. The intense interest Luther often shows in the intricacies of the text of scripture probably reflects the humanist emphasis upon the importance of the literary form of scripture as a key to its experiential meaning. Luther appears to have used the tools of humanism, as he wrestled with his theological riddle.

Nevertheless, scholasticism also played a significant role in Luther's theological breakthrough. One of the ironies of Luther's development seems to be that Luther used a scholastic tool to break free from his original scholastic matrix. The tool in question is a particular way of interpreting scripture, widespread in the medieval period, known as the *Quadriga*, or the 'fourfold sense of scripture'.[10] This way of approaching a biblical text allowed four different meanings of a passage to be identified: the *literal* meaning of the text, and three *spiritual* or non-literal meanings. It was through concentrating upon one of these spiritual senses of scripture (the 'tropological' sense), and playing down the literal sense, that Luther was able to wrest his insight concerning the 'righteousness of God'. Considered *literally*, this righteousness might well refer to God's punishment of sinners – but considered *tropologically* (i.e., non-literally), it referred to God's bestowal of righteousness upon the sinner. And so the scene was set for Luther's break with the theology of the *via moderna*. Curiously, Luther's break with scholasticism came about partly through the use of a scholastic technique. No other Reformer appears to have used this scholastic tool, thus setting Luther apart on this point.

What were the consequences of Luther's breakthrough? Initially, Luther appears to have felt moved to expose the inadequacies of the doctrine of justification associated with the *via moderna*. Working solely within the somewhat restricted circle of the Wittenberg university faculty of theology, Luther mounted a sustained attack on scholasticism. For example, the *Disputation against scholastic theology* of September 1517 is actually directed against one scholastic theologian – Gabriel Biel, representing the *via moderna*. The dean of that faculty, Karlstadt, came to share Luther's views on scholasticism after reading the works of Augustine in early 1517: although he was initially a champion of scholasticism at Wittenberg, he rapidly became one of its most severe critics. Karlstadt and Luther engineered a reform of the theology faculty in March 1518, managing to eliminate virtually anything connected with scholasticism from the curriculum. From now on, theological students at Wittenberg would study Augustine and the Bible, not the scholastics.

But there weren't that many theological students at Wittenberg, and Wittenberg was probably near the top of the league table of insignificant European universities. It is necessary to emphasize how utterly *insignificant* Luther's 'new' insights were at this point. All that we are talking about is alterations to the theological curriculum of an unimportant university, without any fundamental relevance for church or society. Luther was engaged in a minor academic debate, of relevance only to scholastics. How did a minor academic debate become the great popular movement of the Reformation? We have already seen how part of that answer lies in the humanist espousal of Luther as a *cause célèbre* in the aftermath of the Leipzig Disputation (see pp. 44–5). The remainder of that answer lies in the social dimensions of the doctrine of justification, to which we now turn.

The Social Consequences of Luther's 'Discovery'

It might be thought that the question of how sin is forgiven could be relegated to the appropriate sections of theological textbooks. In the late medieval period, however, sin was regarded as a visible and social matter, something which had to be forgiven in a visible and social way. In many ways, the development of the theory of the sacrament of penance in the Middle Ages may be regarded as an attempt to consolidate the social grounding of forgiveness. Forgiveness is not a private matter between the individual and God – it is a public matter involving that individual, the church and society. In 1215 the Fourth Lateran Council declared that 'all believers of both sexes who have reached the age of discretion must faithfully confess their sins in person to their own priest, and attempt to carry out the penance imposed'. Both priest and penance were thus firmly established as part of the medieval process by which God was understood to forgive sins through appointed human representatives and means on earth.[11]

Ecclesiastical vagueness concerning the precise contribution of both penitent and priest in penance inevitably led to the development of a number of highly questionable trends in popular belief. Salvation was widely regarded as something which could be earned or merited through good works. The confused and vague theology of forgiveness of the late medieval period, particularly concerning indulgences, lent weight to the suggestion that it was possible to purchase either or both the forgiveness of sins or the remission of 'purgatorial penalties'. In other words, the eternal penalties resulting from sinful actions could be reduced, if not eliminated, by payment of an appropriate sum of money to the appropriate ecclesiastical figure. Thus Cardinal Albrecht of Brandenburg managed to accumulate a remission of purgatorial penalties reckoned to total 39,245,120 years. If such beliefs were contrary to the teaching of the church, no attempt was made by that church to disabuse its members of such ideas. Indeed, there are reasons for thinking that they were tolerated to the point of being unofficially incorporated into the structures of the church. The power and the income of much of the ecclesiastical establishment and its patrons were actually linked with the continuance of such practices and beliefs.

In the early sixteenth century indulgences were a major source of papal revenue – and, as the somewhat sordid trilateral deal between the Pope, Albrecht of Brandenburg and the banking house of Fuggers indicates, that income found its way into a number of coffers. In a period when ecclesiastical offices were often purchased, rather than earned, the buyers generally felt justified in looking for a return on their investment – and such practices as paying for masses for the dead were encouraged for this reason. As a result, there were a number of vested interests concerned to ensure that the early sixteenth-century vagueness concerning the doctrine of justification was maintained.

The unique and indispensable role of the priest in confession and forgiveness as obviously open to corruption, and the evidence suggests that clerical venality was no small problem on the eve of the Reformation.

Luther's doctrine of justification by faith, with its associated doctrine of the 'priesthood of all believers', thus assumed an importance which far transcended the sphere of academic theology. It cut the ground from under the vested interests we have just noted. Forgiveness was a matter between the believer and God: no others were involved. No priest was required to pronounce that he had been forgiven – the believer could read in scripture the promises of forgiveness to those who confessed their sins, and needed no one to repeat them or execute them. No payment of any kind was required to receive divine forgiveness. The concept of purgatory, upon which so much popular superstition and ecclesiastical exploitation was based, was dismissed as a non-scriptural fiction. With the rejection of the existence of purgatory went a whole attitude to death and dying, and the practices previously associated with them. The new emphasis, derived partly from Renaissance individualism and partly from the New Testament, upon the individual's relation with God effectively marginalized the role of the institution of the church. It was not merely income from indulgences which Luther attacked – it was also the view of the role of the church in forgiveness which lay behind this practice.

What was an indulgence? Originally, an indulgence seems to have been a gift of money to charity as an expression of thankfulness for forgiveness. By the beginning of the sixteenth century, however, this innocent idea had been transformed into an important source of income for a papacy facing a financial crisis, and prepared to be flexible in its theology in order to meet it. Luther's wrath was particularly kindled by the marketing techniques of Johannes Tetzel. For a mere three marks, a sinner could be released from all punishments he would otherwise have faced in purgatory – and many found this an offer difficult to refuse at the price. In an age which knew how to enjoy its venial sins, the possibility of being able to do so without any fear of divine punishment was enormously tempting. Perhaps more sinister was Tetzel's suggestion that it would be possible to release the soul of a loved one from its sufferings in purgatory. The advertising jingle supporting this claim went like this:

> As soon as the coin in the coffer rings
> The soul from purgatory springs!

For Luther, this suggested that God's forgiveness could be purchased outright, degrading Christianity totally. The gospel had been deformed into a sub-Christian cult.

Luther's action in posting the Ninety-Five Theses on indulgences on 31 October 1517 (now celebrated as 'Reformation Day' in Germany) was not merely a protest against Tetzel's indulgence advertisements, which rivalled those of modern detergent manufacturers in terms of their optimistic claims. Nor was it merely a request that the church might clarify its teaching on forgiveness. It marked the appearance of a new theology of forgiveness (or, more accurately, the *re*appearance of an old and apparently forgotten theology of forgiveness) which threatened to remove from the institutional church any role in forgiveness – thus threatening the vested interests of the pope, many clergy, some princes and one rather important banking house. The doctrine of justification by faith alone reaffirmed that God's forgiveness was given, not bought, and was available to any, irrespective of their financial means or social condition. The related doctrine of the 'priesthood of all believers' meant that the believer, with the gracious assistance of God, could do everything necessary to his or her own salvation without needing to involve either priest or church. It is thus little wonder that Luther's views were regarded with such anxiety by the ecclesiastical establishment, and received with great interest by so many laity at the time!

So whereas Luther's initial controversy is with the academic theology of the *via moderna*, events led to him discarding this limited and rather minor sphere of controversy in order to assume the role of a popular reformer. From 1519 onwards, Luther's views on justification increasingly led him to challenge the doctrines and practices of the church of his day, rather than the ideas of the *via moderna*. Where Luther once concerned himself with the intellectual stratosphere, so to speak, he now came down to earth and grounded his ideas in the life of the church. With the publication of the three great reforming manifestos of 1520[12] he demonstrated the power of an idea to captivate the hearts and minds of men and women. No longer are we dealing with a desk-bound academic, but with a charismatic popular reformer.

The social consequences of Luther's doctrine of justification by faith alone may be illustrated with reference to the fate of the lay fraternities. As we noted earlier (p. 20), lay fraternities were associations of lay persons who undertook to provide their members with full funeral rites. The upper classes were able to endow chantries to ensure continued prayers for their souls in purgatory: thus Count Werner of Zimmern had 1,000 requiem masses said for him in 1483. The lower classes, not having access to the funds necessary for such extravagances, clubbed together in fraternities to make sure that the proper rites of passage were said for their members. In addition to this, however, many of the fraternities performed important social roles, such as establishing schools and almshouses for their members, and attempting to care for their members' widows and children. Their *raison d'être*, nevertheless, was fundamentally *religious*, based upon belief in purgatory, the veneration of the saints and the intercession of Mary. The doctrine of justification by faith eliminated the necessity of such fraternities by rejecting the cluster of beliefs concerning death and judgement upon which they were based. The concept of purgatory was dismissed as a non-scriptural fiction which exploited the people's natural and deep-rooted affection for their dead. The doctrine of the priesthood of all believers eliminated the necessity (if not the propriety) of the presence of a priest at such masses. The *raison d'être* of the fraternities was undermined – and with the elimination of any essential *religious* function, the fraternities' *social* roles also collapsed.

Luther's Theology of the Cross

By the year 1520, Luther had developed a specific understanding of the nature of Christian theology, which has now become known as the *theologia crucis*, the 'theology of the cross'.[13] This understanding of theology is particularly important, in that it underlies Luther's political theory, to be discussed in chapter 8. In that it arises directly out of his understanding of the 'righteousness of God', it is appropriate to introduce this theology at this point.

Earlier, we hinted at a fundamental difference between Luther and Augustine concerning *iustitia Dei*, the 'righteousness of God' or the 'justice of God' (the Latin word *iustitia* can be translated in either way). For Augustine, there was a direct correlation between human and divine justice. In other words, the ideas of justice which are embodied in human moral beliefs and legal codes are ultimately based upon divine justice.

Human ideas of justice reflect the divine idea of justice. In making this suggestion, Augustine was drawing partly on the writings of Paul, but mostly on the neo-Platonist world-view of late antiquity.

Luther, however, was convinced that human concepts of justice *were contradicted* by divine justice. His model case for this is given by the fact that God justifies *sinners*. Human concepts of justice demand that God should *punish* sinners – yet the gospel reveals that God *justifies* sinners. God contradicts human preconceptions of what he is like. On the basis of this insight, Luther went on to develop the characteristic themes of the 'theology of the cross' – that God's strength is revealed in what is, by human standards, weakness; his wisdom is revealed in what is, by human standards, stupidity, and so forth. All these statements focus on the cross, where God chose to redeem the world through an act which the world regarded as weak, humiliating and stupid – and thus challenge human standards of power and wisdom.[14] The challenge thus posed to human concepts of justice is incorporated into Luther's political thought.

It is this dialectic between human and divine concepts of justice which underlies Luther's political theory, particularly as it is developed in the doctrine of the 'Two Kingdoms'. We shall return to this point in chapter 8. Our attention now turns to a further development of Luther's doctrine of justification, of particular importance to the Protestant-Roman Catholic debate on justification in the sixteenth century.

The Concept of 'Forensic Justification'

One of the central insights of Luther's doctrine of justification by faith alone is that the individual sinner is incapable of self-justification. It is God who takes the initiative in justification, providing all the resources necessary to justify that sinner. One of those resources is the 'righteousness of God'. In other words, the righteousness on the basis of which the sinner is justified is not his own righteousness, but a righteousness which is given to him by God. Augustine had made this point earlier: Luther, however, gives it a subtle new twist, which leads to the development of the concept of 'forensic justification'.

For Augustine, God bestows justifying righteousness upon the sinner, in such a way that it becomes part of his or her person. As a result, this righteousness, although originating from *outside* the sinner, becomes part of his or her person. For Luther, the righteousness in question remains outside the sinner: it is an 'alien righteousness' (*iustitia aliena*). God treats, or 'reckons', this righteousness *as if* it is part of the sinner's person. These ideas were developed by Luther's follower Philip Melanchthon to give the doctrine now generally known as 'forensic justification'.[15]

Where Augustine taught that the sinner is *made righteous* in justification, Melanchthon taught that he is *counted as righteous* or *pronounced to be righteous*. For Augustine, 'justifying righteousness' is *imparted*; for Melanchthon, it is *imputed*. Melanchthon drew a sharp distinction between the event of being *declared* righteous and the process of being *made* righteous, designating the former 'justification' and the latter 'sanctification' or 'regeneration'. For Augustine, both were simply different aspects of the same thing. According to Melanchthon, God pronounces his verdict – that the sinner is righteous –in the heavenly court (*in foro divino*). This legal approach to justification gives rise to the term 'forensic justification', from the Latin word *forum* ('market place' or 'courtyard').

The importance of this development lies in the fact that it marks a complete break with the teaching of the church up to that point. From the time of Augustine onwards, justification had always been understood to refer to both the event of being declared righteous and the process of being made righteous. Melanchthon's concept of forensic justification diverged radically from this. As it was taken up by virtually all the major Reformers subsequently, it came to represent a standard difference between Protestant and Roman Catholic from that point onwards. In addition to their differences on how the sinner was justified, there was now an additional disagreement on what the word 'justification' designated in the first place. The Council of Trent, the Roman Catholic church's definitive response to the Protestant challenge, reaffirmed the views of Augustine on the nature of justification, and censured the views of Melanchthon as woefully inadequate.

Justification and the Swiss Reformation

As we saw earlier, Luther's doctrine of justification is directed towards the individual believer, clarifying his relationship with both God and the church, in order that his troubled conscience might be relieved. In many ways, it illustrates Luther's concern with the individual and his subjective consciousness, reflecting the rise of individualism associated with the Renaissance. But what of the Swiss Reformation, where more attention was paid to reformation of the *community*?

The European Reformation is often portrayed as a homogeneous phenomenon. In other words, it is presented as being consistent in terms of its underlying ideas and emphases. In fact, this is an unacceptable view of the Reformation, and the role played by the doctrine of justification by faith alone in the Swiss Reformation is a particularly important illustration of this principle. For Luther and the Lutheran Reformation at Wittenberg, this doctrine was of decisive importance: the existence and well-being of the Christian church depended upon it. For Zwingli at Zurich, however, the doctrine was not of importance. Indeed, Zwingli appears to have been suspicious of Luther's doctrine, in that it seemed to threaten morality.

Zwingli saw the Reformation as affecting the corporate life, concerned with church and society rather than just the individual. That Reformation was primarily moral in character: Zwingli was concerned with the moral and spiritual regeneration of Zurich, rather than with the doctrine of justification. The Swiss Reformers knew and disapproved of the indulgence traffic in Germany, but did not attach the same importance to it as did Luther. It is true that such a controversy seemed inevitable in January 1519, as the indulgence seller Bernhardin Sanson arrived at the gates of Zurich. Zwingli had already established himself as a critic of the trade, and the whole purgatorial framework within which it was set. Only too painfully aware of the repercussions of Luther's reaction against Tetzel, the city council refused Sanson admission, thus avoiding confrontation over this issue. Had they allowed him in, the theological course of the Swiss Reformation might have been rather different.

As it happened, the Swiss Reformation was initially primarily concerned with the reform of the morals and practices of the church according to the New Testament. The doctrine of justification did not figure in this programme of reform at all: indeed, the early Reformed theologians, such as Zwingli and Bucer, seem to have regarded Luther's doctrine of justification as a *threat* to morality.[16]

As we have seen, Luther saw repentance as the outcome of justification: an individual is justified and forgiven, and as a result of this he is able to repent fully and begin to do good works. In other words, good works are the consequence, and not the precondition, of divine forgiveness. For Zwingli, however, justification is essentially God's endorsement of the morality of an individual. Good works are the *precondition* of justification. The only person who can be justified is the morally regenerate person. Underlying this theology (which, it need hardly be said, is actually diametrically opposed to Luther's view!) is Zwingli's humanist concern for the promotion of morality. By making justification *dependent* upon moral regeneration, the morality of the community could be upheld. Luther's theology seemed to cut the ground from under morality, by implying (at least, so it seemed to Zwingli and Bucer) that it was *immoral* persons who were justified, thus suggesting that immorality was the best way into the Kingdom of God! In fact, this is not what Luther taught, although it is obvious how this misunderstanding could arise. The early Reformed theologians, especially the great Strasbourg Reformer Martin Bucer, thus developed an understanding of justification which is a curious amalgam of the ideas of Erasmus and Luther, in order to uphold both the graciousness of God and the need for human morality.

The Reformed theologians also tended to regard Luther's concern with personal experience as unacceptably subjective and too orientated towards the individual: their concern was primarily with establishing objective criteria on the basis of which society and the church could be reformed – and they found such objective criteria in scripture. They also had little time for Luther's early preoccupation with scholastic theology, which posed no significant threat to the Swiss Reformation. If the Lutheran church arose out of a concern for the doctrine of justification, the Reformed church was born through a new desire to re-establish the scriptural model of the apostolic church, which we shall explore in more detail in chapter 7. Our attention now turns to one of the leading ideas of Reformed theology, of considerable importance to its political and social theories: the concept of the divine sovereignty.

Divine Sovereignty and Predestination in Reformed Thought

The doctrine of predestination is often thought of as being the central feature of Reformed theology.[17] For many, the term 'Calvinist' is virtually identical with 'placing enormous emphasis upon the doctrine of predestination'. How was it that the concept of grace, which to Luther concerned the justification of the sinner, came to refer to the sovereignty of God, especially as expressed in the doctrine of predestination? And how did this development take place? In the remainder of this chapter, we shall be concerned with the understanding of the doctrine of grace associated with the Reformed church.

Zwingli on the Divine Sovereignty

Zwingli began his epoch-making ministry at Zurich on 1 January 1519. That ministry came close to extinction in August of that same year, when Zurich was struck by a visitation of the plague. The fact that such an outbreak was a commonplace in the early sixteenth century must not be allowed to obscure its seriousness: at least one in four, possibly as many as one in two, died from its effects at Zurich between August 1519 and February 1520. Zwingli's pastoral duties included the consolation of the dying, and it was perhaps inevitable that he himself should contract the disease. As death drew near, Zwingli seems to have been aware that whether he survived or not was a matter for God. He was a helpless plaything in the hands of the Almighty.

We possess a piece of poetry, generally referred to as the *Pestlied*, 'Plague Song', dating from the autumn of 1519. In it, we find Zwingli musing on his destiny. We find him making no appeal to the saints for recovery, and no suggestion that the church can in any way intercede for him. Instead, we find a rugged determination to accept whatever God has in store for him. Whatever God ordains as his lot, Zwingli is prepared to accept:

> Do as you will
> for I lack nothing.
> I am your vessel
> to be restored or destroyed.

It is impossible to read this poem without sensing Zwingli's self-surrender to the divine will. It is probably out of this experience that his conviction arose that he was an instrument in the hand of God, to be yielded completely to God's purposes.

Earlier, we noted how Luther's difficulties concerning the 'righteousness of God' were as much existential as theological. It will be obvious that Zwingli's concern with divine providence also had a strong existentialist dimension. For Zwingli, the question of the omnipotence of God was no longer a textbook question, but an issue which had a direct bearing upon his existence. Whether he lived or died depended, it seemed to Zwingli, upon that providence. This was a question loaded with existential significance for the young preacher, as he lay upon his sickbed wondering what God might have in store for him.

Whereas Luther's theology is at least initially largely shaped by his experience of God's justification of him, a sinner, Zwingli's is almost totally shaped by his sense of the absolute sovereignty of God and of humanity's total dependence upon him.[18] The existential aspects of both thinkers' theology is wrapped up with these experiences. The idea of the absolute sovereignty of God is developed in Zwingli's doctrine of providence, especially the famous sermon *de providentia*, 'on providence'. Many of Zwingli's more critical readers have noted the similarities between Zwingli's ideas and the fatalism of Seneca, and have suggested that Zwingli merely baptizes Senecan fatalism. This suggestion is given some weight through Zwingli's interest in and reference to Seneca in *de providentia*. Whether an individual is saved or condemned is totally a matter for God, who freely makes his decision from eternity. However, it seems that Zwingli's emphasis upon the divine omnipotence and human impotence ultimately derives from his reading of Paul, and is merely reinforced by his reading of Seneca and given existential importance through the close encounter with death of August 1519.

It is instructive to compare Luther and Zwingli's attitude to scripture, which reflects their different approaches to the grace of God. For Luther, scripture is primarily concerned with the gracious promises of God, which culminate in the promise of the justification of the sinner by faith. For Zwingli, scripture is primarily concerned with the law of God, with a code of conduct, with the demands made by a sovereign God of his people. Luther draws a sharp distinction between 'law' and 'gospel', whereas Zwingli regards the two as essentially the same.

It was Zwingli's growing emphasis upon the sovereignty of God which eventually led to his break with humanism. It is notoriously difficult to say when Zwingli stopped being a humanist and started being a Reformer: indeed, there are excellent reasons for suggesting that Zwingli remained a humanist throughout his life. As we saw earlier (pp. 31–2), Kristeller's definition of humanism concerns its *methods* rather than its *doctrines*: if this definition of humanism is applied to Zwingli, he remained a humanist throughout his career. Similar remarks apply to Calvin. But, it may be objected, how can these men be thought of as humanists, when both develop such a rigorous doctrine of predestination? It is thus necessary to remember that at the time of the Renaissance 'humanism' refers to a methodology, not a set of doctrines. It is certainly true that neither Zwingli or Calvin could be thought of as 'humanists' in the twentieth-century sense of the word – but that is irrelevant to the sixteenth century. When it is recalled that numerous writers of antiquity – such as Seneca and Lucretius – developed strongly fatalist philosophies, it can be seen that the case for treating both Reformers as humanists is stronger than might have been thought. Nevertheless, it seems that at some point in his career, Zwingli changed his mind on one central presupposition shared by most of his Swiss humanist contemporaries. If Zwingli remained a humanist after this, he now embraced a somewhat different form of humanism which may of his humanist colleagues regarded as slightly eccentric.

The programme of reform initiated by Zwingli at Zurich in 1519 was essentially humanist. His use of scripture is thoroughly Erasmian, as was his style of preaching, although his political views reflect the Swiss nationalism which Erasmus so detested. Most importantly for our purposes, Reformation is viewed as an educational process, echoing the views of both Erasmus and the Swiss humanist sodalities. Writing to his colleague Myconius on 31 December 1519, reviewing the effects of his first year at Zurich, Zwingli announced that there were 'more than two thousand more or less enlightened individuals in Zurich' as a result. But in a letter of 24 July 1520, we find Zwingli apparently conceding the failure of this humanist conception of Reformation: something more than the educational insights of Quintillian was needed if the Reformation was to succeed. The fate of humanity in general, and the Reformation in particular, is determined by divine providence. It is God, and not humanity, who is the chief actor in the Reformation process. Humanist educational techniques are half-measures, incapable of dealing with the root of the problem.

This scepticism concerning the viability of the humanist reforming programme was made public in March 1525, when Zwingli published his *Commentary on True and False Religion*. Zwingli attacked two presuppositions which were central to the Erasmian reforming programme – the idea of 'free will' (*liberum arbitrium*), which Erasmus had defended vigorously in 1524, and the suggestion that educational methods were capable of reforming corrupt and sinful humanity. What was required, according to Zwingli, was providential divine intervention, without which true Reformation was an impossibility. As is well known, of course, 1525 also saw the publication of Luther's violently anti-Erasmian work *de servo arbitrio*, 'On the bondage of the will',[19] also explicitly attacking Erasmus' doctrine of the 'freedom of the will'. Luther's work is permeated with an emphasis upon the total sovereignty of God, linked with a doctrine of predestination similar to Zwingli's. Many humanists found this emphasis upon human sinfulness and divine omnipotence unacceptable, leading to a certain alienation between Zwingli and many of his former supporters.

Calvin on Predestination

Calvin's thought also reflects a concern with human sinfulness and divine omnipotence, a concern which finds its most complete expression in Calvin's doctrine of predestination. In his early period, Calvin appears to have held mildly humanist reforming views, perhaps similar to those of Lefèvre d'Etaples (Stapulensis). By 1533, however, he appears to have moved over to a more radical position. On 2 November 1533, the rector of the University of Paris delivered an oration to mark the beginning of the new academic year, in the course of which he developed several major themes – such as justification by faith alone – by then associated with the Lutheran Reformation. The rector and Calvin were obliged to flee Paris as a result, in that Calvin appears to have been involved in some way in drafting this oration.[20] But how and when did the young humanist become a Reformer?

The question of the date and nature of Calvin's conversion has intrigued generations of Calvin scholars, even if that intrigue has produced remarkably little in the way of concrete results.[21] It is generally agreed that Calvin switched from a mildly humanist reforming programme to a more radical platform in late 1533 or early 1534. We do not know why. Calvin appears to describe his conversion at two points in his later writings, but we lack the wealth of autobiographical detail provided by Luther. It is, nevertheless, clear that Calvin understands his conversion to be due to divine providence. He asserts that he was so deeply devoted to the 'superstitions of the papacy' that nothing less than an act of God could have freed him. He asserts that God 'tamed his heart and reduced it to obedience'. Once more, we find the same emphasis characteristic of the Reformation: the impotence of humanity and the omnipotence of God. It is these ideas which are linked and developed in Calvin's doctrine of predestination.

Although some scholars have suggested that predestination constitutes the centre of Calvin's thought, it is clear that it does nothing of the sort. It is simply one aspect of his doctrine of salvation. Calvin's chief contribution to the development of the doctrine of grace is the logical rigour with which he approached it. This is perhaps best seen by comparing Augustine and Calvin on the doctrine.

For Augustine, humanity after the Fall is corrupt and impotent, requiring the grace of God to be redeemed. That grace is not given to all. Augustine uses the term 'predestination' to refer to God's action in giving grace to some. It designates the special divine decision and action by which God grants his grace to those who will be saved. But what, it may be asked, happens to everyone else? God passes them over, according to Augustine. He does not actively decide that they will be damned; he simply omits to save them. Predestination, for Augustine, refers only to the divine decision to redeem, and not to the act of abandoning the remainder of fallen humanity.

For Calvin, logical rigour demands that God actively chooses to redeem or to damn. God cannot be thought of as doing something by default: he is active and sovereign in his actions. Therefore God actively wills the salvation of those who will be saved, and the damnation of those who will not. Predestination is thus the 'eternal decree of God, by which he determined what he wished to make of every individual. For he does not create all in the same condition, but ordains eternal life for some and eternal damnation for others'.[22] One of the central functions of the doctrine is to emphasize the graciousness of God. For Luther, God's graciousness is reflected in the fact that he justifies sinners, men and women who are totally unworthy of such a privilege. For Calvin, God's graciousness is demonstrated in his decision to redeem individuals irrespective of their merits: the decision to redeem an individual is made without reference to how worthy that individual might be. For Luther, God's graciousness is demonstrated in that he saves sinners *despite* their demerits; for Calvin, that graciousness is demonstrated in that he saves individuals *irrespective* of their merits. Although Luther and Calvin defend the graciousness of

God in somewhat different manners, the same principle is affirmed by their respective views on justification and predestination.

Although the doctrine of predestination was not central to the thought of Calvin himself, it became the central nucleus of later Reformed theology through the influence of Theodore Beza.[23] From about 1570 onwards, the theme of 'election' came to dominate Reformed theology, and allowed an easy identification of the Reformed congregations and the people of Israel. Just as God had once chosen Israel, so he had now chosen the Reformed congregations as his people. From this moment onwards, the doctrine of predestination begins to assume a major social and political function – a function it did not possess under Calvin. The idea of a covenant between God and his elect, paralleling the covenant between God and Israel in the Old Testament, began to become of major importance to the rapidly expanding Reformed church. The 'covenant of grace' laid down God's obligations to his people, and his people's obligations (religious, social and political) to him. It defined the framework within which individuals and society functioned. The form which this theology took in England – Puritanism – is of particular interest.[24] The sense of being the 'elect people of God' was heightened as the new people of God entered the new promised land – America.[25] Although this development lies outside the scope of this work, it is important to appreciate that the social, political and religious views which characterized the New England settlers derived from the sixteenth-century European Reformation. The international Reformed social vision was grounded in the concept of divine election and the 'covenant of grace'.

In marked contrast, later Lutheranism marginalized Luther's 1525 insights into divine predestination, preferring to work within the framework of a free human response to God, rather than a sovereign divine election of specific individuals.[26] For later sixteenth-century Lutheranism, 'election' meant a human decision to love God, not God's decision to elect certain individuals. Indeed, disagreement over the doctrine of predestination was one of the two major controversies which occupied the polemical writers of both confessions for centuries thereafter (the other controversy concerned the sacraments). Lutherans never had quite the same sense of being the 'elect of God', and were correspondingly modest in their attempts to expand their sphere of influence as a result. The remarkable success of 'international Calvinism' reminds us of the power an idea has to transform both individuals and groups – and the Reformed doctrine of election and predestination was unquestionably the driving force behind the great expansion of the Reformed church in the seventeenth century.

The Doctrine of Grace and the Reformation

'The Reformation, inwardly considered, was just the ultimate triumph of Augustine's doctrine of grace over Augustine's doctrine of the church.'[27] This famous remark summarizes with some brilliance the importance of the doctrine of grace to the development of the Reformation. The Reformers regarded themselves as having recovered Augustine's doctrines of grace from the distortions and perversions of the medieval church. For Luther, Augustine's doctrine of grace, as expressed in the doctrine of justification by faith alone, was the *articulus stantis et cadentis ecclesiae*, 'the article by which the church stands or falls'. And if there were some subtle, and other not-so-subtle, differences between Augustine and the Reformers over the doctrine of grace, the latter felt able to put this down to the superior textual and philological methods at their disposal, regrettably denied to Augustine. For the Reformers, especially Luther, the Christian church was constituted by its doctrine of grace – and any compromise or failure on this matter by an ecclesiastical grouping involved the loss of that grouping's claim to be the Christian church. The medieval church had lost its claim to be 'Christian', thus justifying the action of the Reformers in breaking away from it, in order to re-establish the gospel.

Augustine, however, had developed an ecclesiology, or doctrine of the church, which was opposed to any such development. During the Donatist controversy of the early fifth century, Augustine had emphasized the unity of the church, and argued vigorously against the temptation to form breakaway groups when the main body of the church seemed to be in error. The Reformers felt able to disregard Augustine on this point, holding that his views on grace were far more important that his views on the church. The church, they argued, was a product of the grace of God – and so it was the latter that was of primary importance. The opponents of the Reformation disagreed, arguing that it was the church itself which was the guarantor of the Christian faith.

The scene was thus set for the debate over the nature of the church, to which we shall return in chapter 7. Our attention is now claimed by the second great theme of Reformation thought: the need to return to scripture.

For further reading

For an introduction to the doctrine of justification, see:

Alister McGrath, *Justification by Faith: An Introduction* (Grand Rapids, MI, 1988).

On the history of this doctrine see:

Alister E. McGrath, *Iustitia Dei: A History of the Christian Doctrine of Justification* (2 vols: Cambridge, 1986).

Four excellent introductions to Luther's writings and work are:

Roland Bainton, *Here I Stand: A Life of Martin Luther* (New York, 1959).
Heinrich Bornkamm, *Luther's World of Thought* (St Louis, 1958).
Bernhard Lohse, *Martin Luther: An Introduction to his Life and Writings* (Philadelphia, 1986).
Walther von Loewenich, *Martin Luther: The Man and his Work* (Minneapolis, 1986).

For the most detailed recent analysis of Luther's theological breakthrough in English, see:

Alister E. McGrath, *Luther's Theology of the Cross: Martin Luther's Theological Breakthrough* (Oxford, 1985).

For excellent accounts of Zwingli's life and work, see:

G. R. Potter, *Zwingli* (Cambridge, 1976).
W. P. Stephens, *The Theology of Huldrych Zwingli* (Oxford, 1986).

For excellent accounts of Calvin's life and work, see:

Richard Stauffer, 'Calvin', in *International Calvinism 1541-1715*, ed. Menna Prestwich (Oxford, 1985), pp. 15–38.
François Wendel, *Calvin: The Origins and Development of his Religious Thought* (New York, 1963).

6

The Return to Scripture

At the heart of most religious systems lies a core of written texts, which are regarded as being 'authoritative' – in other words, as having some permanent significance in defining the 'shape' of that religion. In the case of Christianity, the written texts in question are those gathered together as the Bible, and often referred to simply as 'scripture'. As is well known,[1] the Bible is a central document of western civilization, the source of Christian ideas, as well as an influence upon education and culture. The Reformation saw a new importance being attached to scripture – or, perhaps, an ancient view of the importance of scripture being recovered. The principle *scriptura sola*, 'by scripture alone', became one of the great slogans of the Reformers as they sought to bring the practices and beliefs of the church back into line with those of the Golden Age of Christianity. If the doctrine of justification by faith alone was the material principle of the Reformation, the principle of *scriptura sola* was its formal principle. If the Reformers dethroned the pope, they enthroned scripture. Every section of the Reformation movement regarded scripture as the quarry from which their ideas and practices were hewn – yet, as we shall see, scripture proved to be much more difficult to use in this way than might be expected. In this present chapter, we shall consider the Reformation understanding of scripture in some detail, contextualizing it in the world of thought of the late medieval and Renaissance periods.

Scripture in the Middle Ages

To understand the importance of humanism in relation to the development of the ideas of the Reformation, and those ideas themselves, it is necessary to appreciate the way in which scripture was understood and handled in the medieval period. In this section, we shall sketch an outline of the medieval understanding of the importance of scripture.

The Concept of 'Tradition'

For most medieval theologians, scripture was the materially sufficient source of Christian doctrine. In other words, everything that was of essential importance to the Christian faith was contained in scripture. There was no need to look anywhere else for material relevant to Christian theology.[2] There were certainly matters on which scripture had nothing to say – for example, who wrote the Apostles' Creed, at what precise moment during the celebration of the eucharist the bread and wine became the body and blood of Christ, or whether the practice of baptism was intended solely for adult believers. On these matters, the church felt at liberty to attempt to work out what scripture implied, although their judgements were regarded as subordinate to scripture itself.

By the end of the Middle Ages, however, the concept of 'tradition' had come to be of major importance in relation to the interpretation and authority of scripture. Heiko A. Oberman has helpfully indicated that two quite different concepts of tradition were in circulation in the late Middle Ages, which he designates 'Tradition 1' and 'Tradition 2'.[3] In view of the importance of these concepts to the Reformation, we shall examine them briefly.

It was not only the orthodox, but also the heretical, who appealed to scripture for support. John Dryden, writing in the seventeenth century, made this point with force:

> For did not Arius first, Socinus now
> The Son's eternal Godhead disavow?
> And did not these by Gospel texts alone
> Condemn our doctrine and maintain their own?
> Have not all heretics the same pretence,
> To plead the scriptures in their own defence?

In response to various controversies within the early church, especially the threat from Gnosticism, a 'traditional' method of understanding certain passages of scripture began to develop. Second century patristic theologians such as Irenaeus of Lyons began to develop the idea of an authorized way of interpreting certain texts of scripture, which he argued went back to the time of the apostles themselves. Scripture couldn't be interpreted in any random way: it had to be interpreted within the context of the historical continuity of the Christian church. The parameters of its interpretation were historically fixed and 'given'. Scripture must be interpreted within the community of faith. Oberman designates this understanding of tradition as 'Tradition 1'. 'Tradition' here means simply 'a traditional way of interpreting scripture.'

In the fourteenth and fifteenth centuries, however, a somewhat different understanding of tradition developed. 'Tradition' is now understood to be a separate and distinct source of revelation, *in addition to scripture*.[4] Scripture, it was argued, was silent on a number of points – but God had providentially arranged for a second source of revelation to supplement this deficiency: a stream of unwritten tradition, going back to the apostles themselves. This tradition was passed down from one generation to another within the church. Oberman designates this understanding of tradition as 'Tradition 2'.

To summarize. 'Tradition 1' is a *single-source* theory of doctrine: doctrine is based upon scripture, and 'tradition' refers to a 'traditional way of interpreting scripture'. 'Tradition 2' is a *dual-source* theory of doctrine: doctrine is based upon two quite distinct sources, scripture and unwritten tradition. A belief which is not to be found in scripture may thus, on the basis of this dual-source theory, be justified by an appeal to an unwritten tradition. As we shall see, it was primarily against this dual-source theory of doctrine that the Reformers directed their criticisms.

The Vulgate Translation of the Bible

When a medieval theologian refers to 'scripture', he almost invariably means the *textus vulgatus*, 'common text', of Jerome. Although the term 'Vulgate' did not come into general use in the sixteenth century, we are entitled to use the term to refer to the specific Latin translation of the Bible prepared by Jerome in the late fourth and early fifth centuries.[5] This text was passed down to the Middle Ages in a number of forms,[6] with considerable variations between them. For example, Theodulf and Alcuin, noted scholars of the Dark Ages, used quite different versions of the Vulgate text. A new period of intellectual activity opened up in the eleventh century, as the Dark Ages lifted. It was clear that a standard version of this text was required to service the new interest in theology which developed as part of this intellectual renaissance. If theologians were to base their theology upon different versions of the Vulgate, an equally great, if not greater, variation in their conclusions would be the inevitable result. The need for standardization was met by what appears to have been a joint speculative venture by some Paris theologians and stationers in 1226, resulting in the 'Paris version' of the Vulgate text. By then, Paris was recognized as the leading centre of theology in Europe, with the inevitable result that – despite attempts to correct its obvious imperfections – the 'Paris version' of the Vulgate became established as normative. This version, it must be emphasized, was not commissioned or sponsored by any ecclesiastical figure: it appears to have been a purely commercial venture. History, however, concerns the fate of accidents, and it is necessary to note that medieval theologians, attempting to base their theology upon scripture, were obliged to equate scripture with a rather bad commercial edition of an already faulty Latin translation of the Bible. The rise of humanist textual and philological techniques would expose the distressing discrepancies between the Vulgate and the texts it purported to translate – and thus open the way to doctrinal reformation as a consequence.

The Medieval Vernacular Versions of Scripture

During the Middle Ages, a number of vernacular versions of scripture were produced. Although it was once thought that the medieval church condemned this process of translation, it is now known that neither the production of such translations, nor their use by clergy or laity, was ever explicitly forbidden.[7] An important example of such translations is provided by the Wycliffite versions, produced by a group of scholars who gathered around John Wycliffe at Lutterworth, in England.[8] The motivation for the translation of the Bible into English was partly spiritual, partly political. It was spiritual in that the laity could now have access to 'Goddis lawe', and political in that an implicit challenge was posed to the teaching authority of the church. The laity were enabled to detect the obvious differences between the scriptural vision of the church and its somewhat sordid English successor, thus setting the agenda for a programme of reform.

Important though such vernacular versions are, their importance must not be exaggerated. All these versions, it must be remembered, were simply *translations of the Vulgate*. They were not based upon a return to the best manuscripts of scripture, in their original languages, but upon the Vulgate version, with all its weaknesses and errors. The agenda for the Reformation would be set through the application of textual and philological techniques of a sophistication far beyond that of Wycliffe's circle at Lutterworth.

The Interpretation of Scripture

Texts need to be interpreted. There is little point in treating a certain text as authoritative or normative, if there is serious disagreement concerning how that text is to be interpreted. During the later Middle Ages, increasing emphasis came to be placed upon the role of the church as interpreter of scripture. The authority of scripture was guaranteed by the authority of its interpreter – the church, under the divine guidance of the Holy Spirit. As we have seen (pp. 21–5), however, there was such doctrinal confusion and disagreement over the nature and location of theological authority in the later medieval period that it was far from clear who had the ultimate authority to interpret scripture. The pope? A council? Or perhaps even a pious individual who knew his Bible well, as Panormitanus (Nicolo de Tudeschi) suggested, perhaps with his tongue firmly in his cheek. In practice, it seemed to be the pope of the day who held such authority – but there was sufficient confusion concerning this question to allow pluralism to develop virtually unchecked in the later fifteenth century.

The Humanists and the Bible

We have already seen how important the humanist movement was in relation to the study of scripture (pp. 37–40). It may be helpful if we bring together the main elements of the humanist contribution to this important question.

1   The great humanist emphasis upon the need to return *ad fontes* established the priority of scripture over its commentators, particularly those of the Middle Ages. The text of scripture was to be approached directly, rather than through a complicated system of glosses and commentaries.

2   Scripture was to be read directly in its original languages, rather than in Latin translation. Thus the Old Testament was to be studied in Hebrew (except for those few sections written in Aramaic), and the New Testament was to be read in Greek. The growing humanist interest in the Greek language (which many humanists held to be supreme in its capacity to mediate philosophical concepts) further consolidated the importance attached to the New Testament documents. The late Renaissance scholarly ideal was to be *trium linguarum gnarus*, 'expert in three languages (Hebrew, Greek and Latin)'. Trilingual colleges were established at Alcalá in Spain, at Paris and at Wittenberg. The new interest in, and availability of, scripture in its original language soon brought to light a number of serious translation mistakes in the Vulgate, some of considerable importance (see pp. 39–40).

3   The humanist movement made available two essential tools required for the new method of study of the Bible. First, it made available printed texts of scripture in its original languages. For example, Erasmus' *Novum Instrumentum omne* of 1516 allowed scholars direct access to the printed text of the Greek New Testament, and Lefèvre d'Etaples provided the Hebrew text of some Psalms in 1509. Second, it made available manuals of classical languages, allowing scholars to learn languages which they otherwise could not have acquired. Reuchlin's Hebrew primer, *de rudimentis hebraicis* (1506), is an excellent example of this type of material. Greek primers were more common: the Aldine press produced an edition of Lascaris' Greek grammar in 1495; Erasmus' translation of the famous Greek grammar of Theodore of Gaza appeared in 1516, and Melanchthon produced a masterly Greek primer in 1518.[9]

4   The humanist movement developed textual techniques capable of establishing accurately the best text of scripture. These techniques had been used, for example, by Lorenzo Valla to demonstrate the inauthenticity of the famous *Donation of Constantine* (see p. 41). It was now possible to eliminate many of the textual errors which had crept into the Parisian edition of the Vulgate. Erasmus shocked his contemporaries by excluding one verse of the Bible (1 John 5:7), which he could not

find in any Greek manuscript, as a later addition. The verse was certainly there in the Vulgate – but not in the Greek texts which it purported to translate. As this text had become an important proof-text for the doctrine of the Trinity, many were outraged at his action. Theological conservatism here often triumphed over scholarly progress: even the famous King James Version (also known as the Authorized Version) of 1611, for example, included the spurious verse, despite its obvious inauthenticity.[10]

5   The humanists tended to regard ancient texts as mediating an experience, which could be recaptured through the appropriate literary methods. Included in the theme *ad fontes* is the notion of recapturing the experience mediated by the text. In the case of the New Testament, the experience in question was that of the presence and power of the risen Christ. Scripture was thus read with a sense of anticipation – it was believed that the vitality and excitement of the apostolic era could be regained in the sixteenth century, by reading and studying scripture in the right manner.

6   In his *Enchiridion*, which became enormously influential in 1515, Erasmus argued that a biblically-literate laity held the key to the renewal of the church. Both clergy and church were marginalized: the lay reader of scripture had therein a more than adequate guide to the essentials of Christian belief and especially practice. These views, which achieved wide circulation among the lay intelligentsia of Europe, unquestionably prepared the way for the scriptural reforming programme of Luther and Zwingli in the period 1519–25. Even if Luther adopted a theological approach to scripture which contrasted with Erasmus' undoctrinaire attitude, he was widely regarded as building upon a solidly Erasmian foundation.

The Bible and the Reformation

'The Bible,' wrote William Chillingworth, 'I say, the Bible only, is the religion of Protestants.' These famous words of this seventeenth-century English Protestant summarize the Reformation attitude to scripture. Calvin stated the same principle less memorably, if more fully: 'Let this then be a sure axiom: that nothing ought to be admitted in the church as the Word of God, save that which is contained, first in the Law and the Prophets, and secondly in the writings of the Apostles; and that there is no other method of teaching in the church than according to the prescription and rule of his Word.' For Calvin, as we shall see, the institutions and regulations of both church and society were required to be grounded in scripture: 'I approve only of those human institutions which are founded upon the authority of God and derived from Scripture.' Zwingli titled his 1522 tract on scripture *On the Clarity and Certainty of the Word of God*, stating that 'the foundation of our religion is the written word, the scriptures of God.' Such views indicate the remarkably high view of scripture adopted by the Reformers. This view, however, was not without its difficulties, which we propose to explore in the present section.

The Canon of Scripture

Central to any programme which treats scripture as normative is the delimitation of scripture. In other words, what *is* scripture? The term 'canon' (a Greek word meaning 'rule' or 'norm') came to be used to refer to those scriptures recognized as authentic by the church. For medieval theologians, 'scripture' meant 'those works included in the Vulgate'. The Reformers, however, felt able to call this judgement into question. While all the New Testament works were accepted as canonical – Luther's misgivings concerning four of them gaining little support[11] – doubts were raised concerning the canonicity of a group of Old Testament works. A comparison of the contents of the Old Testament in the Hebrew Bible on the one hand, and the Greek and Latin versions (such as the Vulgate) on the other, shows that the latter contain a number of works not found in the former. Following the lead of Jerome, the Reformers argued that the only Old Testament writings which could be regarded as belonging to the canon of scripture were those originally included in the Hebrew Bible. A distinction was thus drawn between the 'Old Testament' and 'Apocrypha': the former consisted of works found in the Hebrew Bible, while the latter consisted of works found in the Greek and Latin bibles (such as the Vulgate), but *not* in the Hebrew Bible.[12] While some Reformers allowed that the apocryphal works were edifying reading, there was general agreement that these works could not be used as the basis of doctrine. Medieval theologians, however, to be followed by the Council of Trent in 1546, defined the 'Old Testament' as 'those Old Testament works contained in the Greek and Latin bibles', thus eliminating any distinction between 'Old Testament' and 'Apocrypha'.

A fundamental distinction thus developed between Roman Catholic and Protestant understandings of what the term 'scripture' actually meant. This distinction persists to the present day. A comparison of Protestant versions of the Bible – the two most important being the *Revised Standard Version* (RSV) and *New International Version* (NIV) – with a Roman Catholic Bible (such as the Jerusalem Bible) will reveal these differences. In fact, it is probably true to say that in modern times the Bible has generally been printed more often without than with the Apocrypha. For the Reformers, *scriptura sola* thus implied not merely one, but *two*, differences from their catholic opponents: not only did they attach a different status to scripture, but they disagreed over what scripture actually was. But what is the relevance of this dispute?

One catholic practice to which the Reformers took particular exception was that of praying for the dead. To the Reformers, this practice rested upon a non-biblical foundation (the doctrine of purgatory), and encouraged popular superstition and ecclesiastical exploitation. Their catholic opponents, however, were able to meet this objection by pointing out that the practice of praying for the dead was explicitly mentioned in scripture, at 2 Maccabees 12:40-6. The Reformers, however, having declared that this book was apocryphal (and hence not part of the Bible), were able to respond that, in their view at least, the practice was not scriptural. This merited the obvious riposte from the catholic side – that the Reformers based their theology on scripture, only after having excluded from the canon of scripture any works which happened to contradict this theology!

One outcome of this debate was the production and circulation of authorized lists of books which were to be regarded as 'scriptural'. The fourth session of the Council of Trent (1546) produced a detailed list, which included the works of the Apocrypha as authentically scriptural, while the Protestant congregations in Switzerland, France and elsewhere produced lists which deliberately omitted reference to these works, or else indicated that they were of no importance in matters of doctrine.

The Authority of Scripture

The Reformers grounded the authority of scripture in its relation to the Word of God. For some, that relation was an absolute identity: scripture *was* the Word of God. For others, the relation was slightly more circuitous: scripture *contained* the Word of God. Nevertheless, there was a consensus that scripture was to be received as if it were God himself speaking. For Calvin, the authority of scripture was grounded in the fact that the biblical writers were 'secretaries (*notaires authentiques*, in the French version of the *Institutes*) of the Holy Spirit'. As Heinrich Bullinger stated it, the authority of scripture was absolute and autonomous: 'Because it is the Word of God, the holy biblical scripture has adequate standing and credibility in itself and of itself.' Here was the gospel itself, able to speak for itself and challenge and correct its inadequate and inaccurate representations in the sixteenth century. Scripture was able both to pass judgement upon the late medieval church (and find it wanting) and also to provide the model for the new Reformed church which would arise in its wake.

A number of points will bring out the importance of the *sola scriptura* principle. First, the Reformers insisted that the authority of popes, councils and theologians is subordinate to that of scripture. This is not necessarily to say that they have *no* authority: as we shall see later, the Reformers allowed certain councils and theologians of the patristic era a genuine authority in matters of doctrine. It *is* to say that such authority is *derived from scripture*, and is thus subordinate to scripture. Luther tends to defend the *sola scriptura* principle by emphasizing the confusion and incoherence of medieval theology, whereas Calvin and Melanchthon argue that the best catholic theology (such as that of Augustine) supports their views on the priority of scripture. Calvin insists that the Bible, as the Word of God, must be regarded as superior to fathers and councils, although he is prepared to treat the latter with respect as aids to the interpretation of scripture:

> For although we hold that the Word of God alone lies beyond the sphere of our judgement, and that fathers and councils are of authority only in so far as they agree with the rule of the Word, we still give to councils and fathers such rank and honour as it is appropriate for them to hold under Christ.

Second, the Reformers argued that authority within the church does not derive from the status of the office-bearer, but from the Word of God which they serve. Traditional catholic theology tended to ground the authority of the office-bearer in the office itself – for example, the authority of a bishop resides in the fact that he is a bishop – and emphasized the historical continuity of the office of bishop with the apostolic era. The Reformers grounded the authority of bishops (or their Protestant equivalent) in their faithfulness to the Word of God. As Calvin stated this point:

> The difference between us and the papists is that they believe that the church cannot be the pillar of the truth unless she presides over the Word of God. We, on the other hand, assert that it is *because* she reverently subjects herself to the Word of God that the truth is preserved by her, and passed on to others by her hands.

Historical continuity is of little importance in relation to the faithful proclamation of the Word of God. The breakaway churches of the Reformation were obviously denied historical continuity with the institutions of the catholic church: no catholic bishop would ordain their clergy, for example. Yet the Reformers argued that the authority and functions of a bishop ultimately derived from faithfulness to the Word of God. Similarly, the decisions of bishops (and also of councils and popes) are authoritative and binding to the extent that they are faithful to scripture. Where the catholics stressed the importance of *historical* continuity, the Reformers emphasized equally the importance of *doctrinal* continuity. While the Protestant churches could not generally provide historical continuity with the episcopacy (except, as in the case of the English or the Swedish reformations, through defections of catholic bishops), they could supply the necessary fidelity to scripture – thus, in their view, legitimating the Protestant ecclesiastical offices. There might not be an unbroken historical link between the leaders of the Reformation and the bishops of the early church – but, the Reformers argued, as they believed and taught the same faith as those early church bishops (rather than the distorted gospel of the medieval church), the necessary continuity was there nonetheless.

The *sola scriptura* principle thus involved the claim that the authority of the church was grounded in its fidelity to scripture. The opponents of the Reformation, however, were able to draw upon a dictum of Augustine: 'I should not have believed the gospel, unless I was moved by the authority of the catholic church.' Did not the very existence of the canon of scripture point to the church having authority over scripture? After all, it was the church who defined what 'scripture' was – and this would seem to suggest that the church had an authority over, and independent of, scripture. Thus John Eck, Luther's opponent at the famous Leipzig Disputation of 1519, argued that 'scripture is not authentic without the authority of the church'. This clearly raises the question of the relation between scripture and tradition, to which we may now conveniently turn.

The Role of Tradition

The *scriptura sola* principle would seem to eliminate any reference to tradition in Christian theology. Christian doctrine, according to the Reformers, is to be based upon scripture, and scripture alone. Where is there any role for tradition in such an understanding of the sources of theology? In fact, however, the magisterial Reformers had a very positive understanding of tradition, as we shall see.

Earlier, we noted the two understandings of tradition characteristic of the late medieval period: 'Tradition 1' and 'Tradition 2' (see p. 97). The *scriptura sola* principle would seem to refer to an understanding of theology which allocates no role whatsoever to tradition – an understanding which we might designate 'Tradition 0'. The three main understandings of the relation between scripture and tradition current in the sixteenth century can be summarized as follows:

Tradition 0: The radical Reformation
Tradition 1: The magisterial Reformation
Tradition 2: The Council of Trent

At first, this analysis might seem surprising. Did not the Reformers *reject* tradition, in favour of the scriptural witness alone? In fact, however, the Reformers were concerned with the elimination of human additions to or distortions of the scriptural witness. The idea of a 'traditional interpretation of scripture' – embodied in the concept of 'Tradition 1' – was perfectly acceptable to the magisterial Reformers, *provided that this traditional interpretation could be justified*.

The only wing of the Reformation to apply the *scriptura sola* principle consistently was the radical Reformation, or 'Anabaptism'. For the radicals (or 'fanatics', as Luther dubbed them), such as Thomas Müntzer and Caspar Schwenkfeld, every individual had the right to interpret scripture as he pleased, subject to the guidance of the Holy Spirit. For the radical Sebastian Franck, the Bible 'is a book sealed with seven seals which none can open unless he has the key of David, which is the illumination of the Spirit'. Unless the Spirit is given to an individual, he cannot interpret scripture – but upon receiving that gift, he may interpret scripture as he pleases. The way was thus opened for individualism, with the private judgement of the individual raised above the corporate judgement of the church. Thus the radicals rejected the practice of infant baptism (to which the magisterial Reformation remained committed) as non-scriptural. (There is no explicit reference to the practice in the New Testament). Similarly, doctrines such as the Trinity and the divinity of Christ were rejected as resting upon inadequate scriptural foundations. 'Tradition 0' places the private judgement of the individual above the corporate judgement of the Christian church concerning the interpretation of scripture. It was a recipe for anarchy – and, as the history of the radical Reformation sadly demonstrates, that anarchy was not slow to develop.

As has often been noted, the magisterial Reformation was theologically rather conservative. Traditional doctrines – such as the divinity of Jesus Christ and the doctrine of the Trinity – were not rejected, on account of the Reformers' conviction that these traditional interpretations of scripture were correct. Equally, many traditional practices (such as infant baptism) were retained, on account of the Reformers' belief that they were consistent with scripture. The magisterial Reformation was painfully aware of the threat of individualism, and attempted to avoid this threat by placing emphasis upon the church's traditional interpretation of scripture, where this traditional interpretation was regarded as correct. Doctrinal criticism was directed against those areas in which catholic theology or practice appeared to have gone far beyond, or to have contradicted, scripture. As most of these developments took place in the Middle Ages, it is not surprising that the Reformers spoke of the period 1200–1500 as an 'era of decay' or a 'period of corruption' which they had a mission to reform. Equally, it is hardly surprising that we find the Reformers appealing to the fathers as generally reliable interpreters of scripture.[13]

This point is of particular importance, and has not received the attention it merits. One of the reasons why the Reformers valued the writings of the fathers, especially Augustine, was that they regarded them as exponents of a biblical theology. In other words, the Reformers believed that the fathers were attempting to develop a theology based upon scripture alone – which was, of course, precisely what they were also trying to do in the sixteenth century. The fathers were thus to be valued as reliable biblical exegetes. Of course, the new textual and philological methods available to the Reformers meant that they could correct the fathers on points of detail – but the Reformers were prepared to accept the 'patristic testimony' as a generally reliable interpretation of scripture. As that testimony included such doctrines as the Trinity and the divinity of Christ, and such practices as infant baptism, the Reformers were predisposed to accept these as authentically scriptural. It will thus be obvious that this high regard for a traditional interpretation of scripture (i.e., 'Tradition 1') gave the magisterial Reformation a strong bias towards doctrinal conservatism.

This understanding of the *sola scriptura* principle allowed the Reformers to criticize their opponents on both sides – on the one, the radicals, on the other the catholics. The catholics argued that the Reformers elevated private judgement above the corporate judgement of the church. The Reformers replied that they were doing nothing of the sort: they were simply restoring that corporate judgement to what it once was, through combating the doctrinal degeneration of the Middle Ages by an appeal to the corporate judgement of the patristic era. The radicals, however, had no place whatsoever for the 'testimony of the fathers'. As Sebastian Frank wrote in 1530: 'Foolish Ambrose, Augustine, Jerome, Gregory – of whom not one even knew the Lord, so help me God, nor was sent by God to teach. Rather, they were all apostles of Antichrist.' 'Tradition 0' had no place for any traditional interpretation of scripture. The magisterial Reformers thus dismissed this radical understanding of the role of scripture as pure individualism, a recipe for theological chaos.

It will therefore be clear that it is obviously totally incorrect to suggest that the magisterial Reformers elevated private judgement above the corporate judgement of the church, or that they descended into some form of individualism. This judgement is unquestionably true of the radical Reformation, the only wing of the Reformation to have been utterly consistent in its application of the *scriptura sola* principle. How often it is that the original radical ideas of a movement such as the Reformation are rejected in favour of more conservative ideas as that movement develops! For the magisterial Reformers, the scripture principle referred primarily to the conviction that all Christian theology and practice was ultimately grounded in the Bible, thus establishing that scripture was the sole normative source of Christian theology. The radical Reformation consistently espoused 'Tradition 0', where the magisterial Reformation espoused 'Tradition 1'. It is true that a certain degree of variation can be detected within the mainstream of the Reformation on this point: Zwingli is closer to the radical position than Calvin is, while Luther is closer to the catholic position. But none, it must be emphasized, was prepared to abandon the concept of a traditional interpretation of scripture, in favour of the radical alternative. As Luther gloomily observed, the inevitable result of such an approach was chaos – a 'new Babel'. Perhaps Luther would have had some sympathy for the views of John Dryden in the following century:

> The Book thus put in every vulgar hand,
> Which each presumed he best could understand,
> The common rule was made the common prey
> And at the mercy of the rabble lay.

The Council of Trent, meeting in 1546, responded to the threat of the Reformation by affirming a two-source theory. This affirmation by the Catholic Reformation of 'Tradition 2' declares that the Christian faith reaches every generation through two sources: scripture and an unwritten tradition. This extra-scriptural tradition is to be treated as having equal authority as scripture. In making this declaration, the Council of Trent appears to have picked up the later, and less influential, of the two main medieval understandings of 'tradition' – leaving the more influential to the Reformers. It is interesting to note that in recent years there has been a certain degree of 'revisionism' within Roman Catholic circles on this point, with several contemporary theologians arguing that Trent *excluded* the view that 'the Gospel is only partly in Scripture and partly in the traditions'.[14]

The Interpretation of Scripture

The general consensus of the magisterial Reformation was that scripture was the container of the Word of God. This Word, although uniquely given at a definite point in the past, could be recovered and appropriated by every generation through the guidance of the Holy Spirit. The early Reformation was characterized by the optimistic belief that it was possible to establish exactly what the Bible said on everything of importance, and make this the basis of a reformed Christianity. The archetypal statement of this exegetical optimism may be found in Erasmus' *Enchiridion*: for Erasmus, the ploughman may read scripture and understand it without any great difficulty. Scripture was clear and persuasive, and could serve as the manifesto of the reforming parties within Christendom.

In his great reforming treatise of 1520, *To the Christian Nobility of the German Nation*, Luther declared that the 'Romanists' had eliminated any threat of reform to the church by constructing three defensive walls around themselves.

> In the first place, when pressed by the temporal power, they have made decrees and declared that the temporal power had no jurisdiction over them, but that, on the contrary, the spiritual power is above the temporal. In the second place, when the attempt is made to reprove them with the Scriptures, they raise the objection that only the pope may interpret the Scriptures. In the third place, if threatened with a council, their story is that no one may summon a council except the pope.[15]

Luther seems to have seen himself as a Joshua with a mission to cast down the three walls of this new Jericho (see Joshua 6:1–20). With three blasts of his reforming trumpet, Luther delineates the broad features of his reforming programme. First, the distinction between the 'spiritual' and 'temporal' powers is abolished. Second, every believing Christian has the right to interpret scripture. Third, any Christian (but especially a German prince!) has the right to summon a reforming council. Luther's programme of reform is initially founded on these three principles, of which the second is of particular interest to us.

> Their claim that only the pope may interpret scripture is an outrageous fancied fable...The Romanists must admit that there are among us good

Christians who have the true faith, spirit, understanding, word, and mind of Christ. Why, then, should we reject the word and understanding of good Christians and follow the pope, who has neither faith nor the Spirit?[16]

Luther appears to suggest that the ordinary pious Christian believer is perfectly capable of reading scripture, and making perfect sense of what he finds within its pages. A similar position is defended by Zwingli in his important treatise of 1522, *On the Clarity and Certainty of the Word of God*. For Zwingli, scripture is perfectly clear. 'The Word of God, as soon as it shines upon an individual's understanding, illuminates it in such a way that he understands it'.

Yet by the end of the 1520s, this exegetical optimism had been discredited to a significant degree, largely through the serious disagreement between Luther and Zwingli over the interpretation of one biblical text: *Hoc est corpus meum*, 'this is my body' (Matthew 26:26). This text was central to the eucharist, and hence of enormous liturgical importance to Reformer and catholic alike. For Luther, this text meant what it said: 'this *is* my body' – in other words, the bread in the eucharist is the body of Christ. For Zwingli, however, its interpretation was somewhat different: 'this *signifies* my body' – in other words, the bread in the eucharist represents the body of Christ. As we shall see in the following chapter, the seriousness of this disagreement between the Reformers over the sacraments did more than divide the magisterial Reformation permanently into two movements: it demonstrated how difficult it was to reach agreement over the interpretation of even those passages of scripture which Luther regarded as most straightforward. The exegetical optimism of the late 1510s and early 1520s was also evident in the suggestion that the ordinary Christian could understand scripture – but by the 1530s, that ordinary Christian could only be relied upon to understand scripture if he was fluent in Hebrew, Greek and Latin, and was familiar with the complexities of linguistic theories.

For the catholic, scripture was difficult to interpret – and God had providentially supplied a reliable interpreter in the form of the church. The Roman Catholic church had the authority to interpret scripture authoritatively. The radical Reformers rejected this totally, as we have seen: every individual believer had the right and the ability to interpret scripture as seemed right to him. The magisterial Reformers found themselves in something of a quandary at this point. They had conceded that scripture is obscure at points, and thus requiring interpretation; their commitment to 'Tradition 1' rather than 'Tradition 0', however, required that they invoke the whole Christian community in the authoritative interpretation of scripture at these points. But how could they do this, without conceding that this authority really lay with the Roman Catholic church? How could an authoritative communal *Protestant* interpretation of scripture be given? We shall examine two means by which the Reformation attempted to overcome this difficulty.

The first means of dealing with the difficulty of interpreting scripture might be designated the 'catechetical' approach. Protestant readers of scripture were provided with a filter, by means of which they might interpret scripture. One example of such a 'filter' is Luther's *Lesser Catechism* (1529), which provided its readers with a framework by which they could make sense of scripture. The most famous guide to scripture, however, is Calvin's *Institutes*, especially the definitive version of 1559. Calvin is known to have initially modelled this work on Luther's catechism. In the preface to the French edition of 1541, Calvin states that the *Institutes* 'could be like a key and an entrance to give access to all the children of God, in order that they might really understand Holy Scripture'. In other words, the reader is expected to use Calvin's *Institutes* as a means to interpret scripture. As the history of the development of the Reformed church in France and the Lowlands indicates, Calvin's approach was remarkably successful. The reader need only have two books – the Bible and Calvin's *Institutes* – to gain full access to the Reformed faith. Calvin's use of scripture in the *Institutes* was so persuasive that it seemed to many that this book held the key to the proper interpretation of scripture. The complex medieval hermeneutical schemes could be dispensed with, in favour of this elegantly-written and lucid work.

The second means of dealing with the problem of the interpretation of scripture might be designated 'the political hermeneutic', and is specifically associated with Zwingli's Reformation at Zurich. This method is of particular importance in relation to the political history of the Reformation. At some point in 1520, the Zurich city council required all its priests to preach according to scripture, avoiding 'human innovations and explanations'. In effect, the decree committed Zurich to the *scriptura sola* principle. By 1522, however, it was clear that this decree had little value: how was scripture to be interpreted? A minor crisis arose in Lent 1522, when some of Zwingli's followers broke the fast traditionally observed at this time of year.[17] During a period in which it was traditional to eat only vegetables or fish, it seems that some of Zwingli's supporters succumbed to the pleasures of some sort of sausage. The city council reaffirmed their commitment to the observance of the Lenten fast a few weeks later on 9 April, and fined Froschauer a trivial amount for allowing it to be broken in his house. There the matter might have rested, except that seven days later Zwingli published (on Froschauer's presses!) a treatise arguing that nowhere in scripture was it required that believers should abstain from meat in Lent. A similar debate also developed during the same year concerning clerical marriage. As tension began to grow in Zurich, it became clear that some means of resolving such ambiguities was needed.

The central difficulty concerned how scripture was to be interpreted. On 3 January 1523 the city council announced that it, as the body entrusted with control of public preaching, had arranged a public disputation for later that same month to determine whether Zwingli's 67 *Schlussreden*, or 'key theses', were in accordance with scripture. This debate is now known as the 'First Zurich Disputation'. The debate, apparently modelled on academic disputations, took place at Zurich town hall on 29 January. It was a personal triumph for Zwingli. More significant, however, was the outcome for the city council, which emerged from the debate as the body entitled to determine what was in accordance with scripture and what was not.[18]

For Zwingli, the city and the church at Zurich were effectively one and the same body – a point which is of particular importance in relation to his theology of the church and sacraments, as we shall see in the following chapter. The city council, therefore, had a right to be involved in theological and religious matters. No longer was the Zurich Reformation to be detained by questions concerning the proper interpretation of scripture – the city council had effectively declared that *it* had the right to interpret scripture for the citizens of Zurich, and given notice that it intended to exercise that right. Scripture might indeed be ambiguous – but the political success of the Reformation at Zurich was virtually guaranteed by the unilateral decision of the city council to act as its interpreter. No appeal need therefore be made to pope or ecumenical council in relation to the interpretation of scripture: the city council was adequate for the needs of Zurich. Similar decisions reached at Basle and Berne on the basis of the Zurich model consolidated the Reformation in Switzerland, and, by allowing Geneva political stability in the mid-1530s, indirectly led to the success of Calvin's Reformation.

It will be obvious that the power struggles within early Protestantism concerned the question of who had the authority to interpret scripture. Whoever was recognized as possessing that authority was *de facto* in control of the ideology – and hence the social and political views – of the various factions of the Reformation. The pope's secular authority was linked with his role as the authoritative interpreter of scripture for Roman Catholics in much the same way. This observation allows us some important insights concerning the social and political dimensions of the Reformation. For example, the radical Reformation axiom, that the enlightened individual had full authority to interpret scripture for himself, is linked with the communism often associated with the movement. All individuals must be regarded as equal. Similarly, the failure of the radical Reformation to produce any first-class theologians – a factor of some importance in relation to the movement's premature degeneration into ideological chaos – reflects a reluctance to allow that any one individual has a right to lay down what others should think, or how they should interpret scripture.

The magisterial Reformation initially seems to have allowed that every individual had the right to interpret scripture, but subsequently became anxious concerning the social and political consequences of this idea. The Peasants' Revolt of 1525 appears to have convinced some, such as Luther, that individual believers (especially German peasants) were simply not capable of interpreting scripture. It is one of the ironies of the Lutheran Reformation, that a movement which laid such stress upon the importance of scripture should subsequently deny its less educated members direct access to that same scripture, for fear that they might misinterpret it (in other words, reach a different interpretation than that of the magisterial Reformers). For example, the school regulations of the Duchy of Württemberg laid down that only the most able school-children were to be allowed to study the New Testament in their final years – provided they studied it in Greek or Latin. The remainder – presumably the vast bulk – of the children were required to read Luther's *Small Catechism* instead. The direct interpretation of scripture was thus effectively reserved for a small and privileged group of people. To put it crudely, it became a question of whether you looked to the pope, to Luther or to Calvin as an interpreter of scripture. The principle of the 'clarity of scripture' appears to have been quietly marginalized, in the light of the use made of the Bible by the more radical elements within the Reformation. Similarly, the idea that everyone had the right and the ability to interpret scripture faithfully became the sole possession of the radicals.

On the basis of the discussion in the present chapter, it will be clear that the Reformation programme of a return to scripture was considerably more intricate than might be expected. The slogan *scriptura sola* turns out to mean something rather different from what might be expected, with the radical Reformation alone conforming to the popular stereotype of the Reformation on this point. Some of the questions raised in this discussion will be highlighted by the Reformation debate over the church and sacraments, to which we now turn.

For further reading

For a general introduction to the place of the Bible in Christianity and especially western European thought, see *The Cambridge History of the Bible*, eds. P. R. Ackroyd *et al.* (3 vols: Cambridge, 1963–9).

For excellent studies of the role of scripture in the medieval period, see:

Gillian R. Evans, *The Language and Logic of the Bible: The Earlier Middle Ages* (Cambridge, 1984).
Beryl Smalley, *The Study of the Bible in the Middle Ages* (Oxford, 3rd edn, 1983).

For the role of scripture in the Reformation, see:

Roland H. Bainton, 'The Bible in the Reformation', in *The Cambridge History of the Bible*, vol. 2, pp. 1–37.
Gillian R. Evans, *The Language and Logic of the Bible: The Road to Reformation* (Cambridge, 1985).
H. Jackson Forstmann, *Word and Spirit: Calvin's Doctrine of Biblical Authority* (Stanford, 1962).
Alister E. McGrath, *The Intellectual Origins of the European Reformation* (Oxford, 1987), pp. 122–74 (with detailed discussion of exegetical and critical methods).
Jaroslav Pelikan, *The Christian Tradition: A History of the Development of Doctrine. 4. Reformation of Church and Dogma (1300-1700)* (Chicago/London, 1984), pp. 203–17.

Also of interest is the role assigned to scripture in sixteenth-century Protestant Confessions (i.e., articles of faith). These Confessions are conveniently brought together, in English translation, in *Reformed Confessions of the Sixteenth Century*, ed. Arthur Cochrane (Philadelphia, 1966). It is important to observe that the early Reformed confessions place affirmation of faith in scripture before faith in God, reflecting the belief that it is only through scripture that a true faith in God is possible. On the canon of scripture, see French Confession (1559), articles 3, 4 (Cochrane, pp. 144–5); Belgic Confession (1561), articles 4, 6 (pp. 190–1); Second Helvetic Confession, article 1 (p. 226). On the authority of scripture, see First Helvetic Confession (1536), articles 1, 2 (Cochrane, pp. 100–1); Geneva Confession (1536), article 1 (p. 120); French Confession (1559), article 5 (pp. 145–6); Belgic Confession (1561), articles 3, 5, 7 (pp. 190–2); Second Helvetic Confession (1566), articles 1, 2 (pp. 224–7).

7

The Doctrine of the Church
and Sacraments

In many ways, the Reformers' views on the church represents their Achilles' heel. The Reformers were confronted with two consistent rival views of the church whose consistency they could not match – those of their catholic and radical opponents. For the former, the church was a visible, historic institution, possessing historical continuity with the apostolic church; for the latter, the true church was in heaven, and no institution of any kind on earth merited the name 'church of God'. The magisterial Reformers attempted to claim the middle ground somewhere between these two rival views, and found themselves involved in serious inconsistencies as a result. If the early Reformers were strong on grace and scripture, they were correspondingly weak on the church and its sacraments. We begin our discussion by considering the most serious disagreement to have erupted within the early reforming movement – the debate between Zwingli and Luther over the sacraments.

The Doctrine of the Sacraments

By the early 1520s, it was clear that the sacramental system of the medieval church was becoming the subject of considerable criticism from reforming factions. The medieval period had witnessed the consolidation of the theology of the sacaments, with seven sacraments being recognized. The Reformers, however, reduced the number of authentic sacraments to two. Henry VIII of England gained (at his own request) from the pope the title *Fidei Defensor*, 'defender of the faith', through his antiLutheran work *Assertio septem sacramentorum*, 'I assert that there are seven sacraments'. But why should the Reformers have been so preoccupied with the theology of the sacraments? To many, it seems a remarkably obscure and irrelevant subject. However, reflection on the context in which the Reformers operated will help explain why this question was so important to the Reformers.

For most lay persons, the main point of contact with the church was through church services on Sundays. The pulpit was one of the most important communication media of the medieval period for this very reason – hence the desire of both Reformers and city councils to control what was said from the pulpit! The main service of the medieval church was, of course, the Mass. This service was said according to a set form of words, in Latin, known as 'the liturgy'. The Reformers objected to this, for two reasons. First, the Mass was said in Latin, which most lay persons couldn't understand. Indeed, it has often been suggested that some of the clergy didn't understand the words either: late Renaissance humanists, fully competent in Latin, occasionally grumbled over priests who couldn't tell the difference between an accusative and an ablative. But second, and more seriously, the way in which the Mass was celebrated appeared to involve a number of assumptions that the Reformers found unacceptable. One such assumption was the theory known as 'transubstantiation', which held that the bread and wine in the Mass, when consecrated, retain their outward appearances, but are transformed respectively into the substance of the body and blood of Jesus Christ.

One of the most effective ways of promoting the cause of the Reformation was therefore to rewrite the liturgy in the vernacular (so that all could understand what was going on), altering it where necessary to eliminate ideas which the Reformers found unacceptable. By attending Sunday services, the laity would thus be exposed to the ideas of the Reformation from two sources – the sermon and the liturgy. Altering the ideas found in the liturgy means, of course, altering the theology of the sacraments, which is precisely what we find happening in the first decade of the Reformation. And it is at this point that we find the most serious disagreement between the magisterial Reformers developing. Luther and Zwingli, the leaders of the two wings of the magisterial Reformation, found themselves totally unable to agree in their views on the sacraments. A number of factors combined to bring about this disagreement: for example, differences in the way in which scripture was interpreted, and the different social contexts of the

Wittenberg and Zurich reformations. In what follows, we shall outline their different understandings of the sacraments, and indicate the importance of these differences for the history of the Reformation.

Luther on the Sacraments

In his reforming treatise of 1520, *The Babylonian Captivity of the Church*, Luther launched a major attack on the catholic understanding of the sacraments. Taking advantage of the latest humanist philological scholarship, he asserted that the Vulgate use of the term *sacramentum* was largely unjustified on the basis of the Greek text. Where the Roman Catholic church recognized seven sacraments, Luther initially recognized three (baptism, eucharist, penance), and shortly afterwards two (baptism and eucharist). According to Luther, the two essential characteristics of a sacrament were the Word of God and an outward sacramental sign (such as water in baptism, and bread and wine in the eucharist): the only true sacraments of the New Testament church were thus baptism and eucharist. He further argued that the medieval sacramental system gave a totally unjustified priority to priests. The sacraments were 'held captive by the church' in three ways:

1 The practice of 'communion in one kind' (in other words, giving the laity only bread, and not wine). According to Luther, this was unjustifiable and without scriptural or patristic precedent. Luther declared that the clerical refusal to offer the chalice (the vessel containing the wine) to the laity was sinful. So influential did Luther's attitude become that the practice of offering the laity the chalice became a hallmark of the Reformation.

2 The doctrine of transubstantiation (which we shall discuss below) seemed to Luther to be an absurdity, an attempt to rationalize a mystery. For Luther, the crucial point was that Christ was really present at the eucharist – not some particular theory as to how he was present. If iron is placed in a fire and heated, it glows – and in that glowing iron, both the iron and heat are present.[1] Why not use some simple everyday analogy such as this to illustrate the mystery of the presence of Christ at the eucharist, instead of rationalizing it using some scholastic subtlety?[2]

> For my part, if I cannot fathom how the bread is the body of Christ, yet I will take my reason captive to the obedience of Christ, and clinging simply to his words, firmly believe not only that the body of Christ

is in the bread, but that the bread is the body of Christ. My warrant for this is the words which say: 'He took bread, and when he had given thanks, he broke it and said, "Take, eat, this (that is, this bread, which he had taken and broken) is my body."' (1 Corinthians 11:23–4.)[3]

It is not the doctrine of transubstantiation which is to be believed, but simply that Christ really is present at the eucharist. The fact is more important than any theory or explanation.

3   The idea that the priest made an offering, or performed a good work or sacrifice, on behalf of the people was equally unscriptural. For Luther, the sacrament was primarily a promise of the forgiveness of sins, to be received through faith by the people.

> You see, therefore, that what we call the mass is a promise of the forgiveness of sins made to us by God, and such a promise as has been confirmed by the death of the Son of God...If the mass is a promise, as has been said, then access to it is to be gained, not with any works, or powers, or merits of one's own, but by faith alone. For where there is the word of the promising God, there must necessarily be the faith of the accepting man. It is plain therefore, that the beginning of our salvation is a faith which clings to the word of the promising God who, without any effort on our part, in free and unmerited mercy takes the initiative and offers us the word of his promise.[4]

Sacraments were concerned with the generation and nourishment of the faith of the people of God, whereas the medieval church tended to treat them as some sort of marketable commodity, capable of earning merit.

Luther was ordained priest in 1507, and celebrated his first Mass at Erfurt on 2 May of that year. He clearly found it a rather trying occasion. We find no hint of any misgivings concerning the traditional catholic understanding of the Mass in his writings, however, until 1519.[5] We have already noted his 'theological breakthrough' of 1515, in which he made his celebrated discovery of the new meaning of the 'righteousness of God' (see pp. 71–8). Although this discovery initially seems to have had no effect on his attitude to the sacraments, it appears that one aspect of his later critique of the medieval theology of the sacraments is foreshadowed in it. Linked with this discovery, significantly, was a new hostility to the use of Aristotelian ideas in theology.[6] In his

Disputation against Scholastic Theology of 1517, Luther makes clear his total rejection of Aristotelianism in theology.

The importance of this anti-Aristotelian development lies in its relation to the medieval doctrine of transubstantiation. This doctrine had been defined by the Fourth Lateran Council (1215), and rested upon Aristotelian foundations – more specifically, on Aristotle's distinction between 'substance' and 'accident'. The *substance* of something is its essential nature, whereas its *accidents* are its outward appearances (for example, its colour, shape, smell and so forth). The theory of transubstantiation affirms that the accidents of the bread and wine (their outward appearance, taste, smell and so forth) remain unchanged at the moment of consecration, while their substance changes from that of bread and wine to that of the body and blood of Jesus Christ. Luther rejected this 'pseudo-philosophy' as absurd, and urged the rejection of the use of such Aristotelian ideas. Aristotle had no place in Christian theology. Nevertheless, it is essential to appreciate that Luther did *not* criticize the underlying basic idea that the bread and wine became the body and blood of Christ: 'no importance attaches to this error, if only the body and blood of Christ are left together with the Word'. Luther's objection was not to the idea of the 'real presence', but to *one specific way of explaining that presence*. God is not merely *behind* the sacraments: he is *in* them as well.

Luther's view that the bread and wine really did become the body and blood of Christ was not the result of sheer theological conservatism. Indeed, Luther pointed out that, if he could have shown that this view was unbiblical, he would have been the first to abandon it. It seemed to him, however, that this was indeed the obvious meaning of biblical texts, such as Matthew 26:26, *hoc est corpus meum*, 'this is my body'.[7] The verse was perfectly clear, and seemed to him to admit no other interpretation. It seemed to Luther that the whole principle of the clarity of scripture (which he regarded as fundamental to his reforming programme at this point) was at stake over the interpretation of this verse. Andreas Karlstadt, his former colleague at Wittenberg – who eventually became his opponent in the 1520s – thought otherwise: it seemed to him that Christ pointed to himself when saying these words. Luther had little difficulty in dismissing this as absurd. He had considerably more difficulty in dealing with Zwingli's assertion that the word 'is' was simply a rhetorical figure of speech (known as *alloeosis*), which really mean 'signifies' or 'represents', and is not to be taken literally.

In common with all the magisterial Reformers, Luther retained the traditional practice of infant baptism. It might be thought that his doctrine of justification by faith alone contradicts this practice. After all, infants have no faith. It must be pointed out, however, that Luther's doctrine of justification by faith does not mean that the individual who has faith is justified for that reason: rather, as we saw earlier (pp. 76–7), it means that God graciously gives faith as a gift. In a paradoxical way, infant baptism is totally consistent with the doctrine of justification by faith, because it emphasizes that faith is not something we can achieve, but something which is given to us graciously. For Luther, the sacraments do not merely strengthen the faith of believers – they were capable of generating that faith in the first place. The sacrament mediates the Word of God, which is capable of evoking faith. For Zwingli, however, the sacraments merely confirmed the Word of God, which required to be preached separately. Thus Luther finds no difficulty with the practice of infant baptism. Baptism does not presuppose faith: rather, it generates faith. 'A child becomes a believer if Christ in baptism speaks to him through the mouth of the one who baptizes, since it is his Word, his commandment, and his Word cannot be without fruit.' Zwingli, in marked contrast, held that sacraments demonstrated the existence of faith, and thus could not use Luther's arguments to justify the practice of infant baptism. As we shall see, he was obliged to justify the practice on rather different grounds.

Luther's views on the 'real presence' were regarded with something approaching disbelief by his reforming colleagues in Zurich, Basle and Strasbourg. It seemed to them that Luther was being inconsistent at this point, making absurd concessions to his catholic opponents. We shall return to Luther's views shortly: let us now consider Zwingli's views, to gain an impression of the astonishing diversity of totally irreconcilable theories of the sacraments current in evangelical circles during the 1520s.

Zwingli on the Sacraments

Like Luther, Zwingli has grave misgivings about the word 'sacrament' itself. He notes that the term has the basic sense of 'oath', and initially treats the sacraments of baptism and eucharist (the remaining five sacraments of the catholic system being rejected) as signs of God's faithfulness to his people. Thus in 1523, he wrote that the word 'sacrament' could be used to refer to those things which 'God has instituted, commanded and ordained with his word, which is as firm and sure as if he had sworn an oath thereto'.[8] Zwingli thus initially treats the sacraments as pledges of God's goodness towards humanity, or signs of his gracious promises of forgiveness. Up to this point, there is a certain degree of similarity between the views of Luther and Zwingli on the functions of sacraments, although, as we shall indicate below, the question of the real presence of Christ in the eucharist divides them radically.

This limited agreement, however, evaporated by 1525. Zwingli retains the idea of a 'sacrament' as an oath or pledge – but whereas he had earlier understood this to be *God's pledge of faithfulness to us*, he now asserted that it refers to *our pledge of obedience and loyalty to one another*. It must be remembered that Zwingli was a chaplain to the army of the Swiss Confederacy (and was present at the disastrous defeat at Marignano in September 1515). Drawing on the military use of oaths, Zwingli argues that a 'sacrament' is basically a declaration of allegiance of an individual to a community. Just as a soldier swears allegiance to his army (in the person of the general) so the Christian swears allegiance to his fellow Christians. Zwingli uses the German term *Pflichtszeichen*, 'a demonstration of allegiance', to designate the essence of a sacrament. A sacrament is thus the means 'by which a man proves to the church that he either aims to be, or already is, a soldier of Christ, and which informs the whole church, rather than himself, of his faith'. In baptism, the believer pledges loyalty to the community of the church; in the eucharist, he demonstrates that loyalty publicly.

Zwingli thus develops the idea that the sacraments are subordinate to the preaching of the Word of God. It is this preaching which brings faith into existence: the sacraments merely provide an occasion by which this faith may be publicly demonstrated. The preaching of the Word of God is of central importance, and the sacraments are like seals on a letter – they confirm its substance.

Zwingli develops the meaning of the eucharist with a further military analogy drawn from his experience as an army chaplain for the Swiss Confederacy:

If a man sews on a white cross, he proclaims that he wishes to be a confederate. And if he makes the pilgrimage to Nähenfels and gives God praise and thanksgiving for the victory vouchsafed to our forefathers, he testifies that he is a confederate indeed. Similarly, the man who receives the mark of baptism is the one who is resolved to hear what God says to him, to learn the divine precepts, and to live his life in accordance with them. And the man who in the remembrance or supper gives thanks to God in the congregation testifies to the fact that from the very heart he rejoices in the death of Christ, and thanks him for it.[9]

The reference is to the victory of the Swiss over the Austrians in 1388 near Nähenfels, in the canton of Glarus. This victory is usually regarded as marking the beginning of the Swiss (or Helvetic) Confederation, and it was commemorated by a pilgrimage to the site of the battle on the first Thursday in April. Zwingli makes two points. First, the Swiss soldier wears a white cross (now incorporated into the Swiss national flag, of course) as a *Pflichtszeichen*, demonstrating publicly his allegiance to the Confederacy. Similarly, the Christian demonstrates his allegiance to the church publicly initially by baptism, and subsequently by attending the eucharist. Baptism is the 'visible entry and sealing into Christ'. Second, the historical event which brought the Confederacy into being is commemorated as a token of allegiance to that same Confederacy. Similarly, the Christian commemorates the historical event which brought the Christian church into being (the death of Jesus Christ) as a token of his commitment to that church. The eucharist is thus a memorial of the historical event leading to the establishment of the Christian church, and a public demonstration of the believer's allegiance to that church and its members.

This understanding of the nature of the eucharist is confirmed by Zwingli's treatment of Matthew 26:26, *hoc est corpus meum*, 'this is my body'. These words were spoken by Christ during the Last Supper, on the day before his death, signifying the manner in which he wished to be remembered by his church. It is as if Christ had said: 'I entrust to you a symbol of this my surrender and testament, to awaken in you the remembrance of me and of my goodness to you, so that when you see this bread and this cup, held forth in this memorial supper, you may remember me as delivered up for you, just as if you saw me before you as you see me now, eating with you.' For Zwingli, Christ's death has the same significance for the church as the battle of Nähenfels has for the Swiss Confederacy. It is the foundational event of the Christian church, central to its identity and self-understanding. Just as the commemoration of Nähenfels does not involve the re-enactment of that battle, so the eucharist involves neither the repetition of the sacrifice of Christ, nor his presence at the commemoration. The eucharist is 'a memorial of the suffering of Christ, and not a sacrifice'. For reasons which we shall explore below, Zwingli insists that the words 'this is my body' cannot be taken literally, thus eliminating any idea of the 'real presence of Christ' at the eucharist. Just as a man, on setting off on a long journey from home, might give his wife his ring to remember him by until his return, so Christ leaves his church a token to remember him by until the day on which he should return in glory.

In 1521 Cornelius Hoen circulated a letter suggesting that the word *est* in *hoc est corpus meum* should not be interpreted literally as 'is', or 'is identical with', but rather as *significat*, 'signifies'. For example, when Christ says 'I am the bread of life' (John 6:48), he is clearly not identifying himself with a loaf of bread, or bread in general. The word 'is' here must be taken in a metaphorical, or nonliteral, sense. One copy of the letter found its way to Luther, who reacted with a notable lack of enthusiasm. Zwingli, who does not appear to have received a copy of the letter until the summer of 1524, was considerably more positive in his reaction. By November and December of that year he was promoting Hoen's ideas with some vigour. In the summer of 1525, the learned Oecolampadius of Basle joined in the discussion, producing a book in which he argued that the writers of the patristic period knew nothing of either transubstantiation or Luther's views on the real presence, but tended towards the view now increasingly being associated with Zwingli.[10]

Zwingli argued that scripture employed many figures of speech. Thus the word 'is' might at one point mean 'is absolutely identical with', and at another it might mean 'represents' or 'signifies'. This point was developed by Oecolampadius in 1527, who asserted that 'in dealing with signs, sacraments, pictures, parables and interpretations, one should and one must understand the words figuratively and not understand the words literally'. Luther responded vigorously to such suggestions in his 1527 treatise *That these words of Christ 'This is my Body' still stand firm against the Fanatics*.

An additional argument used by Zwingli against Luther's views on the real presence concerns the location of Christ. For Luther, Christ is present at the eucharist. Whoever receives the bread and the wine receives Christ. Zwingli, however, points out that both scripture and the creeds affirm that Christ is now 'seated at the right hand of God'. Now Zwingli has not the slightest idea where this might be, and wastes no time speculating on its location – but, he argues, it does mean that wherever Christ is now, he isn't present in the eucharist. He can't be in two places at once. Luther argues that the phrase 'the right hand of God' (as used, for example, at Psalm 8:6 and Luke 10:22) is actually a metaphorical expression, not to be taken literally. It really means 'God's sphere of influence' or 'God's rule'. To say that 'Christ is seated at the right hand of God' does not mean that Christ is now located at a definite location in the stratosphere, but simply that Christ is present wherever God rules. Once more, the question of which scriptural passages were to be interpreted literally and which metaphorically emerged as central to the debate on the real presence.

Zwingli is obliged to face an obvious difficulty in relation to infant baptism. How, it was argued, could he justify baptizing infants, when these had no faith which they could publicly demonstrate? It is clear that Zwingli himself had some misgivings in the late 1510s and early 1520s over this practice.[11] By 1524, however, he appears to have developed a theory of baptism which got round this difficulty altogether. Zwingli pointed out that in the Old Testament infant males were circumcised within days of their birth as a sign of their membership of the people of Israel. Circumcision was the rite laid down by the Old Testament covenant to demonstrate that the circumcised child belonged to the covenant community. The child had been born into a community, to which it now belonged – and circumcision was a sign of belonging to this community.

There had been a long-standing tradition within Christian theology to see baptism as the Christian equivalent of circumcision. Developing this idea, Zwingli argued that baptism was the sign of belonging to a community – the church. The fact that the child was not conscious of this belonging was irrelevant: it *was* a member of the Christian community, and baptism was the public demonstration of this membership. The contrast with Luther on this point will be obvious.

Zwingli takes this argument a stage further. For Zwingli, 'state' and 'church' are virtually equivalent: 'a Christian city is nothing other than a Christian church'. The sacraments thus signified not merely loyalty to the church, but also loyalty to the city community of Zurich.[12] To refuse to allow one's child to be baptized, therefore, was an act of disloyalty to the Zurich city community. The magistrates were thus entitled to expel from Zurich all who refused to allow their children to be baptized. The Anabaptists, as we have seen, regarded infant baptism as unjustifiable. As the radical Reformation posed a major threat to the Reformation at Zurich in the 1520s, on account of both its religious and political views, Zwingli's understanding of baptism as both an ecclesial and civic event provided an excellent means of enforcing political conformity.

Baptism thus became of central importance to Zwingli, in that it provided a criterion by which two totally different concepts of the church might be distinguished. Zwingli's concept of a state or city church was increasingly challenged by the Anabaptists, whose vision of the church involved a return to the simplicities of the apostolic church. For the radicals, the simplicity of that church had been totally destroyed through the conversion of the Roman emperor Constantine in the early fourth century, leading to a close alliance of church and state. The Anabaptists wished to sever this link, whereas Zwingli wished it to be continued in the specific form found at Zurich. Thus Zwingli felt justified in declaring that 'the issue is not baptism, but revolt, faction and heresy'. Baptism represented the criterion which determined whether an individual was a loyal citizen of Zurich, or a traitor to that city. As Anabaptism became an increasing threat to that city in the 1520s, the magistrates at least appreciated the importance of Zwingli's theology at this point. But this point merely emphasizes how closely theology and city and imperial politics were linked in the first era of the Reformation. The very term 'magisterial Reformation' itself points to this close relationship between the magistrates and the Reformation.

The Differences between Luther and Zwingli
Summarized and Evaluated

The debate between Luther and Zwingli is somewhat technical, and may have proved difficult to follow. It may therefore prove helpful if we summarize the main points of difference between them, both recapitulating and extending the above discussion.

1   Both Reformers reject the medieval sacramental scheme. Whereas the medieval period had identified seven sacraments, the Reformers insisted that only two sacraments – baptism and the eucharist – were recognized by the New Testament. Luther was perhaps more conservative in this respect than Zwingli, initially allowing that penance might be considered sacramental, before withdrawing this view in 1520.

2   Luther understands the Word of God and the sacraments to be inseparably linked. Both bear witness to Jesus Christ, and both mediate his power and presence. The sacraments are thus capable of creating, as well as supporting or demonstrating, faith. For Zwingli, it is the Word of God which creates faith, and the sacraments which demonstrate that faith publicly. Word and sacrament are quite distinct, with the former being of greater importance.

3   Although both Reformers retain the traditional practice of infant baptism, they do so for very different reasons. For Luther, sacraments can generate faith – and hence baptism may generate faith in an infant. For Zwingli, sacraments demonstrate allegiance to and membership of a community – and hence baptism demonstrates that an infant belongs to a community.

4   Luther is considerably more traditional in his approach to the celebration of the eucharist than Zwingli. In his major liturgical reforming work *Concerning the order of public worship* (1523), Luther makes it clear that he is prepared to retain the traditional title of 'Mass', providing it is not misunderstood as implying a sacrifice, and to authorize it to be celebrated weekly, preferably in the vernacular, *as the main Sunday service.* Zwingli, however, abolished the title 'Mass', and suggested that the equivalent evangelical rite should be celebrated three or four times a year. No longer was it the centre of Christian worship. Where Luther included a new emphasis upon preaching within the context of the eucharist, Zwingli insisted that this new emphasis should displace the eucharist from its customary weekly Sunday celebration.

5   Luther and Zwingli cannot agree on the meaning of the words *hoc est corpus meum* (Matthew 26:26), central to the eucharist. For Luther, *est* means 'is'; for Zwingli, it means 'signifies'. Two very different ways of interpreting scripture underlie this disagreement.

6   Both Reformers reject the medieval doctrine of transubstantiation.

Luther does so, however, on the basis of its Aristotelian foundations, and is prepared to accept the basic idea which underlies it – the real presence of Christ at the eucharist. Zwingli rejects both the term and the idea. Christ is remembered in his absence at the eucharist.

7   Zwingli asserts that, as Christ now stands at the right hand of God, he cannot be present anywhere else. Luther dismisses Zwingli's assertion as philosophically unsophisticated, and defends the idea of Christ being present without any limits imposed by space or time. Luther's defence of the 'ubiquity of Christ' rested upon some distinctions associated with William of Ockham, which further persuaded Luther's opponents that he had lapsed into some form of new scholasticism.

The dispute between Luther and Zwingli is important at both the theological and political levels. At the theological level, it raised the gravest of doubts concerning the principle of the 'clarity of scripture'. Luther and Zwingli were unable to agree on the meaning of such phrases as 'this is my tody' (which Luther interpreted literally, and Zwingli metaphorically) and 'the right hand of God' (which – with apparent inconsistency on both sides – Luther interpreted metaphorically and Zwingli interpreted literally). The exegetical optimism of the early Reformation may be regarded as foundering on this rock: scripture, it seemed, was far from easy to interpret.

At the political level, the dispute ensured the permanent separation of the two evangelical factions of the Reformation. An attempt to mediate between their rival views took place at the Colloquy of Marburg (1529), attended by such luminaries as Bucer, Luther, Melanchthon, Oecolampadius and Zwingli. By this stage, it was increasingly obvious that unless the Reformation could achieve a significant degree of internal unity, at least some of its gains would be reversed. The catholics had been inhibited from taking military action against the cities of the Reformation due to such long-standing disputes as that between Emperor Charles V and Francis I of France on the one hand, and Pope Clement VII on the other. In 1529, these disputes were resolved within weeks of each other.[13] Suddenly, the two wings of the Reformation faced a powerful political and military threat. The most obvious course of action was to settle their differences – a procedure urged by Bucer, who suggested that differences should be tolerated among evangelicals, provided they agreed to recognize the Bible alone as the normative source of faith. The Protestant landgrave Philip of Hesse, anxious at the new political situation, brought Luther and Zwingli together in the castle hall of Marburg in an attempt to resolve their differences.[14]

That attempt foundered on one point, and one point only. On fourteen articles, Luther and Zwingli felt able to agree. The fifteenth had six points, on which they were able to reach agreement on five. One point, and one point only, remained. But for Luther, Christ was really present at the eucharist, whereas for Zwingli he was present only in the hearts of believers. Philip of Hesse's hope of a united evangelical front against the newly-regrouped catholic forces was dashed, and the political credibility of the Reformation seriously compromised. By 1530, Charles V had begun to re-assert his authority over the German Reformation, helped to no small extent by the political consequences of the differences between Luther and Zwingli over the eucharist.

The Doctrine of the Church

'The Reformation, inwardly considered, was just the ultimate triumph of Augustine's doctrine of grace over Augustine's doctrine of the church.'[15] We have already seen how both wings of the magisterial Reformation laid claim to the insights of Augustine of Hippo concerning grace. Both Luther's doctrine of justification by faith alone, and the emphasis placed by Zwingli and Calvin upon divine predestination, represent slightly different ways of reading Augustine's antiPelagian writings. As we have seen, the Reformation arose within an intellectual context which placed new emphasis upon the importance of this great Christian writer of the late fourth and early fifth centuries, reflected in the publication of the Amerbach edition of Augustine's works in 1506.

The Reformers were convinced that the church of their day and age had lost sight of the doctrine of grace, which Luther regarded as the centre of the Christian gospel. Thus Luther declared that his doctrine of justification by faith alone was the *articulus stantis et cadentis ecclesiae*, 'the article by which the church stands or falls'. Convinced that the catholic church had lost sight of this doctrine, he concluded (with some reluctance, it would seem) that it had lost its claim to be considered as the authentic Christian church. The catholics responded to this suggestion with derision: Luther was simply creating a breakaway faction which had no connection with the church. In other words, he was a schismatic – and had not Augustine condemned schism? Had not Augustine placed enormous emphasis upon the unity of the church, which Luther now threatened to disrupt? Luther, it seemed, could only uphold Augustine's doctrine of grace by rejecting Augustine's doctrine of the church. It is in the context of this tension between two aspects of Augustine's thought, which proved to be incompatible in the sixteenth century, that the Reformation understandings of the nature of the church are to be seen.

The Context of the Reformation Views on the Church

In his period as an academic reformer, Luther shared a profound distaste for schism. Even the row over the Ninety-Five Theses on indulgences of 31 October 1517 did not persuade Luther to break away from the church. In the twentieth century, we have become used to the pheno-menon of 'denominationalism' – but the very idea of the western church breaking up into smaller parts was completely alien to the medieval period. Schism, to put it bluntly, was unthinkable. As Luther himself wrote in early 1519: 'If, unfortunately, there are things in Rome which cannot be improved, there is not – and cannot be! – any reason for tearing oneself away from the church in schism. Rather, the worse things become, the more one should help her and stand by her, for by schism and contempt nothing can be mended.'[16] Luther's views here parallel those of other reforming groups throughout Europe: the church must be reformed from within.

The assumption that the growing alienation of the Wittenberg Reformation from the catholic church was purely temporary seems to underlie much of the thinking of Lutheran writers in the period 1520–41. It seems that the evangelical faction at Wittenberg believed that the catholic church would indeed reform itself, perhaps through convening a reforming council, within a matter of years, thus allowing the Lutherans to rejoin a renewed and reformed church. Thus the Augsburg Confession (1530), setting out the main lines of Lutheran belief, is actually remarkably conciliatory towards catholicism. Such hopes of reunion were, however, dashed in the 1540s. In 1541, the Colloquy of Regensburg[17] seemed to offer the hope of reconciliation, as a group of Protestant and catholic theologians met to discuss their differences. Those discussions ended in failure. In 1545, the Council of Trent finally met to hammer out the response of the catholic church to the Reformation. Some, such as Cardinal Reginald Pole, had hoped that the Council would prove to be conciliatory towards the Protestants: in the event, however, the Council identified and condemned the leading ideas of Protestantism. Any hopes of reconciliation had been dashed. The Protestant churches now had to recognize that their existence was not temporary, but permanent. They had to justify their existence *as Christian churches* alongside a body which seemed to have a much stronger claim to that title – the Roman Catholic church itself.

On this basis of this historical preamble, it will be obvious that the Reformers' concern with the theory of the church dates from the 1540s. It is a question which preoccupied the second, rather than the first, generation of Reformers. If Luther was concerned with the question, 'How may I find a gracious God?', his successors were obliged to deal with the question which arose out of this – 'Where can I find the true church?' Supreme among second-generation Reformers, of course, is John Calvin, and it is in his writings that we find perhaps the most important contributions to this debate.

The Nature of the Church

The early Reformers were convinced that the medieval church had become corrupted and its doctrine distorted either through a departure from scripture on the one hand, or through human additions to scripture on the other. Luther's early views on the nature of the church reflect his emphasis on the Word of God: the Word of God goes forth conquering, and wherever it conquers and gains true obedience to God *is* the church.

> The sure mark by which the Christian congregation can be recognized is that the pure gospel is preached there. For just as the banner of an army is the sure sign by which one can know what kind of lord and army have taken to the field, so too the gospel is the sure sign by which one knows where Christ and his army are encamped...Likewise, where the gospel is absent and human teachings rule, there no Christians live

but only pagans, no matter how numerous they are and how holy and upright their life may be.[18]

An episcopally ordained ministry is therefore not necessary to safeguard the existence of the church, whereas the preaching of the gospel is essential to the identity of that church. 'Where the word is, there is faith; and where faith is, there is the true church.' The visible church is constituted by the preaching of the Word of God: no human assembly may claim to be the 'church of God' unless it is founded on this gospel. We have already seen (p. 105) how this understanding of the church is functional, rather than historical: what legitimates a church or its office-bearers is not *historical* continuity with the apostolic church, but *theological* continuity. It is more important to preach the same gospel as the apostles than to be a member of an institution which is historically derived from them. A similar understanding of the church may be found with Philip Melanchthon, Luther's colleague at Wittenberg, who conceived of the church primarily in terms of its function of administering the means of grace.

Luther's vision of the church possessed the great virtue of simplicity. Simplicity, however, frequently amounts to inadequacy. As it became increasingly clear that Luther and Zwingli could not agree over what the gospel was (their eucharistic disagreement highlighting this point), the credibility of Luther's vision of the church became undermined. More serious, however, was the challenge posed by the radical Reformation, to which we may now turn.

For the radicals, such as Sebastian Franck, the apostolic church had been totally compromised through its close links with the state, dating back to the conversion of the Emperor Constantine. As an institution, the church was corrupted by human power struggles and ambition. Frank wrote thus:

> I believe that the outward Church of Christ, including all its gifts and sacraments, because of the breaking in and laying waste by antichrist right after the death of the apostles, went up into heaven, and lies concealed in the Spirit and in truth. I am thus quite certain that for fourteen hundred years now there has existed no gathered Church nor any sacrament.

Just as most of the radicals were utterly consistent in their application of the *scriptura sola* principle, so they were equally consistent in their views on the institutional church. The true church was in heaven, and its institutional parodies were on earth.[19]

Luther was thus forced to deal with two difficulties. If the church was not institutional, but was defined by the preaching of the gospel, how could he distinguish his views from the radicals? He himself had conceded that 'the church is holy even where the fanatics [Luther's term for the radicals] are dominant, so long as they do not deny the word and the sacraments'. Alert to the political realities of his situation, he countered by asserting the need for an institutional church. Just as he tempered the radical implications of the *scriptura sola* principle by an appeal to tradition (see pp. 106–9), so he tempered his potentially radical views on the nature of the true church by insisting that it had to be viewed as an historical institution. The institution of the church is the divinely instituted means of grace. But by countering the radicals by asserting that the church was indeed visible and institutional, Luther found himself having difficulty in distinguishing his views from those of his catholic opponents. He himself fully appreciated this problem:

> We on our part confess that there is much that is Christian and good under the papacy; indeed, everything that is Christian and is good is to be found there and has come to us from this source. For instance, we confess that in the papal church there are the true Holy Scriptures, true baptism, the true sacrament of the altar, the true keys to the forgiveness of sins, the true office of the ministry, the true catechism in the form of the Lord's Prayer, the Ten Commandments and the articles of the Creed.[20]

Luther is thus obliged to assert that 'the false church has only the appearance, although it also possesses the Christian offices'. In other words, the medieval church may have *looked like* the real thing, but it was really something rather different.

The logic of the situation became impossible, especially when Luther was confronted with two further problems. The first was posed by St Paul's letters in the New Testament to the Corinthians and Galatians. St Paul wrote to these churches, accusing them of having departed from the gospel – yet he still addresses them as Christian churches. How could Luther go further than Paul in this matter? At worst, the Roman church was like the Galatian church – having departed from the gospel at points, it could still be treated as a Christian church.

The second problem was posed by an aspect of Augustine's theory of the church, going back to the Donatist controversy of the early fifth century.[21] The Donatists were a breakaway movement in the north African church, who insisted that the catholic church of their day had become compromised through its attitude to the Roman authorities during a period of persecution. Only those who were truly holy could be recognized as members of the true church. Augustine argued the catholic case: the church must be recognized as having a mixed membership, both saints and sinners. The righteous and the wicked coexisted within the same church, and no human had the authority to weed out the wicked from the church.

Augustine drew upon the parable of the tares (Matthew 13:24–31) to make this point. In this parable, the owner of a field arrives one morning to find both wheat and weeds ('tares', in older English) growing side by side. Selective herbicides being unknown, he is reluctant to try to remove the weeds: by doing so, he would inevitably damage some of the wheat as well. His solution to his problem is to wait until the wheat is ready to harvest, and then separate them. According to Augustine, this parable applies to the church. Like the field in the parable, the church contains both wheat and weeds, the just and the wicked, which coexist until the day of judgement. On that day, God will judge between them – and no human is permitted to pre-empt God's judgement. The church will thus contain both good and evil until the end of time. Augustine argues that the term 'catholic' (which literally means 'whole'), as applied to the church, describes its mixed membership of saints and sinners.

The 'Donatist' and 'Augustinian' views of the church are thus very different. The difference is not merely of purely theological relevance, but affects their social function. This point was made with clarity by Max Weber in his pioneering work *The Protestant Ethic and the Spirit of Capitalism*, and was popularized by Ernst Troeltsch. According to Troeltsch, the sociological distinction involved is between a 'church' on the one hand, and a 'sect' on the other:

> The Church is that type of organization which is overwhelmingly conservative, which to a certain extent accepts the secular order, and dominates the masses; in principle, therefore, it is universal, i.e., it desires to cover the whole of the life of humanity. The sects, on the other hand,

are comparatively small groups; they aspire after personal inward perfection, and they aim at a direct personal fellowship between the members of each group. From the very beginning, therefore, they are forced to organize themselves in small groups, and to renounce the idea of dominating the world.[22]

For Augustine, Christianity is embodied as a church; for the Donatists, as a sect. It is thus Augustine's view of the church which ensures its social importance.

Luther accepted Augustine's view of the church as a 'mixed' body, whereas the radicals developed a Donatist view of the church as a body of the just, and the just alone. Like the Donatists, the radicals demanded moral perfection of their members. The church and the world were opposed to one another as light and darkness, and they had no time for what they regarded as the political compromises of Luther and Zwingli. For Luther, however, corrupt churchmen are found in the church 'just as mouse droppings are found among peppercorns, or tares among the grain'. It is one of the ecclesiastical facts of life, recognized by Augustine, which Luther endorses. The magisterial Reformation thus leads to the establishment of a church, whereas the radical Reformation leads to the formation of sects. The sociological distinction between the two movements reflects their different understandings of the nature of the church. Theology and sociology are closely linked at this point. (Earlier, we noted the famous maxim which represents the Reformation as the triumph of Augustine's doctrine of grace over his doctrine of the church: it is necessary at this point to note that Luther and the other magisterial Reformers retained at least this aspect of Augustine's theory of the church.) But what basis does Luther then have for breaking away from the catholic church? Does not this aspect of his theory of the church necessarily imply that there will always be corruption in the true church? On the basis of Augustine's theory, corruption in the catholic church does not necessarily mean that it is a 'false church'.

If any Reformer wrestled with the problem posed by the doctrine of the church, it was Calvin. The first major discussion of the theory of the church is to be found in the second edition of his *Institutes of the Christian Religion*, published in 1539. Although Calvin deals with the subject in the first edition of the *Institutes* (1536), he was then quite innocent of any experience of ecclesiastical management or responsibility, which accounts for the curiously unfocused nature of his discussion. By the time of the second edition of this work, Calvin had gained more experience of the problems presented to the new evangelical churches.

For Calvin, the marks of the true church were that the Word of God should be preached, and that the sacraments be rightly administered. Since the Roman Catholic church did not conform to even this minimalist definition of the church, the evangelicals were perfectly justified in leaving it. And as the evangelical churches conform to this definition of a church, there was no justification for further division within them. This point is of particular importance, reflecting Calvin's political judgement that further fragmentation of the evangelical congregations would be disastrous to the cause of the Reformation.

By 1543, Calvin had gained considerably more experience of ecclesiastical responsibility, particularly during his period at Strasbourg. Bucer, the intellectual force behind the Reformation at Strasbourg, had a considerable reputation as an ecclesiastical administrator, and it is probable that Calvin's later theory of the church reflects his personal influence. For example, a distinction which Calvin now employs – between the visible and the invisible church – is certainly to be found in Bucer's writings. Scripture, according to Calvin, uses the word 'church' in two different senses. At some points, it uses the word to refer to the invisible totality of the elect, living and dead; at others, to refer to the 'visible' church, as it is represented by living congregations in the present. Calvin now argues that there are specific scriptural directions regarding the right order of ministry in the visible church, so that a specific form of ecclesiastical order now becomes an item of doctrine. In other words, he includes a specific form of ecclesiastical administration (and he here borrows the term *administratio* from the field of secular government) in 'the gospel purely preached'.

Calvin's minimalist definition of the church now takes on a new significance. The true church is to be found where the gospel is rightly preached, and the sacraments rightly administered – and understood to be included within this definition is a specific form of ecclesiastical institution and administration. Calvin refers to the 'order by which the Lord willed his church to be governed', and develops a detailed theory of church government based upon his exegesis of the New Testament, drawing extensively upon the terminology of the imperial

Roman adminstration. Contrary to what the radicals asserted, Calvin insists that a specific form of church structure and administration is laid down by scripture. Thus Calvin he that the ministerial government of the church is divinely ordained, as is the distinction between 'minister', 'elder', 'deacon' and 'people'.

The precise details of Calvin's regulations for church government need not concern us.[23] What is of particular importance is the new development which is obvious in the theory of the church. Luther had defined the church in terms of the ministry of the Word of God, which was of little help in distinguishing the magisterial Reformation from the catholic position on the other hand, and the position of the radicals on the other. Calvin, while retaining an emphasis on the importance of the ministry of the Word of God, now insisted that this same Word of God specified one particular form of church government. This was a bold new step in the interpretation of scripture; it also gave Calvin a criterion by which to judge (and find wanting) his catholic and radical opponents. Where Luther was vague, Calvin was precise. By the time of Calvin's death (1564), the Reformed church was as institutionalized as its catholic rival, and had become its most formidable opponent.

For further reading

For the Reformers' views on the sacraments, see:

Timothy George, 'The Presuppositions of Zwingli's Baptismal Theology', in *Prophet, Pastor, Protestant: The Work of Huldrych Zwingli after Five Hundred Years*, eds E. J. Furcha and H. Wayne Pipkin (Allison Park, PA, 1984), pp. 71–87.

Brian Gerrish, 'Gospel and Eucharist: John Calvin on the Lord's Supper', in *The Old Protestantism and the New: Essays in the Reformation Heritage* (Chicago, 1982), pp. 106–17.

Basil Hall, '*Hoc est corpus meum*: The Centrality of the Real Presence for Luther', in *Luther: Theologian for Catholics and Protestants*, ed. George Yule (Edinburgh, 1985), pp. 112–44.

Killiam McDonnell, *John Calvin, The Church and the Eucharist* (Princeton, 1967).

David C. Steinmetz, 'Scripture and the Lord's Supper in Luther's Theology', in *Luther in Context* (Bloomington, Ind., 1986), pp. 72–84.

W. P. Stephens, *The Theology of Huldrych Zwingli* (Oxford, 1986), pp. 180–259.

For the Reformers' views on the church, see:

Paul D. L. Avis, *The Church in the Theology of the Reformers* (London, 1981).

Rupert E. Davies, *The Problem of Authority in the Continental Reformers* (London, 1946).

F. H. Littel, *The Anabaptist View of the Church* (Boston, 2nd edn, 1958).

J. T. McNeill, 'The Church in Sixteenth-Century Reformed Theology', *Journal of Religion* 22 (1942), pp. 251–69.

W. P. Stephens, *The Holy Spirit in the Theology of Martin Bucer* (Cambridge, 1970), pp. 156–66.

——, *The Theology of Huldrych Zwingli*, pp. 260–81.

8

The Political Thought of the Reformation

In the previous chapter, we noted two distinct theological views of the church associated with the Reformation, each resulting in a different sociological role for that body: the Augustinian model, which corresponds sociologically to a 'church'; and the Donatist model, which corresponds sociologically to a 'sect' (see pp. 135–6). The magisterial Reformers adopted the former model, and their radical opponents the latter model. For the radical Menno Simons, the church was 'an assembly of the righteous', at odds with the world. This notion of the church as a faithful remnant in conflict with the world harmonized with the Anabaptist experience of persecution by the forces of Antichrist, personified in the magistracy. Where the radicals with their rigorous views on church membership had no time for compromises with the state or city authorities,[1] however, the magisterial Reformers depended upon precisely such compromises. Indeed, the very phrase 'magisterial Reformation' points to the close co-operation of Reformer and magistrate in the propagation and defence of the Reformation.

We have already noted (pp. 5–6) the rise in power of secular governments throughout Europe in the early sixteenth century. The Concordat of Bologna, for example, had given to the King of France the right to appoint all the senior clergy of the French church. The ascendancy of the catholic church in both France and Spain was maintained primarily through state interests. The political realities of the early sixteenth century demanded a similar liason between the states or cities and the churches of the Protestant Reformation. It must not, however, be thought that the 'magisterial Reformers were political puppets: their understanding of the role of the city or state authorities in reforming the church reflects their theological presuppositions. In what follows, we shall examine the political views of the four major magisterial Reformers: Luther, Zwingli, Bucer and Calvin.

Luther's Doctrine of the Two Kingdoms

The medieval period witnessed the development of the 'doctrine of the two estates' – the *temporal* and the *spiritual*. According to this view, actively promoted by supporters of papal political manoeuvring, the clergy belonged to the 'spiritual estate', and the laity to the 'temporal' estate. These two estates, or realms or spheres of authority, were quite distinct. Although the spiritual estate could (and did) intervene in the affairs of the temporal estate, the latter was not permitted to interfere with the former. Underlying this theory is a long history of papal controversy with secular rulers, particularly during the period of the Avignon papacy.[2]

Viewed pragmatically, this understanding of the spheres of influence of the secular and ecclesiastical powers meant that the reformation of the church was a matter purely for that church itself: laity, whether peasants or secular rulers such as the emperor himself, did not possess the necessary authority to bring about the reform of the church. As we saw earlier (p. 110), this is the first of Luther's 'three walls' of the modern-day Jericho which he proposed to demolish. Convinced that the church had locked itself into its position, Luther developed the doctrine of the 'priesthood of all believers' in his famous reforming treatise of 1520, *To the Christian Nobility of the German Nation*:

> It is pure invention that pope, bishop, priests and monks are called the spiritual estate, while princes, lords, artisans and farmers are called the temporal estate. . . All Christians are truly of the spiritual estate, and there is no difference between them except that of office. . . We are all consecrated priests through baptism, as St Peter says in 1 Peter 2:9.[3]

While fully recoizing the need for administration within the church, Luther insists that the difference is purely one of office and not status. All believers, by virtue of their baptism, belong to the spiritual estate. (Notice that Luther is able to assume that all Germans are baptized). 'Christ does not have two bodies, one temporal, the other spiritual.

There is but one head and one body.'[4] Laity have thus a right to demand a general council to reform the church – and, tongue placed firmly in his cheek, Luther reminds his readers that it was the Roman emperor Constantine (a lay man if ever there was one) who was responsible for calling the most important council in the history of the church (Nicea, in 325). Why should not the German nobility call for a council to reform the church in 1520?

Having thus abolished the medieval distinction between the 'temporal' and 'spiritual' estates, Luther proceeds to develop an alternative theory of spheres of authority, based upon a distinction between the 'Two Kingdoms' or the 'Two Governments'.[5] It is this doctrine of the 'Two Kingdoms' which is central to Luther's social thought, and with which we are concerned in the present section.

Luther draws a distinction between the 'spiritual' and the 'worldly' government of society. God's *spiritual* government is effected through the Word of God and the guidance of the Holy Spirit. The believer who 'walks by the Spirit' needs no further guidance from anyone as to how he should act: he is perfectly in tune with the divine will, and acts accordingly. Just as a good tree needs no instructions to bear good fruit, so the true believer needs no legislation to guide his conduct. Just as a tree bears fruit naturally, so the believer naturally acts morally and responsibly.[6] Luther also emphasizes the difference between human and divine conceptions of 'righteousness' or 'justice', a theme which we noted earlier as characteristic of his 'theology of the cross' (p. 83). God's standards of justice call those of the world into question.[7]

God's *worldly* government is effected through kings, princes and magistrates, through the use of the sword and the civil law. They have no authority in matters of doctrine. 'When temporal princes and lords try to change and be master of the Word of God in such a high-handed manner – something which is as fobidden to them as it is to the meanest beggar – they are seeking to be God themselves.' Their proper sphere of authority concerns the affairs of the world, the things of Caesar rather than of God. Although these temporal rulers are involved in the secular world, they are nevertheless performing the work of God. Whether these princes or magistrates are true believers or not, they still perform a divine role (Luther appeals to Romans 13:1–7 and 1 Peter 2:13–14 in support of this contention). God has ordained that order shall be imposed upon creation, for the maintenance of peace, the repression of sin. There are three hierarchies, or 'orders', within a Christian society: the household or family, with the father as the head (reflecting the paternalism of Luther's age); the princes and magistrates, who exercise secular authority; and the clergy, who exercise spiritual authority. All these are founded on the Word of God, and reflect the divine will for the structuring and preservation of the worldly realm.

Luther recognizes that his Augustinian view of the relation between church and society implies that there are 'mouse-droppings among the peppercorns, tares among the grain': in other words, the good and the evil coexist within both church and society. This is not to say that 'good' and 'evil' cannot be *distinguished*: it is simply to recognize, with the pragmatism for which Luther is noted, that they cannot be *isolated*. The good can be ruled by the Spirit, but the evil must be ruled by the sword. Luther insisted that the great masses of baptized Germans were not true Christians. Thus Luther recognizes that it is utterly unrealistic to hope that society could be governed by the precepts of the Sermon on the Mount. Perhaps everyone ought to be – but not everyone would be. Spirit and sword must coexist in the government of a Christian society.

Nevertheless, Luther's social ethic seems to suggest that two totally different moralities exist side by side: a private Christian ethic, reflecting the rule of love embodied in the Sermon on the Mount, and challenging human conceptions of righteousness; and a public morality, based upon force, which endorses human conceptions of righteousness. Christian ethics is grounded in the doctrine of justification by faith alone, in which the believer gratefully responds to God's grace with good works; public morality is based upon fear and coercion, in which the citizen obeys the law for fear of the consequences of failing to do so. The Sermon on the Mount is a splendid moral guide for the individual Christian – but its moral demands are not necessarily applicable to the public morality. It will therefore be obvious that Luther puts the Christian who is also a public figure (such as a prince or magistrate) in the virtually impossible position of having to employ two different ethics, one for his private life and the other for his public life.

God thus governs the church by the Holy Spirit through the gospel, in a manner from which all coercion is excluded; and he governs the world by the sword of secular authority. The magistrates are entitled to use the sword to enforce the law, not because violence is inherently justified, but on account of the intractability of human sin. Were there no human sin, no coercion would be necessary: all would recognize the wisdom of the gospel, and modify their behaviour accordingly. God establishes political order in order to restrain human greed and wickedness, themselves the result of sin.

The spiritual authority of the church is thus persuasive, not coercive, and concerns the individual's soul, rather than his body or goods. The temporal authority of the state is coercive, rather than persuasive, and concerns the individual's body and goods, rather than his soul. Luther's fundamental criticism of the medieval papacy was that it had confused these two separate realms of authority, especially through its system of Canon Law. Although Luther carefully distinguishes these two realms of authority, both in terms of their scope and source, he insists that they are not in opposition to one another, but are merely different aspects of the same thing – God's rule over his fallen and sinful world.

Luther's political theology is thus pragmatic. Recognizing the political realities of his situation at Wittenberg, and his reliance upon the political support of the German princes, Luther reinforces their political authority by grounding it in the divine providence. God governs the world, including the church, through the princes and magistrates. The church is in the world, and so must submit itself to the order of the world.

But what, it may reasonably be asked, happens if the state becomes tyrannical? Have Christians the right to intervene, and actively oppose the state? Luther thought not, at least in the 1520s. As the Peasants' Revolt loomed on the horizon, it seems that the deficiencies of his political thought became obvious. Secular rulers possessed their office by divine right. Thus in his *Admonition to Peace* (1525), Luther criticizes the German lords for their tyranny over the peasants – but upbraids the peasants for even contemplating revolt against their masters. 'The fact that the rulers are wicked and unjust does not excuse disorder and rebellion, for the punishing of wickedness is not the responsibility of everyone, but of the worldly rulers who bear the sword.'[8] The peasants, by assuming the role of judges and avenging what they regarded as wrong, are in effect assuming the place of God:

It is true that the rulers do wrong when they suppress the gospel and oppress you in temporal matters. But you do far greater wrong when you not only suppress God's word, but read it underfoot, invade his authority and law, and put yourselves above God. Besides, you take from the rulers their authority and right...What do you expect God and the world to think when you pass judgement and avenge yourselves on those who have injured you and even upon your rulers, whom God has appointed.[9]

This understanding of the relation of church and state has been the subject of intense criticism. Luther's social ethic has been described as 'defeatist' and 'quietist', encouraging the Christian to tolerate (or at least fail to oppose) unjust social structures. Luther preferred oppression to revolution. It also seemed to draw a cynical distinction between a private morality which is identifiably Christian, and the public morality which is not. The Peasants' War seemed to show up the tensions within Luther's social ethic: the peasants were supposed to live in accordance with the private ethic of the Sermon on the Mount, turning the other cheek to their oppressors – while the princes were justified in using violent coercive means to re-establish social order.[10] And although Luther maintained that the magistrate had no authority in the church, except as a Christian believer, the technical distinction involved was so tenuous as to be unworkable. The way was opened to the eventual domination of the church by the state which was to become a virtually universal feature of Lutheranism. The failure of the German church to oppose Hitler in the 1930s is widely seen as reflecting the inadequacies of Luther's political thought. Even Hitler, it appeared to the German Christians, was an instrument of God.[11]

David C. Steinmetz has helpfully pointed out that five central premises can be discerned as underlying Luther's confused political theology:[12]

1   Christian ethics, but not human morality, is grounded in the doctrine of justification by faith alone.
2   All Christians have a civic and social responsibility to perform. Some Christians may discharge these responsibilities by holding public office.
3   The morality of the Sermon on the Mount applies to the life of every Christian, but not necessarily to every decision which Christians may make if they hold public office.
4   The state has been divinely ordained to achieve certain purposes, which the church cannot, and should not attempt to, achieve. In

other words, their spheres of influence and authority are different, and must not be confused.

5   God rules the church through the gospel, but is obliged to rule the sinful world through law, wisdom, natural law and coercion.

Luther is no political thinker, and his limited and deficient experiments in this field are best regarded as an attempt to accommodate to the political realities of his time.[13] For the consolidation of the German Reformation, the full support of the German princes and magistrates was essential. Luther appears to have been prepared to lend these rulers religious dignity, in return for their continued support for the Reformation. The end justified the means. Luther appeals to a specific power group: had a different group held political power, he would almost certainly have appealed to it instead, and justified its existence. Thus Luther is clearly a monarchist, whereas Zwingli argues that all monarchs eventually degenerate into tyrants. For Zwingli, aristocracy (even when it degenerates into oligarchy) is to be preferred to monarchy. One wonders what would have happened if Luther had been a reformer in oligarchical Zurich, and Zwingli in electoral Wittenberg. The 'ifs' of history, even if unanswerable, are at least intriguing!

It is interesting to note the position of Martin Bucer on this point. Bucer's sphere of influence was twofold. The pioneer of the Reformation in the great imperial city of Strasbourg, he ended his days at Cambridge attempting to give a new sense of direction to the faltering English Reformation. Now Strasbourg was governed by a city council, and England by a monarch. Whereas Luther's theology reflects a monarchical, and Zwingli's an oligarchical, form of government, Bucer was thus obliged to tread warily, lest he offend either one of two governments. It is thus perhaps no cause for surprise that we find Bucer affirming that the precise form of temporal authority adopted is a matter of indifference. Temporal authority may be individual or corporate, based upon a hereditary monarchy or an elected assembly: the essential point is that whoever exercises such authority should be godly, open to the guidance of the Holy Spirit. A similar position was developed by John Calvin in the 1536 *Institutes*: any form of government whatever – whether it is a monarchy, an aristocracy or a democracy – is equally legitimate and equally competent to perform its divinely appointed office. Perhaps aware of the impact his ideas were to have in a variety of different political contexts, Calvin affirms (despite his obvious misgivings concerning monarchy) that a scripturally determined understanding of the nature of the church is consistent with whatever form of civil government happens to be established.

Zwingli on the State and Magistrate

We have already noted the strong link in Zwingli's thought between the church and state, evident in his baptismal views (see pp. 126–7). From the beginning of his reforming ministry at Zurich, Zwingli appears to have recognized the political realities of the situation: Zurich could not be reformed without the consent and active involvement of the city council. For Zwingli, 'church' and 'state' were simply different ways of looking at the city of Zurich, rather than separate entities.[14] The life of the state does not differ from the life of the church, in that each demands what the other demands. Both the preacher and the ruler were under obligation to God, in that they had both been entrusted with establishing the rule of God over the city. Zwingli regarded Zurich as a theocracy, in the sense that the whole life of the city community was under the rule of God: minister and magistrate alike were charged with expounding and enforcing that rule.

There are obvious parallels between the theories of government associated with Luther and Zwingli. It may be helpful to list them.

1 Both maintain that the need for such government is the result of sin. As Zwingli put it, 'If all men rendered to God what they owed him, we should need neither prince nor ruler – indeed, we should never have left paradise.'

2 Both recognize that not all members of the community are Christians. While the proclamation of the gospel may convert some, there are those who will never be converted. (Both Luther and Zwingli, it must be remembered, were strongly predestinarian in their views). As government takes in the whole community, it is legitimate for the government to use force where this is necessary.

3 Those who exercise authority within the community do so with the authority of God. God exercises his authority through the magistrates.

4   Against the radicals, both Luther and Zwingli insist that Christians
    may hold public office. For the radicals, holding such office involved
    political compromises, thus corrupting the Christian. For Luther
    and Zwingli, a believer was more likely to exercise power respons-
    ibly and charitably than anyone else, and was to be encouraged to
    gain office for that reason. Zwingli insists that, without the fear
    of God, a ruler will become a tyrant. Where Plato wished his kings
    to be philosophers, Zwingli wished his aristocrats to be Christians.
5   Both Luther and Zwingli draw a distinction between private and
    public morality. The commands of the Sermon on the Mount (for
    example, not to resist evil, or to turn the other cheek) apply to
    the Christian as a private individual, but not to the Christian as
    the holder of a public office. Thus Zwingli points out that Christ
    himself attacked the Pharisees, and did not turn his other cheek when
    brought before the High Priest.
6   Both Luther and Zwingli distinguish the types of righteousness
    associated with the Christian and the state. Zwingli argues that the
    gospel is concerned with the promotion of inner righteousness,
    arising from the transformation of the individual through the hearing
    of the gospel, whereas the state is concerned with the promotion
    of outward righteousness, arising from the individual being con-
    strained to keep the law. The gospel alters human nature, whereas
    the state merely restrains human greed and sin, having no positive
    power to alter human motivation. Luther emphasizes the tension
    between human and divine righteousness: whereas Zwingli states
    that divine righteousness is interior and human righteousness exterior,
    Luther suggests that they are also mutually contradictory. The
    righteousness which Christians are commanded to seek is dia-
    metrically opposed to the more cynical standards of righteousness
    employed by rulers.

For Zwingli, the city council derived its authority from God, whose
Word they were not in a position to judge or challenge. This insight
appears to have been of theoretical, rather than practical, importance.
The First Zurich Disputation of 19 January 1523 (see p. 113) effectively ensured that the city council was recognized as having the authority
to interpret scripture. While Zwingli clearly understood the council
to be *under* the Word of God, the city council appears to have

manoeuvred itself into a position by which it was really *over* the Word of God. Whoever interprets the Word of God effectively has authority over it – whether that interpreter is the pope or a city council. This led to the complaint that Zwingli allowed 'matters which ought to belong to the whole church to be dealt with by the Two Hundred [the city council] when the church of the whole city and neighborhood is seven thousand, more or less'.

But what form of government is to be preferred? Zwingli draws a distinction between three political systems: monarchy, aristocracy and democracy. In his discussion of these systems, he displays a political realism which seems to owe virtually nothing to any specifically Christian insight. In many ways, his discussion of the question reflects those of the classic era, with an emphasis upon historical rather than theoretical analysis. Monarchy is an arbitrary form of government, in which the ruler is selected on the basis of inadequate criteria. Monarchs are prone to degenerate into tyranny, and are difficult to replace when inadequate. And, Zwingli points out, there are obvious shortcomings in entrusting authority to one single individual. Democracy, in contrast, places authority in the hands of the whole people, but can easily degenerate into chaos. When this happens, individual interests are placed above those of the state, and the *res publica* suffers as a result. Aristocracy, however, possesses both a representative element and an accountability to the people, avoiding the shortcomings of both monarchy and democracy. It is the *via media* between these two deficient forms of government.

This attitude contrasts sharply with Luther's preference for a monarchical form of government. It also allows us to understand Zwingli's more positive attitude towards the resistance of tyranny. For Zwingli, tyranny was not to be tolerated. Although Zwingli occasionally denies that rulers may be killed, there are a number of passages which clearly imply that tyrannicide is acceptable.[15] Christians are under obligation to obey God, rather than men – and just that obedience may involve deposing or killing rulers. Zwingli is careful to lay down the conditions under which a ruler may be deposed. Murder, war and uprising are declared to be unacceptable: peacable means must be employed wherever possible. As Zwingli favors an aristocratic (or, at worst, an oligarchic) form of government, he is able to point to a number of peaceful means by which such rulers may be deposed – for example, by the election of a replacement. Luther's situation was somewhat different: one disadvantage of a monarchical system of government is that the prince rules for life, making regicide one of the few options available for his removal. Zwingli, however, is able to advocate less drastic electoral means of deposing unsatisfactory rulers, thus protecting more tender consciences.

Bucer and Calvin on Magistrate and Ministry

The consolidation of the magisterial Reformation owed much to the close integration of the roles of preacher and magistrate in the imperial city of Strasbourg under Martin Bucer.[16] Having been expelled from Geneva in 1538, it was to Bucer's Strasbourg that Calvin turned to receive both political refuge and ecclesiastical experience. While Bucer's relationship with the city council of Strasbourg was occasionally stormy, he nevertheless regarded that council as entrusted with a God-given task to reform the church. In view of the importance of Bucer's views, we may consider them before passing on to consider those of Calvin himself.

Bucer points out that in the New Testament period, the temporal authorities were non-Christian. God was therefore obliged to use other means – such as the agency of the Holy Spirit – to preserve and develop his church. But, Bucer argues, such has been the impact of the Christian faith since those early days that temporal authorities are now themselves Christian: God therefore uses them in the sixteenth century, even if he used different means in the first.

> At the time of the apostles and martyrs, the Lord wanted to accomplish everything by the power of his Spirit, so that the whole world might see that the crucified one was Lord, and that he rules in heaven over all. Therefore he allowed kings and all those who were powerful to act in complete defiance against him and his people. But when he had converted the authorities, he wished them truly to serve him with their office and power, which derives from him, and is committed to them only for the good of Christ's flock.

Whereas it is the task of the minister to preach the Word of God, that of the magistrate is to govern according to it. This might seem to suggest that preachers have authority over the magistrate: however, in that the magistrates were responsible for the appointment of preachers, the possibility of tension was lessened. For Bucer, it is axiomatic that the magistracy is godly, and open to the promptings of the Holy Spirit. The history of the Reformation at Strasbourg suggests that the members of the city council were actually primarily concerned with the well-being of Strasbourg, and indirectly themselves. Bucer, however, appears to have regarded 'city' and 'church' as so closely linked that this instinct for self-preservation directly advanced the cause of the Reformation.

Bucer's ideas were developed by John Calvin on his return to Geneva in September 1541. The rulers of Geneva, having broken free from external rule in 1536, found themselves without any coherent system of church order. All the ecclesiastical changes of the 1530s had been destructive, eventually leading to something approaching chaos. A comprehensive set of ecclesiastical ordinances were required, and Calvin was recalled to Geneva to help with this task. The magistrates were prepared to let Calvin have his way (within reason) in his organization of the Genevan church, provided that their civil authority was not affected. Calvin's original idea was that ecclesiastical discipline should rest with a body to be known as the Consistory, made up of pastors and twelve magistrates of their choice. This Consistory would have the right, for example, to excommunicate anyone whose moral conduct or religious beliefs were unacceptable. The magistrates, scenting a challenge to their authority, vigorously affirmed their right over all temporal matters. A compromise was reached, which Calvin interpreted as a recognition of the right of the Consistory to recommend excommunication, and the magistrates interpreted as a recognition of their authority to excommunicate. The history of Geneva over the next fifteen years indicated how unsatisfactory this compromise turned out to be.

For all its compromises made in the face of the political realities of Geneva, the fundamental basis of Calvin's understanding of the relation of church and state is clear. While the political authority must not be allowed to abolish the spiritual, the Anabaptist view that the spiritual authority abrogates the political is unequivocally rejected. When the present order passes away at the last day, there will be no need for a political authority – but while human beings remain tied to this earth, the political authority is essential in order 'to foster and maintain the external worship of God, to defend sound doctrine and the condition of the church, to adapt our conduct to human society, to form our manners to civil justice, to reconcile us to one another, to cherish peace and common tranquility'.[17]

Calvin thus assigns to the magistrates two roles: the maintenance of political and ecclesiastical order, and making provision for the teaching of right doctrine. Both the political and spiritual authorities are to use their distinctive resources committed to them by God for the disciplining of the same body of people.

> For the church has not the right of the sword to punish or restrain, has no power to coerce, no prison nor other punishments which the magistrate is wont to inflict. Then the object in view is not to punish the sinner against his will, but to obtain a profession of penitence by voluntary chastisement. The two things, then, are widely different, because neither does the church assume anything to herself which is proper to the magistrate, nor is the magistrate competent to what is done by the church.[18]

The political authority was to use its right to coercion (generally through the threat of exile or execution: Geneva did not have a long-term prison) and the spiritual authority its teaching ministry for the promotion of virtue. Calvin also stated that the ministry had the right to explain to the magistracy what the Word of God required in a given situation, suggesting that the ministry was the legislative, and the magistracy the executive, of the Genevan theocracy. However, the magistracy appears to have felt able to resist the ministry sufficiently frequently to weaken the latter's role in the government of the city.

For Calvin, both magistrates and ministers were committed to the same task, the difference between them lying in the tools they had available and their respective spheres of authority.[19] Their responsibilities are complementary, rather than competitive. Both magistrates and ministers were agents and servants of the same God, committed to the same cause, differing only in their spheres and means of action. Where the Anabaptists regarded church discipline as a matter for that church itself,[20] Calvin regarded it as a matter of public concern, within the legitimate authority of the magistracy. Although Calvin's Geneva was troubled more than once through tensions between the two authorities, spiritual and political, the strong sense of social organization which became an essential part of 'Calvinism' may be traced back to Calvin's

Geneva. When the Puritans set foot in the New World, they brought with them not merely a religion, but a social vision, whose roots lay in a small town in modern-day Switzerland.

One further aspect of Calvin's political thought is of interest. Like Zwingli, Calvin had a profound mistrust of monarchy. Monarchs are prone to fall into tyranny; they are motivated by their personal concerns, rather than the well-being of their people. Even the Old Testament kings were prone to this tendency; their sixteenth-century equivalents were even worse. Although Calvin tends to condemn monarchs rather than monarchy, his misgivings concerning the very idea of absolute rule by one individual are unmistakable.[21] The subsequent challenge posed by 'Calvinism' to monarchies throughout Europe, evident in the challenge to and subsequent execution of Charles I of England (1649), is an adequate testimony to the subsequent importance of the Genevan political theology. The relative merits of Lutheranism and 'Calvinism' were often assessed on the basis of their political views, the former being regarded as monarchical and the latter as republican. The political circumstances of the founders of these religious sytems seem to have become elevated into fundamental beliefs of those systems.

On the basis of the above analysis, it will be obvious that the phrase 'Calvin's Geneva' is profoundly misleading. Calvin was no Genevan dictator, ruling the population with a rod of iron. Calvin was not even a citizen of Geneva for most of his time there, and was thus denied access to political authority. His status was simply that of a pastor who was in no position to dictate to the magisterial authorities who administered the city. Indeed, those authorities retained to the end the right to dismiss Calvin, even if they chose not to exercise them. As a member of the Consistory, he was certainly able to make representations to the magistracy on behalf of the ministers – representations which were, however, frequently ignored. In any case, Calvin had no *legal* right to act independently of the ministry, whose collegiality he is anyhow known to have valued and respected. Calvin's influence over Geneva ultimately rested, not in his formal legal standing (which was insignificant) but in his considerable personal authority as a preacher and pastor.

For further reading

Heinrich Bornkamm, *Luther's World of Thought* (St Louis, 1958), pp. 218–72.

——, *Luther's Doctrine of the Two Kingdoms* (Philadelphia, 1966).

Harro Höpfl, *The Christian Polity of John Calvin* (Cambridge, 1985).

David C. Steinmetz, 'Luther and the Two Kingdoms', in *Luther in Context* (Bloomington, Ind., 1986), pp. 112–25.

W. P. Stephens, *The Theology of Huldrych Zwingli* (Oxford, 1986), pp. 282–310.

T. F. Torrance, *Kingdom and Church: A Study in the Theology of the Reformation* (Edinburgh, 1956).

Appendix 1

A Glossary of Theological and Historical Terms

The standard theological reference work in English, to which the reader is referred for further discussion, is *The Oxford Dictionary of the Christian Church* (Oxford: Oxford University Press, 2nd edn revised, 1984). The third edition of this work is expected to be published in 1990. Much useful information may be found in an older reference work: *The New Schaff-Herzog Encyclopedia of Religious Knowledge* (12 vols; Grand Rapids, Mich.: Baker Book House, 1957), with especially useful information on sixteenth-century Lutheran and Reformed controversies. A specialized glossary of late medieval theological terms may be found in Heiko A. Oberman, *The Harvest of Medieval Theology: Gabriel Biel and Late Medieval Nominalism* (Cambridge, Mass.: Harvard University Press, 1963), pp. 459–76. Glossaries of terms relating to the doctrine of justification may be found in Alister E. McGrath, *Iustitia Dei: A History of the Christian Doctrine of Justification* (2 vols; Cambridge: Cambridge University Press, 1986), vol. 1, pp. 188–90.

Adiaphora

Literally, 'matters of indifference'. Beliefs or practices which the Reformers regarded as being tolerable, in that they were neither explicitly rejected nor stipulated by scripture. For example, what ministers wore at church services was often regarded as a 'matter of in difference'. The concept is of importance in that it allowed the Reformers to adopt a pragmatic approach to many beliefs and practices, thus avoiding unnecessary confrontation.

Anabaptism

Literally, 're-baptizer'. A term used to refer to the radical wing of the Reformation, based on thinkers such as Menno Simons or Balthasar Hubmaier. See p. 11.

antiPelagian writings

The writings of Augustine relating to the Pelagian controversy, in which he defended his views on grace and justification. See 'Pelagianism'.

Apostolic era

For humanists and reformers alike, the definitive period of the Christian church, bounded by the resurrection of Jesus Christ (c. AD 35) and the death of the last apostle (c. AD 90?). The ideas and practices of this period were widely regarded as normative in humanist and reforming circles.

Augustinianism

A term used in two major senses. First, it refers to the views of Augustine of Hippo concerning the doctrine of salvation, in which the need for divine grace is stressed (see pp. 55–7). In this sense, the term is the antithesis of Pelagianism. Second, it is used to refer to the body of opinion within the Augustinian Order during the Middle Ages, irrespective of whether these views derive from Augustine or not. See further David C. Steinmetz, *Luther and Staupitz: An Essay in the Intellectual Origins of the Protestant Reformation* (Durham, NC, 1980), pp. 13–16.

Calvinism

An ambiguous term, used with two quite distinct meanings. First, it refers to the religious ideas of religious bodies (such as the Reformed church) and individuals (such as Theodore Beza) who were pro foundly influenced by John Calvin, or by documents written by him. Second, it refers to the religious ideas of John Calvin himself. Although the first sense is by far the more common, there is a growing recognition that the term is misleading. See p. 10.

Catechism

A popular manual of Christian doctrine, usually in the form of question and answer, intended for religious instruction. With its considerable emphasis upon religious education, the Reformation saw the appearance of a number of major catechisms, most notably Luther's Lesser Catechism (1529), and the celebrated Heidelberg Catechism (1563).

Christology

The section of Christian theology dealing with the identity of Jesus Christ, particularly the question of the relation of his human and divine natures. Apart from a disagreement between Luther and Zwingli at Marburg in 1529, Christology, like the doctrine of the Trinity, was of little relevance to the Reformation.

Cinquecènto

The 1500s – i.e., the sixteenth century. See p. 28.

Confession

Although the term refers primarily to the admission to sin, it acquired a rather different technical sense in the sixteenth century – that of a document which embodies the principles of faith of a Protestant church. Thus the Augsburg Confession (1530) embodies the ideas of early Lutheranism, and the First Helvetic Confession (1536) those of the early Reformed church. The term 'Confessionalism' is often used to refer to the hardening of religious attitudes in the later sixteenth century, as the Lutheran and Reformed churches became involved in a struggle for power, especially in Germany.

Ecclesiology

The section of Christian theology dealing with the theory of the church (Latin *ecclesia* = 'church'). At the time of the Reformation, controversy centered upon the question of whether the Protestant churches could be regarded as continuous with mainstream Christianity – in other words, were they a reformed version of Christianity, or something completely new, having little or no connection with the previous 1,500 years of Christian history?

Evangelical

A term used to refer to the nascent reforming movements, especially in Germany and Switzerland, in the 1510s and 1520s. The term was later replaced by 'Protestant' in the aftermath of the Diet of Speyer.

évangeliques

A term often used to refer to the French reforming movement, especially in the 1520s and 1530s, centring upon figures such as Margaret of Navarre and Guillaume Briçonnet.

Evangelism

A term often used in English-language scholarship to refer to the Italian reforming movement in the period 1511–45, centring upon figures such as Gasparo Contarini and Reginald Pole.

Exegesis

The science of textual interpretation, usually referring specifically to the Bible. The term 'biblical exegesis' basically means 'the process of interpreting the Bible'. See pp. 110–15. The specific techniques employed in the exegesis of scripture are usually referred to as 'hermeneutics'.

Fathers

An alternative term for 'patristic writers'.

Hermeneutics

The principles underlying the interpretation, or exegesis, of a text, particularly of scripture. The first phase of the Reformation witnessed the development of a number of ways of interpreting scripture, deriving from both humanism and scholasticism. Zwingli initially used a hermeneutical scheme deriving from Erasmian humanism, and Luther a scheme deriving from scholastic theology. See pp. 110–15.

Justification by faith, doctrine of

The section of Christian theology dealing with how the individual sinner is able to enter into fellowship with God. See pp. 68–9. Although of major importance to Martin Luther and his colleagues at Wittenberg, the doctrine was of little interest to the Swiss Reformers, such as Zwingli. See pp. 84–6.

Liturgy

The written text of public services, especially of the eucharist. As liturgy was predetermined by theology in the Reformation, the reform of the liturgy was regarded as being of particular importance. See pp. 118–19.

Lutheranism

The religious ideas associated with Martin Luther, particularly as expressed in the Lesser Catechism (1529) and the Augsburg Confession (1530). A series of internal disagreements within Lutheranism after Luther's death (1546) between hardliners (the so-called 'Gnesio-Lutherans' or 'Flacianists') and moderates ('Philippists'), led to their resolution by the Formula of Concord (1577), which is usually regarded as the authoritative statement of Lutheran theology.

Magisterial Reformation

A term used to refer to the Lutheran and Reformed wings of the Reformation, as opposed to the radical wing (Anabaptism). See pp. 7–8.

Nominalism

Strictly speaking, the theory of knowledge opposed to realism. The term is, however, still used occasionally to refer to the *via moderna*. See pp. 53–5.

Patristic

An adjective used to refer to the first centuries in the history of the church, following the writing of the New Testament (the 'patristic period'), or thinkers writing during this period (the 'patristic writers'). For the Reformers, the period thus designated seems to be c.100–451 (in other words, the period between the closing of the New Testament and the Council of Chalcedon). The Reformers tended to regard the New Testament and, to a lesser extent, the patristic periods as normative for Christian belief and practice.

Pelagianism

An understanding of how humans are able to merit their salvation which is diametrically opposed to that of Augustine of Hippo, placing considerable emphasis upon the role of human works and playing down the idea of divine grace. See pp. 55–7.

Protestantism

A term used in the aftermath of the Diet of Speyer (1529) to designate those who 'protested' against the practices and beliefs of the Roman Catholic church. Prior to 1529, such individuals and groups had referred to themselves as 'evangelicals'.

Quattrocènto

The 1400s – i.e., the fifteenth century.

Radical Reformation

A term used with increasing frequency to refer to the Anabaptist movement – in other words, the wing of the Reformation which went beyond what Luther and Zwingli envisaged. See p. 11.

Sacrament

In purely historical terms, a church service or rite which was held to have been instituted by Jesus Christ himself. Although medieval theology and church practice recognized seven such sacraments, the Reformers argued that only two (baptism and eucharist) were to be found in the New Testament itself. The theory of the sacraments proved intensely divisive, with the Reformers unable to reach agreement among themselves concerning what the sacraments actually achieved. See pp. 117–30 for further discussion.

Schism

A deliberate break with the unity of the church, condemned vigorously by influential writers of the early church, such as Cyprian and Augustine. The Reformers were branded as 'schismatics' by their opponents. The Reformers thus found themselves in the difficult situation of upholding Augustine's views on grace, but disregarding his views on schism. See pp. 93–4; 130–6.

schola Augustiniana moderna

A form of late medieval scholasticism which laid emphasis upon Augustine's doctrine of grace, while adopting a nominalist position on the question of universals. See pp. 60–1.

Scotism

The scholastic philosophy associated with Duns Scotus. See p. 54.

Scripture Principle

The theory, especially associated with Reformed theologians, that the practices and beliefs of the church should be grounded in scripture. Nothing that could not be demonstrated to be grounded in scripture could be regarded as binding upon the believer. The phrase *sola scriptura*, 'by scripture alone', summarizes this principle. See pp. 104–9.

Septuagint

The Greek translation of the Old Testament, dating from the third century BC.

Sermon on the Mount

The standard way of referring to Christ's moral and pastoral teaching in the specific form which it takes in chapters 5–7 of Matthew's gospel.

Sodality

A term used generally to refer to the humanist groups associated with many northern European cities and universities in the late fifteenth and early sixteenth centuries. For example, the *sodalitas Collimitiana* at Vienna centred around Georg Collimitius, and the *sodalitas Staupitziana* at Nuremberg centred around Johannes von Staupitz.

Soteriology

The section of Christian theology dealing with the doctrine of salvation (Greek: *soteria*).

Thomism, *via Thomae*

The scholastic philosophy associated with Thomas Aquinas. See p. 54.

Transubstantiation

The medieval doctrine according to which the bread and the wine are transformed into the body and blood of Christ in the eucharist, while retaining their outward appearance. See p. 121.

Trecènto

The 1300s – i.e., the fourteenth century.

Turmerlebnis

A German term, literally meaning 'tower experience', often used to designate Luther's moment of breakthrough. See pp. 73. In a later (confused) reference, Luther mentions that his theological breakthrough took place in a tower of the Augustinian monastery at Wittenberg – hence the reference to the 'tower'.

via antiqua

A term used to designate forms of scholastic philosophy, such as Thomism and Scotism, which adopted a realist position on the question of universals. See pp. 55–7.

via moderna

A term used broadly in two senses. First, forms of scholastic philosophy which adopted a nominalist position on the question of universals, in opposition to the realism of the *via antiqua*. See pp. 55–7. Second, and more importantly, the form of scholasticism (formerly known as 'Nominalism') based upon the writings of William of Ockham and his followers, such as Pierre d'Ailly and Gabriel Biel. See pp. 57–60.

Vulgate

The Latin translation of the Bible, largely deriving from Jerome, upon which medieval theology was largely based. Strictly speaking, 'Vulgate' designates Jerome's translation of the Old Testament (except the Psalms, which was taken from the Gallican Psalter); the apocryphal works (except Wisdom, Ecclesiasticus, I and II Maccabees, and Baruch, which were taken from the Old Latin Version); and all the New Testament. The recognition of its many inaccuracies was of fundamental importance to the Reformation. See pp. 97–8.

Zwinglianism

The term is used generally to refer to the thought of Huldrych Zwingli, but is often used to refer specifically to his views on the sacraments, especially on the 'real presence' (which for Zwingli was more of a 'real absence'). See pp. 123–6.

Appendix 2

English Translations of Major Primary Sources

John Calvin

Calvin's most important work is the 1559 edition of the *Institutes of the Christian Religion*. This is available in a number of English translations, of which the two following are particularly recommended:
Institutes of the Christian Religion, trans. Henry Beveridge (2 vols: Grand Rapids, 1975).
Institutes of the Christian Religion, ed. J. T. McNeill, trans. Ford Lewis Battles (2 vols: Library of Christian Classics 20–1: Philadelphia/London, 1975).
The 1536 edition of the *Institutes* is also available in English translation:
Institution of the Christian Religion, trans. F. L. Battles (Atlanta, 1975).
   Many of Calvin's remaining works, particularly his tracts and New Testament commentaries, were translated into English by the Calvin Translation Society during the nineteenth century:
Calvin's Tracts (3 vols: Edinburgh, 1844–51)
Calvin's Commentaries (47 vols: Edinburgh, 1843–59)
A new translation of the New Testament commentaries is also available:
Calvin's Commentaries, eds D. W. Torrance and T. F. Torrance (Edinburgh, 1959–).
The following translations should also be noted:
Calvin's Commentary on Seneca's 'De Clementia', ed. F. L. Battles and A. M. Hugo (Leiden, 1969).
John Calvin and Jacopo Sadoleto: A Reformation Debate. Sadoleto's Letter to the Genevans and Calvin's Reply (New York, 1966).
Jean Calvin: Three French Treatises, ed. F. H. Higman (London, 1970).
Calvin's Theological Treatises, ed. J. K. S. Reid (Library of Christian Classics 22: Philadelphia, 1954).

Desiderius Erasmus of Rotterdam

The most comprehensive English edition of Erasmus' works is *The Collected Works of Erasmus* (81 vols: Toronto, 1969–), still in progress. This series, when complete, will be the definitive English-language edition of Erasmus. The following are of particular interest to the historian of the Reformation:

The Correspondence (vols. 1–22), especially letters 993–1251 (vols 7–8), which deal with the period 1519–21, during which the 'Lutherana tragoedia' began to dominate Erasmus' concerns.

The New Testament Scholarship (vols 41–60), which did much to lay the intellectual foundations of the Reformation. These volumes should be read in conjunction with Erika Rummel, *Erasmus' Annotations on the New Testament: From Philologist to Theologian* (Erasmus Study 8: Toronto, 1986).

Martin Luther

The most widely-used English translation of Luther's works is the so-called 'American edition': *Luther's Works* (55 vols: St Louis/Philadelphia, 1955–75). In addition to a companion volume, this edition includes most of Luther's exegetical works (vols 1–30), as well as tracts, sermons and political writings (vols 31–54). The exegetical works are arranged in the order in which the scriptural books are found in the Bible, rather than in the order in which Luther wrote them.

A useful anthology is *Martin Luther: Selections from his Writings*, ed. John Dillenberger (New York, 1962). The three 'Reformation treatises' of 1520 are conveniently collected together in *Three Treatises* (Philadelphia, 1973).

Huldrych Zwingli

The most complete English translation to date are the three volumes of *The Latin Works of Huldreich Zwingli*, as follows:

The Latin Works and Correspondence of Huldreich Zwingli, vol. I: 1510-1522, ed. S. M. Jackson (New York, 1912).

The Latin Works of Huldreich Zwingli, vol. II, ed. W. J. Hinke (Philadelphia, 1922); reprinted as *Zwingli on Providence and Other Essays* (Durham, NC, 1983).

The Latin Works of Huldreich Zwingli, vol. III, ed. C. N. Heller (Philadelphia, 1929); reprinted as *Commentary on True and False Religion* (Durham, NC, 1981).

These have been supplemented by:

Huldrych Zwingli Writings: The Defense of the Reformed Faith, ed. E. J. Furcha (Allison Park, PA, 1984).

Huldrych Zwingli Writings: In Search of True Religion, ed. H. Wayne Pipkin (Allison Park, PA, 1984).

Two other collections are worth noting:

The Selected Works of Huldrych Zwingli, ed. S. M. Jackson (Philadelphia, 1901; reprinted 1972).

Zwingli and Bullinger, ed. G. W. Bromiley (Library of Christian Classics 24: Philadelphia, 1953).

Appendix 3

Standard Abbreviations of Major Journals and Sources

The following abbreviations are encountered regularly in the literature dealing with the history and thought of the Reformation period. The situation is made more complicated than necessary through absence of general agreement on the standard abbreviations for certain works. Where several abbreviations are in use, the preferred abbreviation is indicated.

The most helpful guide to the abbreviations used to designate the secondary literature is Siegfried Schwertner, *Internationales Abkürzungsverzeichnis für Theologie und Grenzgebiete* (Berlin/New York: de Gruyter, 1974). ['International Glossary of Abbreviations for Theology and Related Subjects', often abbreviated as *IATG*].

Primary Sources

The reader will find it helpful to read these notes in conjunction with Appendixes 2 and 4.

CR   *Corpus Reformatorum* (Berlin/Leipzig/Zurich, 1834–). The standard edition of the works of Melanchthon (vols 1–28), Calvin (vols 29–87), and Zwingli (vols 88–). The Calvin section is sometimes (confusingly) referred to as *OC*. See notes on Calvin and Zwingli in Appendix 4.

CWE   *Complete Works of Erasmus* (Toronto, 1969–). This series, which is still in progress, has become the standard English translation of Erasmus' works.

EE   *Erasmi Epistolae*, ed. P. S. Allen (Oxford, 1905–58). The standard edition of Erasmus' correspondence.

LB   Desiderii Erasmi Opera Omnia, ed. J. LeClerc (Leiden, 1703-6; reprinted London, 1962). The Leiden (Lugduni Batavorum) edition of Erasmus' works.

LCC   Library of Christian Classics (London/Philadelphia, 1953–). Includes useful translations of Bucer, Zwingli and Melanchthon, as well as of Calvin's 1559 *Institutes*.

LW   Luther's Works, eds Jaroslav Pelikan and Helmut Lehmann (55 vols: St Louis/Philadelphia, 1955–75). The 'American edition' of Luther's works in English translation.

OC   Opera Calvini. An alternative, and somewhat confusing, reference to the Calvin section of *Corpus Reformatorum*: see *CR*.

OS   Opera Selecta Ioannis Calvini, ed. Peter Barth (5 vols: Munich, 1926–36). A useful critical edition of Calvin's major works, including both the 1536 and 1559 editions of the *Institutes*.

S   Huldrich Zwingli's Werke, eds M. Schuler and J. Schulthess (8 vols: Zurich, 1828–42). The first edition of Zwingli's works, now being supplanted gradually by the *Corpus Reformatorum* edition.

SS   An alternative abbreviation for the Schuler–Shulthess edition of Zwingli's works: see *S*.

WA   D. Martin Luthers Werke: Kritische Gesamtausgabe, ed. J. K. F. Knaake, G. Kawerau *et al.* (Weimar, 1883–). The definitive 'Weimar edition' of Luther's works, which also includes his correspondence (*WABr*), his German Bible (*WADB*) and his 'Table-Talk' (*WATr*).

WABr   D. Martin Luthers Werke: Briefwechsel (15 vols: Weimar, 1930–78). The correspondence section of the Weimar edition of Luther's works.

WADB   D. Martin Luthers Werke: Deutsches Bibel (Weimar, 1906–). The 'German Bible' section of the Weimar edition of Luther's works.

WATr   D. Martin Luthers Werke: Tischreden (6 vols: Weimar, 1912–21). The 'Table-Talk' section of the Weimar edition of Luther's works.

Z   Huldreich Zwinglis sämtliche Werke, ed. E. Egli *et al.* (Corpus Reformatorum, vols 88– : Berlin/Leipzig/Zurich, 1905–). The best critical edition of Zwingli's works, still in progress, replacing the Schuler–Schulthess edition of the nineteenth century. Two other methods of referring to this edition should be noted. First, *CR*, followed by a volume number of 88 or greater – this refers the reader to the appropriate volume in the section of *Corpus Reformatorum* series devoted to Zwingli. Second, *CR (Zwingli)*, which refers the reader to the *Corpus Reformatorum* series, vols. 88–. Thus *CR (Zwingli) 1* is a reference to the first volume in the Zwingli section of the *Corpus Reformatorum* series – i.e., volume 88. See further Appendix 4.

ZW Alternative abbreviation for *Huldreich Zwinglis sämtliche Werke*: preferred abbreviation is *Z*.

Secondary Sources

ADB Allgemeine Deutsche Biographie (55 vols: Leipzig, 1875-1912; reprinted Berlin, 1967–71).

AGBR Aktensammlung zur Geschichte der Basler Reformation in den Jahren 1519 bis Anfang 1534 (3 vols: Basle, 1921–37).

AGZR Aktensammlung zur Geschichte der Zürcher Reformation in den Jahren 1519-33, ed. Emil Egli (Zurich, 1879; reprinted Aalen, 1973).

ARG Archiv für Reformationsgeschichte

BHR Bibliothèque d'humanisme et Renaissance

CIC Corpus Iuris Canonici (2 vols: Leipzig, 1879; reprinted Graz, 1959).

CICiv Corpus Iuris Civilis (3 vols: Berlin, 1872–1908).

EThL Ephemerides Theologicae Lovanienses

FcS Franciscan Studies

FS Franziskanische Studien

HThR Harvard Theological Review

JThS Journal of Theological Studies

QFRG Quellen und Forschungen zur Reformationsgeschichte (Gütersloh, 1911–).

RGG Religion in Geschichte und Gegenwart (6 vols: Tübingen, 3rd edn, 1957–65).

RGST Reformationsgeschichtliche Studien und Texte (Münster, 1906–).

RThAM Recherches de théologie ancienne et médiévale

SJTh Scottish Journal of Theology

SMRT Studies in Medieval and Reformation Thought, ed. H. A. Oberman (Leiden, 1966–).

ZKG Zeitschrift für Kirchengeschichte

ZKTh Zeitschrift für katholische Theologie

ZThK Zeitschrift für Theologie und Kirche

*Zwa   Zwingliana: Beiträge zur Geschichte Zwinglis, der Reformation, und
des Protestantismus in der Schweiz*

Note that some writers prefer to abbreviate 'Theology' and derived
words as 'T' rather than 'Th' – thus *SJTh, JThS* and *HThR* are often
abbreviated as *SJT, JTS* and *HTR.*

Appendix 4

How to Refer to Major Primary Sources

Major studies of Reformation personalities or ideas frequently assume that their readers know how to interpret references to primary source materials. Experience suggests that this is a wildly optimistic assumption. This appendix aims to enable the reader to handle the most commonly encountered methods of referring to such material for the four major figures for which this is usually necessary: Calvin, Erasmus, Luther and Zwingli.

Abbreviations used in referring to primary sources may be found in Appendix 3. English translations of major works may be found in Appendix 2.

John Calvin

Calvin's *Institutes of the Christian Religion* is almost invariably referred to in the edition of 1559. This edition is divided into four main sections (books), each dealing with a broad general theme. Each book is then divided into chapters, each of which is further subdivided into sections. A reference to the 1559 edition of this work will therefore include *three* numbers, identifying the *book*, the *chapter* and the *section*. The book number is usually given in capital Roman numerals, the chapter in small Roman numerals, and the section in Arabic numerals. Thus book two, chapter twelve, section one, would probably be referred to as II.xii.1, although a reference might read II, 12, 1 or 2.12.1.

In addition, reference may be given to an edition (for example, the *Corpus Reformatorum* or *Opera Selecta*) or an English translation. For example, the reference *Institutio* III.xi.1; *OS* 4.193.2–5 is a reference to book three, chapter eleven, section one of the 1559 edition of the *Institutes*, specifically the section to be found on lines 2–5 of page 193 of the fourth volume of the *Opera Selecta*. Similarly a reference to *Institutes* IV.v.5; tr. Beveridge, 2.243 is to the fifth section of the fifth chapter of book four of the *Institutes*, as it is found on page 243 of volume two of the celebrated translation by Henry Beveridge (see Appendix 2).

Reference to Calvin's commentaries and sermons usually involves the *Corpus Reformatorum* edition, which is referred to simply by volume and page number. Thus *CR* 50.437 is a reference to page 437 of volume 50. The volume number will be in the range 1–59. Occasionally, unfortunately, confusion can result from an irritating practice, fortunately generally confined to older studies of Calvin. The *Corpus Reformatorum* edition consists of the works of Melanchthon (vols 1–28), Calvin (vols 29–87) and Zwingli (vols 88–). Volume one of Calvin's works is thus volume 29 within the series – and older works sometimes refer to Calvin's works using this higher volume number. If you find reference to this edition of Calvin with a volume number in the region 60–87, you should subtract 28 to obtain the correct volume number. If you find an isolated reference to Calvin, especially in an older work, which doesn't seem to make sense – subtract 28, and try again!

Desiderius Erasmus

The two most commonly encountered editions of Erasmus' Latin works are the Leclerc edition, published at Leiden in 1703 (reprinted in 1963), and the Allen edition of the correspondence.

The Leclerc edition is almost invariably referred to in the following manner. An initial number denotes the *volume*, and a second number the *column* (each page is divided into two columns, numbered individually). This is then followed by a *letter* (A–F), which indicates the position of the section being referred to in the column. These letters are printed on the page of the Leclerc edition for ease of reference. The following references are given to illustrate this: *LB* V.153 F; *LB* X.1754 C–D; and *LB* II.951 A–B. The first reference is to column 153 of volume 5, the letter F indicating that the section is at the bottom of the column. The second reference is to column 1754 of volume 10, the letters C–D indicating that the section being referred to is to be found towards the middle of the column. The final reference is to column 951 of volume 2, the letters A–B indicating that the section is towards the top of the page.

The Allen edition of the correspondence is generally referred to by first identifying the *volume*, followed by the *page* and *line* numbers – thus *EE* 2.491.133–9 refers to lines 133–9 on page 491 of the second of the twelve volumes of the Allen edition of the correspondence. Occasionally, reference is made to the *letter number* – thus *EE* 2, no. 541, is a reference to letter number 541 (from Erasmus to Capito, dated 26 February 1517), to be found in the second volume of the Allen edition.

Martin Luther

The only critical edition of Luther's works now generally referred to is the great 'Weimar edition', begun in 1883 as part of the celebrations of the 400th anniversary of the German Reformer's birth. The edition is divided into four main sections:

1   The main body of the work, containing his major theological writings (abbreviated as *WA*).
2   The correspondence (abbreviated as *WABr*). In catalogues, this section is generally designated by the German word *Briefwechsel*.
3   The so-called 'Table-Talk' (abbreviated as *WATr*). In catalogues, this section is generally designated by the German word *Tischreden*. This material was not written by Luther himself, but consists of reports of Luther's meal-time conversations with his friends. The reliability of this material has frequently been challenged.
4   The 'German Bible' (abbreviated as *WADB*). In catalogues, this section is generally designated by the German words *Deutsches Bibel*. The first stage in deciphering a reference to the Weimar edition is thus to determine which of the four sections of the work is being referred to. For most purposes, it is likely to be the main body of the work which is being referred to.

The main body of the work is relatively simple to handle. Reference is invariably given by volume number, page number, and line number – in that order. There is some variation in the method of referring to the volume number, some writers using Roman and others Arabic numerals. Thus *WA* 4.25.12–17 and *WA* IV.25.12–17 are both references to lines 12–17 of page 25 of the fourth volume of the main body of the work. The only difficulty to note is that some volumes are divided into parts. Where this applies, the *part* number follows immediately after the *volume* number. Three main systems are encountered for designating the part number. The references *WA* 55 II.109.9, *WA* LV/2.109.9 and *WA* 55^2.109.9 all refer to line nine of page 109 of the second part of volume 55 of the Weimar edition.

The correspondence (*WABr*) and German Bible (*WADB*) are generally referred to in much the same way. Thus *WABr* 1.99.8–13 is a reference to lines 8–13 of page 99 of the first volume of the correspondence. In the case of the Table-Talk (*WATr*), however, a slightly different means of reference is generally employed. The Table-Talk is divided into nearly six thousand sections, and the general practice is to refer to the volume number, followed by the section number. Thus *WATr* 2.2068 is a reference to section 2068, which may be found in the second of the six volumes of the Weimar edition of the Table-Talk. On a few rare occasions, these sections are further subdivided: the subdivisions are identified by letter – for example, *WATr* 3.3390b.

Huldrych Zwingli

Reference in all modern studies is to the excellent *Corpus Reformatorum* edition, generally designated simply as *Z* (for other designations, see Appendix 3). Several works not in this modern edition are to be found in the Schuler–Schulthess edition. The student must therefore be able to deal with both these editions.

The *Corpus Reformatorum* edition is referred to by by volume number, page number and line number. Volume 6 is subdivided, with the subdivisions usually being designated by small Roman letters. Thus *Z* III.259.32 refers to line 32 on page 259 of volume 3, and *Z* VI iii.182.3–5 to lines 3–5 on page 182 of the third part of volume 6, of the *Corpus Reformatorum* edition. In older works, reference is occasionally made to the Zwingli section of the *Corpus Reformatorum* edition using a volume number of 88 or greater. This is because the *Corpus Reformatorum* edition brings together the works of three Reformers (the others being Melanchthon and Calvin, who take up volumes 1–87). To convert from this older system, subtract 87 from the volume number. Thus *CR* 90.259.32 is equivalent to *Z* III.259.32.

The Schuler–Schulthess edition is referred to by volume number, page number and line number. Volumes 2 and 6 are subdivided, with the sub-divisions being designated by small Roman letters. Thus *S* IV.45.26–8 refers to lines 26–8 on page 45 of volume 4; *S* VI i.602.48 refers to line 48 on page 602 of the first part of volume 6.

Appendix 5

Referring to the Psalms in the Sixteenth Century

Several major works of the sixteenth-century Reformers take the form of commentaries on the Psalter, or on individual Psalms – for example, Martin Luther's famous lectures of 1513–15, generally known as *Dictata super Psalterium*. The student is likely to be confused by a major difficulty encountered in referring to the Psalms. Most sixteenth-century writers used the Latin version of the Bible known as the Vulgate. For reasons which defy a simple explanation, the numeration of the Psalms in the Vulgate is different from that found in the Hebrew text, and hence in modern English versions. Thus when Luther refers to Psalm 70, he means *Psalm 70 according to the numbering used in the Vulgate* – which is Psalm 71 in modern English editions. This obviously raises two difficulties. First, how can we convert from the Vulgate numbers to those found in the English Bible? And second, how can we refer to the Psalms to take account of this difference in numeration? We shall deal with these questions separately.

The Vulgate Psalm Numbers

We can tabulate the differences between the Vulgate and modern English versions of the Psalter as follows:

Vulgate	English Versions
1–8	1–8
9.1–21	9
9.22-39	10
10–112	11–113

113.1–8	114
113.9–26	115
114	116.1–9
115	116.10–19
116–45	117 46
146	147.1–11
147	147.12–20
148–50	148–50

It will thus be clear that the Vulgate and English Psalm numbers are identical only in the case of eleven Psalms (1–8, 148–50).

Thus when Luther refers to Psalm 22, he actually intends Psalm 23. Some modern English translations alter references to the Psalms to make allowance for the numeration difference – but when dealing with the original text, the student must be prepared to adjust the Psalm numbers accordingly. If you find a reference to a Psalm which doesn't make sense, try altering the numbers according to the above table.

Referring to Psalms

It is now virtually universal practice within the learned literature dealing with the Reformation (and especially Luther) to refer to Psalms in the following manner. If there is a difference between the Psalm numbers in the English and Vulgate texts, *the Vulgate number is given first, followed by the English number in parentheses*. Thus a discussion of 'Luther's exposition of Psalm 70 (71)' means Psalm 70 *according to the Vulgate numeration* and Psalm 71 *according to the English numeration*. Similarly, a reference to Psalm 22 (23).3 is a reference to verse 3 of Psalm 22 *following the Vulgate numeration*, and Psalm 23 *following the English numeration*. Occasionally the situation is further complicated through some Psalms having different verse numbers in the Vulgate and English versions. A reference to 'Psalm 84.11 (85.10)' thus means Psalm 84, verse 11 in the Vulgate version; Psalm 85, verse 10, in the English version.

Appendix 6

Updating Reformation Bibliographies

The present work includes a comprehensive bibliography of important works dealing with Reformation thought. Bibliographies, however, go out of date quickly, particularly in a field such as Reformation studies in which so much scholarly activity is taking place. The student may therefore wonder how such a bibliography may be kept up to date. It is hoped that the following suggestions will be helpful.

The *Archiv für Reformationsgeschichte* Literature Supplement

The leading journal in the field of Reformation studies is *Archiv für Reformationsgeschichte* ('Archive for Reformation History'), published annually in October. Since 1972 this journal has included a supplementary Literature Review (*Literaturbericht*), which provides details of several thousand important books or articles published recently relating to the history or the thought of the Reformation. Some are annotated, either in English or German. The review is divided into sections and subsections, the classification being given in German. An English version of its most important sections follows:

1	General
2	Religion and Culture
2.1	Before the Reformation
2.2	Luther
2.3	Zwingli
2.4	Calvin
2.5	Protestantism
3	Spirit and Culture

The student should select the section or subsections of particular interest to him, and work his way through the publications listed thereunder.

Review Articles and Published Bibliographies

A number of review articles or bibliographies are published regularly. The annual *Luther-Jahrbuch*, *Zwingliana*, and the November issue of *Calvin Theological Journal* include invaluable reports on recent works on Luther, Zwingli and Calvin respectively. The journal *Ephemerides Theologicae Lovaniensis* publishes an annual bibliography of works, including many relevant to the study of the Catholic Reformation. The student is also recommended to check library catalogues under the 'Bibliography' sections of noted Reformers – such as Luther, Calvin or Zwingli – where he will find works such as the following:

A. Erichson, *Bibliographia Calviniana* (Nieuwkoop, 3rd edn, 1965).
W. Niesel, *Calvin-Bibliographie (1901-1959)* (Munich, 1961).
H. W. Pipkin, *A Zwingli Bibliography* (Pittsburg, PA, 1972).

It is also useful to look through recent numbers of leading history or theology journals – such as *Church History*, *Journal of Ecclesiastical History* or *Journal of Theological Studies* – with two objectives in mind. First, look for reviews of recent books. If a book *has* been reviewed by one of these journals, it is likely to be important. Second, look for review articles – in other words, articles which summarize recent work in a given field. An example of such a review is Robert White, 'Fifteen Years of Calvin Studies in French (1965–1980)', *Journal of Religious History* 21 (1982), pp. 140–61.

Finally, the student is recommended to browse through the bibliography section of any recent publication dealing with the Reformation, and note works of relevance which appeared recently. Writers using the Harvard (author-and-date) system make this a particularly easy task, in that the date of publication of the work is immediately obvious.

Journal Literature Searches

A number of major journals publish important articles in English dealing with Reformation thought. You are recommended to gain access to each number of these journals as it is published, and note any studies of relevance to your particular interest. The following list of major journals is arranged in descending order of importance:

Archiv für Reformationsgeschichte
Sixteenth Century Journal
Church History
Journal of Ecclesiastical History
Harvard Theological Review
Journal of Theological Studies

Readers with a particular interest in the radical Reformation should also gain access to the *Mennonite Quarterly Review*. *Archiv für Reformationsgeschichte* publishes articles in either English or German in about equal number; those published in German, however, helpfully include an abstract in English.

Readers with a knowledge of German should also check the ollowing journals:

Zeitschrift für Kirchengeschichte
Zeitschrift für Theologie und Kirche
Kerygma und Dogma

Abstracting Services

A number of organizations and journals provide abstracts of articles and/or books, arranged by subject. Two major publications are provided by the American Theological Library Association:

Religion Index One: Periodicals
Index to Book Reviews in Religion

These works are to be found in most North American university and college libraries. The following are also useful:

Guide to Social Science and Religion in Periodical Literature
Religious and Theological Abstracts
Social Sciences and Humanities Index.

Cataloguing practices vary from one library to another. In the event of difficulty in locating these reference works, you should consult your librarian.

Appendix 7

Chronology of Political and Intellectual History

1348 First German university founded at Prague.

1365 University of Vienna founded.

1378–1417 The Great Schism in the western church, with antipopes in Avignon and Rome.

1386 University of Tübingen founded. Reform of statutes of University of Vienna, leading to dominance of the *via moderna*.

1388 University of Cologne founded.

1392 University of Erfurt founded.

1409 University of Leipzig founded.

1414–18 Council of Constance, ending the Great Schism.

1425 University of Louvain founded.

1453 The Fall of Constantinople: increased migration westwards of Greek-speaking scholars and their manuscripts.

1457 University of Freiburg-im-Breisgau founded.

1460 University of Basle founded.

1472 University of Ingolstadt founded.

1474 Condemnation of the *via moderna* at Paris: migration of those sympathetic to the *via moderna* to German universities.

1477 Outbreak of war between France and the house of Hapsburg.

1481 French decree against the *via moderna* rescinded.

1483 Martin Luther born, 10 November.

1484 Huldrych Zwingli born, 1 January. Gabriel Biel appointed to chair at Tübingen.

1491 Johan Froben starts printing at Basle.

1492 Christobal Colon (Columbus) discovers the Americas.

1498 Zwingli begins his studies at University of Vienna.

1501 Luther begins his studies at University of Erfurt.

1502 University of Wittenberg founded.

1503 First edition of Erasmus' *Enchiridion*.

1505 Luther enters the Augustinian monastery at Erfurt, 17 July.

1506 Publication of Amerbach edition of the works of Augustine.

1508 Reform of statutes of University of Wittenberg. Luther lectures in moral philosophy at University of Wittenberg.

1512 Luther begins lecturing on the Bible at Wittenberg. Philip Melanchthon arrives at Tübingen.

1515 Publication of the *Letters of Obscure Men*, ridiculing the Cologne Dominicans. Publication of third edition of Erasmus' *Enchiridion*. Defeat of the Swiss Confederation at the Battle of Marignano, September: Zurich announces it will henceforth enter into no further foreign alliances.

1516 Publication of Erasmus' *Novum Instrumentum omne*. Luther and Karlstadt clash over the interpretation of Augustine, 25 September.

1517 Karlstadt defends 151 Augustinian theses, 26 April. Luther posts 95 theses on indulgences, 31 October.

1518 Karlstadt reforms theological curriculum at Wittenberg, with new emphasis upon Augustine and the Bible, March. Christoph Froschauer begins printing at Zurich. Luther's Heidelberg Disputation, April. Luther appears before Cajetan at Augsburg, October–November.

1519 Charles V elected emperor. Leipzig Disputation between Luther, Karlstadt and Eck, July. Luther condemned by the University of Cologne, 30 August. Luther condemned by the University of Louvain, 7 November.

1520 Luther condemned by the University of Paris, 15 April. Papal bull *Exsurge Domine* threatens Luther with excommunication, 15 June. Luther publishes his three reforming treatises: *Address to the German Nobility, The Babylonian Captivity of the Church, The Freedom of a Christian.* Zurich city council issues mandate declaring that all preaching must be based upon scripture. Luther publicly burns the papal bull and works of canon law.

1521 Diet of Worms; Luther placed under the ban of the Empire, 8 May. Luther placed in protective custody in the Wartburg.

1522 Unrest at Wittenberg leads to Luther's return. Breaking of the Lenten Fast at Zurich.

1523   First Zurich Disputation, placing city council in charge of scriptural preaching at Zurich, 29 January. Basle city council issues mandate on preaching according to scripture, based on Zurich's 1520 mandate. Second Zurich Disputation, on the mass and images in churches, 26-8 October.

1524   Battle of Novara, 30 April. Zurich city council issues decree permitting removal of images from churches, 15 June.

1525   Anabaptism becomes an important movement: first baptisms at Zurich, 21 January. Battle of Pavia, 25 February. Zwingli's *Commentary on true and false religion*, criticising Erasmus, published. The Twelve Articles of Memmingen set out the grievances of the German peasantry: mob violence results. Zurich abolishes the mass, 12 April. Luther writes *Against the murderous and Thieving Hordes of Peasants*, 4 May. Thomas Müntzer and 53 supporters of the Peasants' Revolt publicly executed, 27 May. Luther's *de servo arbitrio* published, confirming a serious rift with Erasmus.

1526   Diet of Speyer, June–August.

1527   Sack of Rome by the troops of Charles V.

1528   Berne accepts Zwinglian Reformation, including the abolition of the mass, 7 February. St Gall abolishes the mass, 17 July.

1529   Diet of Speyer, ending toleration of Lutheranism in Catholic districts, 21 February. Protest of six princes and fourteen cities against the Diet of Speyer, giving rise to the term 'Protestant'. Treaty of Barcelona, between Charles V and Pope Clement VII, 29 June. Peace of Cambrai: Francis I of France and Charles V agree peace, 3 August. Philip of Hesse convenes abortive Colloquy of Marburg, 1–4 October. Charles V and Venice agree peace at Bologna, 28 December.

1530   Pope Clement VII crowns Charles V emperor at Bologna.

1531   Founding of the Schmalkaldic League for the defence of Protestantism, 27 February. Death of Zwingli in battle at Cappel, 11 October.

1533   Nicolas Cop's All Saints Day oration at Paris, 1 November.

1534   Affair of the Placards provokes Francis I to action against French evangelicals, 18 October.

1536   First edition of Calvin's *Institutes* published, March. Bucer and Luther reach agreement on the eucharist, May. Calvin summoned to Geneva by Farel, July.

1538 Calvin expelled from Geneva.

1539 Second edition of Calvin's *Institutes*.

1540 Bigamy of Philip of Hesse.

1541 Colloquy of Regensburg (Ratisbon), April–May. Calvin returns to establish his theocracy at Geneva, September.

1545 Council of Trent opens, 13 December.

1546 Death of Luther, 18 February. Outbreak of Schmalkaldic War.

1547 Defeat of Schmalkaldic League at Mühlberg, 24 April.

Notes

Chapter 1 Introduction

1 'The one definite thing which can be said about the Reformation in England is that it was an act of State...The Reformation in England was a parliamentary transaction': F. M. Powicke, *The Reformation in England* (London, 1941), pp. 1, 34. See further A. G. Dickens, 'The Reformation in England', in *Reformation Studies* (London, 1982), pp. 443–56; J. J. Scarisbrick, *The Reformation and the English People* (Oxford, 1985), pp. 61–84.

Chapter 2 Late Medieval Religion

1 Bernd Moeller, 'Piety in Germany around 1500', in *The Reformation in Medieval Perspective*, ed. Steven E. Ozment (Chicago, 1971), pp. 50-75.
2 H. J. Cohn, 'Anticlericalism in the German Peasants' War, 1525', *Past and Present* 83 (1979), pp. 3–31.
3 Gerald Strauss, *Manifestations of Discontent in Germany on the Eve of the Reformation* (Bloomington, Ind., 1971); A. G. Dickens, 'Intellectual and Social Forces in the German Reformation', in *Reformation Studies* (London, 1982), pp. 491–503.
4 See Gerald Strauss, *Luther's House of Learning: Indoctrination of the Young in the German Reformation* (Baltimore, 1978).

Chapter 3 Humanism and the Reformation

1 See Wallace K. Ferguson, *The Renaissance in Historical Thought* (New York, 1948).
2 Jacob Burckhardt, *The Civilization of the Renaissance in Italy* (New York, 1935), p. 143.
3 See the invaluable study of Peter Burke, *The Italian Renaissance: Culture and Society in Italy* (Oxford, revised edn, 1986).
4 See W. Rüegg, *Cicero und der Humanismus* (Zurich, 1946), pp. 1–4; A. Campana, 'The Origin of the Word "Humanist"', *Journal of the Warburg and Courtauld Institutes* 9 (1946), pp. 60–73.
5 Charles Trinkaus, 'A Humanist's Image of Humanism: The Inaugural Orations of Bartolommeo della Fonte', *Studies in the Renaissance* 7 (1960), pp. 90–147; H. H. Gray, 'Renaissance Humanism: The Pursuit of Eloquence', in *Renaissance*

Essays, eds P. O. Kristeller and P. P. Wiener (New York, 1968), pp. 199–216.

6 Hans Baron, *The Crisis of the Early Italian Renaissance: Civic Humanism and Republican Liberty in an Age of Classicism and Tyranny* (Princeton, NJ, revised edn, 1966).

7 Jerrold E. Seigel, ' "Civic Humanism" or Ciceronian Rhetoric? The Culture of Petrarch and Bruni', *Past and Present* 34 (1966), pp. 3-48.

8 For an excellent biography, see Roland H. Bainton, *Erasmus of Rotterdam* (New York, 1969).

9 The word *enchiridion* literally means 'in the hand', and came to have two meanings: a *weapon* held in the hand (i.e, a dagger), or a *book* held in the hand (i.e., a 'handbook').

10 On the Vulgate, see chapter 6, and R. Loewe, 'The Medieval History of the Latin Vulgate', in G. W. H. Lampe (ed.), *Cambridge History of the Bible II: The West from the Fathers to the Reformation* (Cambridge, 1969), pp. 102–54.

11 The full extent of humanist influence upon the Reformers goes further than suggested by this brief summary. The reader is referred to Alister E. McGrath, *The Intellectual Origins of the European Reformation* (Oxford, 1987), for a discussion of two major points: (1) the influence of humanism upon the text of scripture (pp. 122–39); (2) the influence of humanism upon the interpretation of scripture (pp. 152–74). On the full importance of the 'patristic testimony' for the Reformation, see McGrath, *Intellectual Origins of the European Reformation*, pp. 175–90.

12 In fact, of course, a few 'pseudo-Augustinian' works managed to get through the humanists' process of sieving: the Amerbach edition of Augustine's works includes *de vera et falsa poenitentia*, 'on true and false penitence', which contradicts Augustine at points.

13 For further details, see McGrath, *Intellectual Origins of the European Reformation*, pp. 43–59.

14 For further details, see McGrath, *Intellectual Origins of the European Reformation*, pp. 59–68.

Chapter 4 Scholasticism and the Reformation

1 David Knowles, *The Evolution of Medieval Thought* (London, 1976), pp. 71–288; Paul Vignaux, *Philosophy in the Middle Ages* (New York, 1959), pp. 69–90.

2 On Aquinas, see Etienne Gilson, *The Christian Philosophy of St Thomas Aquinas* (New York, 1956).

3 See Charles G. Nauert, 'The Clash of Humanists and Scholastics: An Approach to Pre-Reformation Controversies', *Sixteenth Century Journal* 4 (1973), pp. 1–18; James Overfield, 'Scholastic Opposition to Humanism in Pre-Reformation Germany', *Viator* 7 (1976), pp. 391–420. A particularly helpful essay on this theme is A. H. T. Levi, 'The Breakdown of Scholasticism and the Significance of Evangelical Humanism', in *The Philosophical Assessment of Theology*, ed. G. R. Hughes (Georgetown, 1987), pp. 101–28.

4 On the problem of universals, see John Hospers, *An Introduction to Philosophical Analysis* (Englewood Cliffs, NJ, 2nd revised edn, 1976), pp. 354–67. On realism

and nominalism in the Middle Ages, see Etienne Gilson, *History of Christian Philosophy in the Middle Ages* (London, 1978), pp. 489–98; M. H. Carré, *Realists and Nominalists* (Oxford, 1946).

5 On Thomism, see Gilson, *History of Christian Philosophy in the Middle Ages*, pp. 361–83. On Scotism, see Gilson, *History of Christian Philosophy in the Middle Ages*, pp. 454–71.

6 For the historical development of the Pelagian controversy, and the issues involved, see Peter Brown, *Augustine of Hippo: A Biography* (London, 1975), pp. 340–407; Gerald Bonner, *St Augustine of Hippo: Life and Controversies* (Norwich, 2nd edn, 1986), pp. 312–93.

7 See Alister E. McGrath, *Iustitia Dei: A History of the Christian Doctrine of Justification* (2 vols: Cambridge, 1986), vol. 1, pp. 128–45; Brown, *Augustine of Hippo*, pp. 398–407.

8 For what follows, see McGrath, *Iustitia Dei*, vol. 1, pp. 119–28; 166–72.

9 See Francis Oakley, *The Political Thought of Pierre d'Ailly: The Voluntarist Tradition* (New Haven, 1964).

10 See William J. Courtenay, 'The King and the Leaden Coin: The Economic Background of Sine Qua Non Causality', *Traditio* 28 (1972), pp. 185–209.

11 For the personalities involved, see William J. Courtenay, *Adam Wodeham: An Introduction to His Life and Writings* (Leiden, 1978).

12 See Heiko A. Oberman, *Masters of the Reformation: The Emergence of a New Intellectual Climate in Europe* (Cambridge, 1981), pp. 64–110.

13 Heiko A. Oberman, 'Headwaters of the Reformation: *Initia Lutheri - Initia Reformationis*', reprinted in *The Dawn of the Reformation: Essays in Late Medieval and Early Reformation Thought* (Edinburgh, 1986), pp. 39–83.

14 Oberman, 'Headwaters of the Reformation', p. 77.

15 McGrath, *Intellectual Origins of the European Reformation*, pp. 108–15.

16 Karl Reuter, *Das Grundverständnis der Theologie Calvins* (Neukirchen, 1963); *Vom Scholaren bis zum jungen Reformator: Studien zum Werdegang Johannes Calvins* (Neukirchen, 1981).

17 Alister E. McGrath, 'John Calvin and Late Medieval Thought: A Study in Late Medieval Influences upon Calvin's Theological Development', *Archiv für Reformationsgeschichte* 77 (1986), pp. 58–78; idem, *Intellectual Origins of the European Reformation*, pp. 94–107.

18 See P. O. Kristeller, 'The Contribution of Religious Orders to Renaissance Thought and Learning', *American Benedictine Review* 21 (1970), pp. 1–55.

Chapter 5 The Doctrine of Grace

1 For an elementary introduction to these ideas, see Alister McGrath, *Understanding Jesus* (Grand Rapids, MI, 1987), pp. 123–36.

2 For the background, see Krister Stendahl, 'The Apostle Paul and the Introspective Conscience of the West', in *Paul among Jews and Gentiles* (Philadelphia, 1983), pp. 78–96.

3 See Alister E. McGrath, *Luther's Theology of the Cross: Martin Luther's Theological Breakthrough* (Oxford, 1985), pp. 72–92; 100–28.

4 McGrath, *Luther's Theology of the Cross*, pp. 88–9.

5 McGrath, *Luther's Theology of the Cross*, pp. 106–13, for texts and analysis.

6 See Alister E. McGrath, *Iustitia Dei: A History of the Christian Doctrine of Justification* (2 vols: Cambridge, 1986), vol. 1, pp. 51–70.

7 For full Latin text and English translation, see McGrath, *Luther's Theology of the Cross*, pp. 95–8. For an English translation, see *Luther's Works* (55 vols: St Louis/Philadelphia, 1955–75), vol. 34, pp. 336–8. We have paraphrased Luther somewhat and omitted some of his more technical phrases for the sake of clarity.

8 For the debate, see McGrath, *Luther's Theology of the Cross*, pp. 95–147, especially pp. 142–7. A significant minority opinion places the breakthrough in 1518–19. A useful essay, worth consulting, is Brian A. Gerrish, 'By Faith Alone: Medium and Message in Luther's Gospel', in *The Old Protestantism and the New: Essays on the Reformation Heritage* (Chicago, 1982), pp. 69–89.

9 For details of Luther's doctrine of justification by faith, see McGrath, *Iustitia Dei*, vol. 2, pp. 10–20.

10 For further details, see Alister E. McGrath, *The Intellectual Origins of the European Reformation* (Oxford, 1987), pp. 152–67.

11 For further discussion, see John Bossy, *Christianity in the West 1400–1700* (Oxford, 1987), pp. 35–56; David C. Steinmetz, 'Luther against Luther', in *Luther in Context* (Bloomington, Ind., 1986), pp. 1–11; Thomas N. Tentler, *Sin and Confession on the Eve of the Reformation* (Princeton, 1977).

12 *To the Christian Nobility of the German Nation, The Babylonian Captivity of the Church* and *The Freedom of a Christian*. These works are collected together in *Martin Luther: Three Treatises* (Philadelphia, 1973).

13 For a full discussion, see Walther von Loewenich, *Luther's Theology of the Cross* (Minneapolis, 1976); McGrath, *Luther's Theology of the Cross*, pp. 148–75.

14 For contemporary expositions of this theme, and its social and political relevance, see Jürgen Moltmann, *The Crucified God* (London, 1974); Alister McGrath, *The Enigma of the Cross* (London, 1987).

15 On this, see McGrath, *Iustitia Dei*, vol. 2, pp. 1–3, 20–5; idem, *Justification by Faith: An Introduction*, pp. 47–62.

16 McGrath, *Iustitia Dei*, vol. 2, pp. 32–9.

17 A view which received its most important statement in Alexander Schweizer, *Die protestantischen Centraldogmen in ihrer Entwicklung innerhalb der reformirten Kirche*, 'The Protestant Central Dogmas in their Evolution within the Reformed Church', (2 vols: Zurich, 1854–6).

18 See W. P. Stephens, *The Theology of Huldrych Zwingli* (Oxford, 1986), pp. 86–106.

19 On this work, see Harry J. McSorley, *Luther - Right or Wrong* (Minneapolis, 1969).

20 Although doubt was cast upon Calvin's role in drafting Nicolas Cop's All Souls' Day oration, new manuscript evidence has been uncovered suggesting that he was positively implicated. See Jean Rott, 'Documents strasbourgeois concernant

Calvin. Un manuscrit autographe: la harangue du recteur Nicolas Cop', in *Regards contemporains sur Jean Calvin* (Paris, 1966), pp. 28–43.

21 See, for example, Harro Höpfl, *The Christian Polity of John Calvin* (Cambridge, 1982), pp. 219–26.

22 *Institutes* III.xxi.5. See further R. T. Kendall, *Calvin and English Calvinism to 1649* (Oxford, 1979), pp. 13–28; Höpfl, *Christian Polity of John Calvin*, pp. 227–39.

23 For details of this important alteration, and an analysis of its consequences, see *The History of Christian Theology I: The Science of Theology*, ed. Paul Avis (Grand Rapids, MI, 1986), pp. 157–9.

24 See McGrath, *Iustitia Dei*, vol. 2, pp. 111–21.

25 For Calvinism in England and America at this time, see Patrick Collinson, 'England and International Calvinism, 1558–1640', in *International Calvinism 1541-1715*, ed. Menna Prestwich (Oxford, 1985), pp. 197–223; W. A. Speck and L. Billington, 'Calvinism in Colonial North America', in *International Calvinism*, ed. Prestwich, pp. 257-83.

26 See McGrath, *Iustitia Dei*, vol. 2, pp. 39–53, especially pp. 48–51.

27 B. B. Warfield, *Calvin and Augustine* (Philadelphia, 1956), p. 322.

Chapter 6 The Return to Scripture

1 See the magisterial collection of studies assembled in *The Cambridge History of the Bible*, eds P. R. Ackroyd *et al.* (3 vols: Cambridge, 1963–69).

2 See Alister E. McGrath, *The Intellectual Origins of the European Reformation* (Oxford, 1987), pp. 140–51. Two major studies of this theme should be noted: Paul de Vooght, *Les sources de la doctrine chrétienne d'après les théologiens du XIVe siècle et du début du XVe* (Paris, 1954); Hermann Schüssler, *Der Primät der Heiligen Schrift als theologisches und kanonistisches Problem im Spätmittelalter* (Wiesbaden, 1977).

3 Heiko A. Oberman, 'Quo vadis, Petre? Tradition from Irenaeus to *Humani Generis*', in *The Dawn of the Reformation: Essays in Late Medieval and Early Reformation Thought* (Edinburgh, 1986), pp. 269–96.

4 See George H. Tavard, *Holy Writ or Holy Church? The Crisis of the Protestant Reformation* (London, 1959).

5 See J. N. D. Kelly, *Jerome: Life, Writings and Controversies* (London, 1975). Strictly speaking, 'Vulgate' designates Jerome's translation of the Old Testament (except the Psalms, which was taken from the Gallican Psalter); the apocryphal works (except Wisdom, Ecclesiasticus, I and II Maccabees, and Baruch, which were taken from the Old Latin Version); and all the New Testament.

6 See Raphael Loewe, 'The Medieval History of the Latin Vulgate', in *Cambridge History of the Bible*, vol. 2, pp. 102–54.

7 See McGrath, *Intellectual Origins*, pp. 124–5 and references therein.

8 Henry Hargreaves, 'The Wycliffite Versions', in *Cambridge History of the Bible*, vol. 2, pp. 387–415.

9 See Basil Hall, 'Biblical Scholarship: Editions and Commentaries', in *Cambridge History of the Bible*, vol. 3, pp. 38–93.

10 See Roland H. Bainton, *Erasmus of Christendom* (New York, 1969), pp. 168–71.

11 Roland H. Bainton, 'The Bible in the Reformation', in *Cambridge History of the Bible*, vol. 3, pp. 1–37; especially pp. 6–9.

12 For further discussion of the problem of the Old Testament canon, see Roger T. Beckwith, *The Old Testament Canon of the New Testament Church* (London, 1985).

13 See Pierre Fraenkel, *Testimonia Patrum: The Function of the Patristic Argument in the Theology of Philip Melanchthon* (Geneva, 1961); McGrath, *The Intellectual Origins of the European Reformation*, pp. 175–90.

14 E.g., Tavard, *Holy Writ or Holy Church?*, p. 208.

15 Martin Luther, *Three Treatises* (Philadelphia, 1975), pp. 10-11.

16 *Three Treatises*, pp. 20–1.

17 For the details, see G. R. Potter, *Zwingli* (Cambridge, 1976), pp. 74–96.

18 See Heiko A. Oberman, *Masters of the Reformation* (Cambridge, 1981), pp. 187–209.

Chapter 7 The Doctrine of the Church and Sacraments

1 See Basil Hall, '*Hoc est corpus meum*: The Centrality of the Real Presence for Luther', in *Luther: Theologian for Catholics and Protestants*, ed. George Yule (Edinburgh, 1985), pp. 112–44, for further details.

2 For an analysis of the reasons underlying Luther's rejection of Aristotle at this point, see Alister E. McGrath, *Luther's Theology of the Cross: Martin Luther's Theological Breakthrough* (Oxford, 1985), pp. 136–41.

3 Martin Luther, *Three Treatises* (Philadelphia, 1975), p. 150.

4 Luther, *Three Treatises*, pp. 155–6.

5 See Hall, '*Hoc est corpus meum*: The Centrality of the Real Presence for Luther'.

6 See Alister E. McGrath, *Luther's Theology of the Cross: Martin Luther's Theological Breakthrough* (Oxford, 1985), pp. 136–41.

7 Other important texts used by Luther include 1 Corinthians 10:16–33; 11:26–34. See David C. Steinmetz, 'Scripture and the Lord's Supper in Luther's Theology', in *Luther in Context* (Bloomington, Ind., 1986), pp. 72–84.

8 See W. P. Stephens, *The Theology of Huldrych Zwingli* (Oxford, 1986), pp. 180–93.

9 'On Baptism', in *Zwingli and Bullinger*, ed. G. W. Bromiley (Library of Christian Classics 24: Philadelphia, 1953), p. 131.

10 Gordon Rupp, *Patterns of Reformation* (London, 1969), pp. 23-30.

11 See Timothy George, 'The Presuppositions of Zwingli's Baptismal Theology', in *Prophet, Pastor, Protestant: The Work of Huldrych Zwinglli after Five Hundred Years*, eds E. J. Furcha and H. Wayne Pipkin (Allison Park, PA, 1984), pp. 71–87, especially pp. 79–82.

12 On this point, and its political and institutional importance, see Robert C. Walton, 'The Institutionalization of the Reformation at Zürich', *Zwingliana* 13 (1972), pp. 497–515.

13 Pope Clement VII accepted peace at Barcelona on 29 June; the King of France came to terms with Charles V on 3 August. The Colloquy of Marburg took place on 1-5 October.

14 For an account of the Colloquy of Marburg, see G. R. Potter, *Zwingli* (Cambridge, 1976), pp. 316–42.

15 B. B. Warfield, *Calvin and Augustine* (Philadelphia, 1956), p. 322.

16 See Scott H. Hendrix, *Luther and the Papacy: Stages in a Reformation Conflict* (Philadelphia, 1981).

17 Also known as 'Ratisbon'. For details, see Peter Matheson, *Cardinal Contarini at Regensburg* (Oxford, 1972); Dermot Fenlon, *Heresy and Obedience in Tridentine Italy: Cardinal Pole and the Counter Reformation* (Cambridge, 1972).

18 *Luther's Works*, vol. 39, p. 305.

19 For a full discussion, see F. H. Littel, *The Anabaptist View of the Church* (Boston, 2nd edn, 1958).

20 *Luther's Works*, vol. 41, pp. 231–2.

21 See Geoffrey G. Willis, *Saint Augustine and the Donatist Controversy* (London, 1950); Gerald Bonner, *St Augustine of Hippo: Life and Controversies* (Norwich, 2nd edn, 1986), pp. 237–311.

22 Ernst Troeltsch, *The Social Teaching of the Christian Churches* (2 vols: London, 1931), vol. 1, p. 331. For variations of this analysis, see Howard Becker, *Systematic Sociology* (Gary, Ind., 1950), pp. 624-42; Joachim Wach, *Types of Religious Experience: Christian and NonChristian* (Chicago, 1951), pp. 190–6.

23 See J. K. S. Reid, 'Diakonia in the Thought of Calvin', in *Service in Christ: Essays presented to Karl Barth on his 80th Birthday*, ed. James I. McCord and T. H. L. Parker (London, 1966), pp. 101–9; Harro Höpfl, *The Christian Polity of John Calvin* (Cambridge, 1985), pp. 77-127.

Chapter 8 The Political Thought of the Reformation

1 The case of Thomas Müntzer illustrates this point: see Gordon Rupp, *Patterns of Reformation* (London, 1969), pp. 157–353. More generally, the development of the radical Reformation in the Low Countries should be noted: W. E. Keeney, *Dutch Anabaptist Thought and Practice, 1539-1564* (Nieuwkoop, 1968).

2 See W. Ullmann, *Medieval Papalism: The Political Theories of the Medieval Canonists* (London, 1949); M. J. Wilks, *The Problem of Sovereignty: The Papal Monarchy with Augustus Triumphus and the Publicists* (Cambridge, 1963).

3 Martin Luther, *Three Treatises* (Philadelphia, 1975), p. 12.

4 *Three Treatises*, p. 15.

5 There is a considerable degree of ambiguity in Luther's use of terms such as 'kingdom' and 'government': see W. D. J. Cargill Thompson, 'The Two Kingdoms' and the 'Two Regiments': Some Problems of Luther's *Zwei-Reiche-Lehre*', in *Studies in the Reformation: Luther to Hooker* (London, 1980), pp. 42–59.

6 See *Temporal Authority: To what extent should it be obeyed?*, in *Luther's Works* (55 vols: St Louis/Philadelphia, 1955-75), vol. 45, pp. 75–129, especialy pp. 90–5. The 1519 sermon *Two Kinds of Righteousness* clarifies this distinction: *Luther's Works*, vol. 31, pp. 293–306.

7 See F. Edward Cranz, *An Essay on the Development of Luther's Thought on Justice,*

Law and Society (Cambridge, Mass., 1959), for a full analysis of this point.

8 *Luther's Works*, vol. 46, p. 25.

9 *Luther's Works*, vol. 46, p. 27.

10 See David C. Steinmetz, 'Luther and the Two Kingdoms', in *Luther in Context* (Bloomington, Ind., 1986), pp. 112–25.

11 See the famous letter of Karl Barth (1939), in which he asserted that 'The German people suffer... from the mistake of Martin Luther regarding the relation of Law and Gospel, of temporal and spiritual order and power': quoted by Helmut Thielicke, *Theological Ethics* (3 vols: Grand Rapids, 1979), vol. 1, p. 368.

12 See Steinmetz, 'Luther and the Two Kingdoms', p. 114.

13 See the useful study of W. D. J. Cargill Thompson, 'Luther and the Right of Resistance to the Emperor', in *Studies in the Reformation*, pp. 3–41.

14 See R. N. C. Hunt, 'Zwingli's Theory of Church and State', *Church Quarterly Review* 112 (1931), pp. 20–36; Robert C. Walton, *Zwingli's Theocracy* (Toronto, 1967); W. P. Stephens, *The Theology of Huldrych Zwingli* (Oxford, 1986), pp. 282–310.

15 See Stephens, *Theology of Huldrych Zwingli*, p. 303, n. 87.

16 W. P. Stephens, *The Holy Spirit in the Theology of Martin Bucer* (Cambridge, 1970), pp. 167–72. On Bucer's political theology in general, see T. F. Torrance, *Kingdom and Church: A Study in the Theology of the Reformation* (Edinburgh, 1956), pp. 73–89.

17 See Torrance, *Kingdom and Church*, pp. 157–60.

18 *Institutes of the Christian Religion* IV.xi.3; trans. Beveridge (2 vols: Grand Rapids, 1975), vol. 2, p. 441.

19 For a careful study, see Harro Höpfl, *The Christian Polity of John Calvin* (Cambridge, 1985), pp. 152–206. Additional information may be found in Gillian Lewis, 'Calvinism in Geneva in the Time of Calvin and Beza', in *International Calvinism 1541-1715*, ed. Menna Prestwich (Oxford, 1985), pp. 39–70.

20 K. R. Davis, 'No Discipline, no Church: An Anabaptist Contribution to the Reformed Tradition', *Sixteenth Century Journal* 13 (1982), pp. 45–9.

21 Nevertheless, it must be noted that Calvin was in the habit of dedicating works to European monarchs, in the hope of winning them to the Reformation cause. Among the dedicatees of Calvin's published works were Edward VI and Elizabeth I of England and Christopher III of Denmark.

Select Bibliography

Roland H. Bainton, *Here I Stand: A Life of Martin Luther* (New York, 1959).

——, *Erasmus of Christendom* (New York, 1969).

H. Baron, *The Crisis of the Early Italian Renaissance: Civic Humanism and Republican Liberty in an Age of Classicism and Tyranny* (Princeton, NJ, revised edn, 1966).

N. Birnbaum, 'The Zwinglian Reformation in Zurich', *Past and Present* 15 (1959), pp. 27–47.

Heinrich Boehmer, *Martin Luther: Road to Reformation* (New York, 1957).

Heinrich Bornkamm, *Luther's World of Thought* (St Louis, 1958).

——, *Luther's Doctrine of the Two Kingdoms* (Philadelphia, 1966).

John Bossy, *Christianity in the West 1400-1700* (Oxford/New York, 1987).

W. J. Bouwsma, 'The Two Faces of Humanism: Stoicism and Augustinianism in Renaissance Thought', in *Itinerarium Italicum: The Profile of the Italian Renaissance in the Mirror of its European Transformations*, ed. H. A. Oberman with T. A. Brady (Leiden, 1975), pp. 3–60.

Peter Burke, *The Italian Renaissance: Culture and Society in Italy* (Oxford, revised edn, 1987).

A. G. Dickens, *The Counter Reformation* (London, 1968).

A. G. Dickens and John M. Tonkin, *The Reformation in Historical Thought* (Cambridge, Mass., 1985).

Gerhard Ebeling, *Luther: An Introduction to His Thought* (Philadelphia, 1970).

G. R. Elton, *Reform and Renewal* (Cambridge, 1973).

W. K. Ferguson, *The Renaissance in Historical Thought: Five Centuries of Interpretation* (Boston, 1948).

Brian A. Gerrish, 'The Word of God and the Word of Scripture: Luther and Calvin on Biblical Authority', in *The Old Protestantism and the New: Essays on the Reformation Heritage* (Chicago, 1982), pp. 51–68.

Peter J. Klassen, *The Reformation: Change and Stability* (St Louis, 1980).

P. O. Kristeller, 'Renaissance Aristotelianism', *Greek, Roman and Byzantine Studies* 6 (1965), pp. 157–74.

——, 'The European Diffusion of Italian Humanism', in *Renaissance Thought II: Humanism and the Arts* (New York, 1965), pp. 69–88.

——, *Renaissance Thought and Its Sources* (New York, 1979).

Walther von Loewenich, *Martin Luther: The Man and His Work* (Minneapolis, 1986).

Bernhard Lohse, *Martin Luther: An Introduction to his Life and Writings* (Philadelphia, 1986).

Alister E. McGrath, *Luther's Theology of the Cross: Martin Luther's Theological Breakthrough* (Oxford, 1985).

——, *Iustitia Dei: A History of the Christian Doctrine of Justification* (2 vols: Cambridge, 1986).

——, *The Intellectual Origins of the European Reformation* (Oxford, 1987).

Bernd Moeller, *Imperial Cities and the Reformation: Three Essays* (Philadelphia, 1972).

Heiko A. Oberman, *The Harvest of Medieval Theology: Gabriel Biel and Late Medieval Nominalism* (Cambridge, Mass., 1963).

——, *Forerunners of the Reformation: The Shape of Late Medieval Thought Illustrated by Key Documents* (Philadelphia, 1981).

——, *Masters of the Reformation: The Emergence of a New Intellectual Climate in Europe* (Cambridge, 1981).

——, *The Dawn of the Reformation: Essays in Late Medieval and Early Reformation Thought* (Edinburgh, 1986).

S. E. Ozment (ed.), *The Reformation in Medieval Perspective* (Chicago, 1971).

——, *The Reformation in the Cities: The Appeal of Protestantism to Sixteenth-Century Germany and Switzerland* (New Haven, Conn., 1975).

——, *The Age of Reform 1250-1550: An Intellectual and Religious History of Late Medieval and Reformation Europe* (New Haven, Conn., 1980).

——, *Reformation Europe: A Guide to Research* (St Louis, 1982).

Menna Prestwich (ed.), *International Calvinism 1541-1715* (Oxford, 1985).

George C. Sellery, *The Renaissance: Its Nature and Origins* (Madison, 1962).

R. J. Sider, *Andreas Bodenstein von Karlstadt: The Development of His Thought 1517-1525* (Leiden, 1974).

B. Smalley, *The Study of the Bible in the Middle Ages* (Oxford, 3rd edn, 1983).

L. W. Spitz, *The Religious Renaissance of the German Humanists* (Cambridge, Mass., 1963).

——, 'The Course of German Humanism', in *Itinerarium Italicum: The Profile of the Italian Renaissance in the Mirror of its European Transformations*, ed. H. A. Oberman with T. A. Brady (Leiden, 1975), pp. 371–436.

D. C. Steinmetz, *Misericordia Dei: The Theology of Johannes von Staupitz in its Late Medieval Setting* (Leiden, 1968).

——, *Luther and Staupitz: An Essay in the Intellectual Origins of the Protestant Reformation* (Durham, NC, 1980).

W. P. Stephens, *The Theology of Huldrych Zwingli* (Oxford, 1986).

C. Trinkaus, *In Our Image and Likeness: Humanity and Divinity in Italian Humanist Thought* (2 vols: Chicago, 1970).

F. Wendel, *Calvin: The Origins and Development of His Religious Thought* (New York, 1963).

George H. Williams, *The Radical Reformation* (Philadelphia, 1962).

Supplementary Annotated
Bibliography

Annotations

1   Background to Reformation
2   Late Medieval Religion
3   Humanism
4   Scholasticism
5   Doctrine of Grace
6   Doctrine of Scripture
7   Church and Sacraments
8   Social and Political Theory

2 G. Alberigo, 'Il movimento conciliare (xiv–xv sec.) nella ricerca storica recente', *Studi Medievali* 19 (1978), pp. 913–50.

8 J. W. Allen, *A History of Political Thought in the Sixteenth Century* (London, 1977).

3 M. J. B. Allen, 'Marsilio Ficino on Plato, the Neoplatonists and the Christian Doctrine of the Trinity', *Renaissance Quarterly* 37 (1984), pp. 555–84.

7 L. G. M. Alting von Geusau, *Die Lehre von der Kindertaufe bei Calvin* (Bilthoven/Mainz, 1963).

3 H. Ankwick-Kleehoven, *Der Wiener Humanist Johannes Cuspinian, Gelehrter und Diplomat zur Zeit Kaiser Maximilians* (Graz, 1959).

2 R. Bäumer, 'Die Reformkonzilien des 15. Jahrhunderts in der neueren Forschung', *Annuarium Historiae Conciliorum* 1 (1969), pp. 153–64.

2 ——, 'Die Zahl der allgemeinen Konzilien in der Sicht von Theologen des 15. und 16. Jahrhunderts', *Annuarium Historiae Conciliorum* 1 (1969), pp. 288–313.

4 K. Bannach, *Die Lehre von der doppelten Macht Gottes bei Wilhelm von Ockham: Problemgeschichtliche Voraussetzungen und Bedeutung* (Wiesbaden, 1975).

28 Hans Baron, 'Religion and Politics in the German Imperial Cities during the Reformation', *English Historical Review* 52 (1937), pp. 405–27; 614–33.

3 ——, '"Leonardi Bruno: "Professional Rhetorician" or "Civic Humanist"?', *Past and Present* 36 (1967), pp. 21–37.

36 G. Bauch, 'Die Anfänge des Studiums der griechischen Sprache und Literatur in Nord-Deutschland', *Gesellschaft für deutsche Erziehungs- und Schulgeschichte* 6 (1896), pp. 47–98.

3 ——, *Die Rezeption des Humanismus in Wien* (Breslau, 1903).

[36] ——, 'Die Einführung des Hebräischen in Wittenberg mit Berücksichtigung der Vorgeschichte des Studiums der Sprache in Deutschland', *Monatschrift für Geschichte und Wissenschaft des Judentums* 48 (1904), pp. 22–32; 77–86; 145–60; 214–23; 283–99; 328–40; 461–90.

[K.] Bauer, *Die Wittenberger Universitätstheologie und die Anfänge der Deutschen Reformation* (Tübingen, 1928).

[45] O. Bayer, *Promissio: Geschichte der reformatorischen Wende in Luthers Theologie* (Göttingen, 1971).

[36] J. H. Bentley, 'Erasmus' *Annotationes in Novum Testamentum* and the Textual Criticism of the Gospels', *Archiv für Reformationsgeschichte* 67 (1976), pp. 33–53.

[8] A. Biéler, *La pensée economique et sociale de Calvin* (Geneva, 1959).

[3] P. Bietenholz, *Der italienische Humanismus und die Blütezeit des Buchdrucks in Basel* (Basle, 1959).

[2] L. Binz, *Vie religieuse et réforme ecclésiastique dans le diocèse de Genève pendant la Grand Schisme* (Geneva, 1973).

[28] A. J. Black, *Monarchy and Community: Political Ideas in the Later Conciliar Controversy* (Cambridge, 1970).

[2] ——, *Council and Commune: The Conciliar Movement and the Council of Basel* (London, 1979).

[3] J. Bohatec, *Budé und Calvin: Studien zur Gedankenwelt des französischen Frühhumanismus* (Graz, 1950).

[3] C. Bonorand, *Vadians Weg vom Humanismus zur Reformation und seine Vorträge über die Apostelgeschichte* (Vadian-Studien 7: St Gallen, 1962).

[3] ——, 'Die Bedeutung der Universität Wien für Humanismus und Reformation, insbesondere in der Ostschweiz', *Zwingliana* 12 (1964–8), pp. 162–80.

[3] ——, *Aus Vadians Freundes- und Schülerkreis in Wien* (Vadian-Studien 8: St Gallen, 1965).

[3] ——, *Vadian und die Ereignisse in Italien im ersten Drittel des 16. Jahrhunderts* (Vadian-Studien 13: St Gallen, 1985).

[4] E. Borchert, *Der Einfluß des Nominalismus der Spätscholastik nach dem Traktat de communicatione idiomatum des Nikolaus Oresme* (Münster, 1940).

[7] S. N. Bosshard, *Zwingli-Erasmus-Cajetan: Die Eucharistie als Zeichen der Einheit* (Wiesbaden, 1978).

[5] C. Boyer, 'Luther et le "De spiritu et litera" de Saint Augustin', *Doctor Communis* 21 (1968), pp. 167–87.

[6] L. E. Boyle, 'Innocent III and Vernacular Versions of Scripture', in *The Bible in the Medieval World*, ed. K. Walsh and D. Wood (Studies in Church History: Subsidia 4: Oxford, 1985), pp. 131–55.

[28] T. A. Brady, *Ruling Class, Regime and Reformation at Strassburg, 1520-1555* (Leiden, 1977).

[3] V. Branca, 'Ermolao Barbaro and Late Quattrocento Venetian Humanism', in *Renaissance Studies*, ed. J. R. Hale (Totowa, NJ, 1973), pp. 218–43.

[2] W. Brandmüller, *Das Konzil von Pavia-Siena 1423-1424* (2 vols: Münster, 1968–73).

[3]   Q. Breen, *John Calvin: A Study in French Humanism* (Hamden, 2nd edn, 1968).

[7]   Peter N. Brooks, *Thomas Cranmer's Doctrine of the Eucharist* (London, 1965).

[1]   E. Buechler, *Die Anfänge des Buchdrucks in der Schweiz* (Berne, 2nd edn, 1951).

[3]   H. O. Burger, *Renaissance, Reformation, Humanismus* (Bad Homburg, 1969).

[3]   A. Campana, 'The Origin of the Word "Humanist"', *Journal of the Warburg and Courtauld Institutes* 9 (1946), pp. 60–73.

[3]   S. I. Camporeale, *Lorenzo Valla: umanesimo e teologia* (Florence,1972).

[3]   D. Cantimori, 'Sulla storia del concetto di Rinascimento', *Annali della scuola normale superiore di Pisa: lettere, storia e filosophia*, 2nd series, 1 (1932), pp. 229–68.

[3]   G. Cervani, 'Il Rinascimento italiano nella interpretazione di Hans Baron', *Nuova rivista storica* 39 (1955), pp. 492–503.

[36] J. Chomorat, 'Les *Annotations* de Valla, celles de Erasme et la grammaire', in *Etudes de l'exégèse au XVIe siècle*, ed. O. Fatio and P. Fraenkel (Geneva, 1978), pp. 202–28.

[12] M. U. Chrisman, *Lay Culture, Learned Culture: Books and Social Change in Strasbourg, 1480-1599* (New Haven/London, 1982).

[6]   C. Christ, 'Das Schriftverständnis von Zwingli und Erasmus im Jahre 1522', *Zwingliana* 16 (1983), pp. 111–25.

[6]   K. W. Clark, 'Observations on the Erasmian Notes in Codex 2', *Texte und Untersuchungen* 73 (1959), pp. 755–6.

[4]   W. J. Courtenay, 'Covenant and Causality in Pierre d'Ailly', *Speculum* 46 (1971), pp. 94–119.

[4]   ——, 'The King and the Leaden Coin: The Economic Background to Sine Qua Non Causality', *Traditio* 28 (1972), pp. 185–209.

[4]   ——, 'Nominalism and Late Medieval Thought: A Bibliographical Essay', *Theological Studies* 33 (1972), pp. 716–34.

[4]   ——, 'John of Mirecourt and Gregory of Rimini on whether God can undo the Past', *RThAM* 39 (1972), pp. 224–56; 40 (1973), pp. 147–74.

[24] ——, 'Nominalism and Late Medieval Religion', in *The Pursuit of Holiness in Late Medieval and Renaissance Religion*, ed. C. Trinkaus and 'H. A. Oberman (Leiden, 1974), pp. 26–59.

[4]   ——, *Adam Wodeham: An Introduction to his Life and Writings* (Leiden, 1977).

[4]   ——, 'Late Medieval Nominalism Revisited: 1972–1982', *Journal of the History of Ideas* 44 (1983), pp. 159–64.

[7]   J. Courvoisier, 'Réflexions à propos de la doctrine eucharistique de Zwingle et Calvin', in *Festgabe Leonhard von Muralt* (Zurich, 1970), pp. 258–65.

[7]   ——, *De la Réforme au Protestantisme: essai d'ecclesiologie réformé* (Paris, 1977).

[12] N. Z. Davis, 'Some Tasks and Themes in the Study of Popular Religion', in *The Pursuit of Holiness in Late Medieval and Renaissance Religion*, ed. C. Trinkaus and H. A. Oberman (Leiden, 1974), pp. 307–36.

[4]   M. Del Pra, 'Linguaggio e conoscenza assertiva nel pensiero di Roberto Holkot', *Rivista critica di storia della filosofia* 11 (1956), pp. 15–40.

[4]   ——, 'La teoria del "significato totale" delle propositione nel pensiero di Gregorio da Rimini', *Rivista critica di storia della filosofia* 11 (1956), pp. 287–311.

[8] D. Demandt, 'Zur Wirtschaftsethik Huldrych Zwinglis', in *Beiträge zur Wirtschafts- und Sozialgeschichte des Mittelalters*, ed. K. Schulz (Cologne, 1976), pp. 306–21.

[4] W. Dettloff, *Die Lehre von der Acceptatio Divina bei Johannes Duns Scotus mit besonderer Berücksichtigung der Rechtfertigungslehre* (Werl, 1954).

[4] ——, *Die Entwicklung der Akzeptations- und Verdienstlehre von Duns Skotus bis Luther* (Münster, 1963).

[1] A. G. Dickens, 'Intellectual and Social Forces in the German Reformation', in *Reformation Studies* (London, 1982), pp. 491–503.

[4] J. P. Donnelly, *Calvinism and Scholasticism in Vermigli's Doctrine of Man and Grace* (Leiden, 1976).

[12] L. G. Duggan, 'The Unresponsiveness of the Late Medieval Church: A Reconsideration', *The Sixteenth Century Journal* 9 (1978), pp. 3–26.

[6] G. Ebeling, 'Die Anfänge von Luthers Hermeneutik', in *Lutherstudien I* (Tübingen, 1971), pp. 1–68.

[4] W. Eckermann, *Wort und Wirklichkeit: Das Sprachverständnis in der Theologie Gregors von Rimini und seine Weiterwirkung in der Augustinerschule* (Würzburg, 1978).

[68] E. Egli, 'Zur Einführung des Schriftprinzips in der Schweiz', *Zwingliana* 1 (1903), pp. 332–9.

[4] F. Ehrle, *Der Sentenzenkommentar Peters von Candia des Pisaner Papstes Alexanders V: Ein Beitrag zur Scheidung der Schulen in der Scholastik des vierzehnten Jahrhunderts und zur Geschichte des Wegestreits* (Münster, 1925).

[12] E. L. Eisenstein, *The Printing Press as an Agent of Change* (2 vols: Cambridge, 1979).

[2] O. Engels, 'Zur Konstanzer Konzilsproblematik in der nachkonziliaren Historiographie des 15. Jahrhunderts', in *Von Konstanz nach Trient: Beiträge zur Kirchengeschichte von den Reformkonzilien bis zum Tridentinum*, ed. R. Bäumer (Paderborn, 1972), pp. 233–59.

[3] H. Entner, 'Der Begriff "Humanismus" als Problem der deutschen Literaturgeschichtsschreibung', *Klio* 40 (1962), pp. 260–70.

[23] ——, 'Probleme der Forschung zum deutschen Frühhumanismus 1400–1500', *Wissenschaftliche Zeitschrift der Ernst-Moritz-Arndt-Universität Greifswald* 15 (1966), pp. 587–90.

[234] J. Etienne, *Spiritualisme érasmien et théologiens louvainistes: un changement de problématique au début du XVIe siècle* (Louvain/Gembloux, 1956).

[6] G. R. Evans, *The Language and Logic of the Bible: The Earlier Middle Ages* (Cambridge, 1984).

[6] ——, *The Language and Logic of the Bible: The Road to Reformation* (Cambridge, 1985).

[78] A. Farner, *Die Lehre von Kirche und Staat bei Zwingli* (Tübingen, 1930).

[456] H. Feld, *Martin Luthers und Wendelin Steinbachs Vorlesungen über den Hebräerbrief: Eine Studie zur Geschichte der neutestamentlichen Exegese und Theologie* (Wiesbaden, 1971).

[46] ——, *Die Anfänge der modernen biblischen Hermeneutik in der spätmittelalterlichen Theologie* (Wiesbaden, 1977).

6   P. Fraenkel, *Testimonia Patrum: The Function of the Patristic Argument in the Theology of Philip Melanchthon* (Geneva, 1961).

12 W. Friedensburg, *Urkundenbuch der Universität Wittenberg I: (1502-1611)* (Magdeburg, 1926).

4   A. L. Gabriel, "Via Antiqua" und "Via Moderna" and the Migration of Paris Students and Masters to the German Universities in the Fifteenth Century', in *Antiqui und Moderni: Traditionsbewußtsein und Fortschrittbewußtsein im späten Mittelalter*, ed. A. Zimmermann (Berlin/New York, 1974), pp. 439–83.

3   F. Gaeta, *Lorenzo Valla: filologia e storia nell'umanesimo* (Naples, 1955).

4   G. Gál, 'Adam of Wodeham's Question on the "complexe significabile" as the Immediate Object of Scientific Knowledge', *FcS* 37 (1977), pp. 66–102.

3458 A. Ganoczy, *Le jeune Calvin: genèse et évolution de sa vocation réformatrice* (Wiesbaden, 1966).

34 E. Garin, 'Le traduzioni umanistiche di Aristotele nel secolo XV', *Atti e memorie dell'Accademia fiorentini di scienze morali 'La Columbaria'* 16 (1951), pp. 55–104.

3   D. Geanokoplos, 'The Discourse of Demetrius Chalcondyles on the Inauguration of Greek Studies at the University of Padua in 1463', *Studies in the Renaissance* 21 (1974), pp. 119–44.

7   T. George, 'The Presuppositions of Zwingli's Baptismal Theology', in *Prophet, Pastor, Protestant: The Work of Huldrych Zwingli after Five Hundred Years*, eds E. J. Furcha and H. Wayne Pipkin (Allison Park, Penn., 1984), pp. 71–87.

5   B. A. Gerrish, 'By Faith Alone: Medium and Message in Luther's Gospel', in *The Old Protestantism and the New: Essays on the Reformation Heritage* (Chicago, 1982), pp. 69–89.

23 J. de Ghellinck, 'La première édition imprimée des *Opera omnia S. Augustini*', in *Miscellanea J. Gessler I* (Antwerp, 1948), pp. 530–47.

36 B. Girardin, *Rhétorique et théologique: Calvin, le commentaire de l'epître aux Romains* (Paris, 1979).

2   A. Godin, *L'homélaire de Jean Vitrier: spiritualité franciscaine en Flandre au XVIᵉ siècle* (Geneva, 1971).

6   ——, 'Fonction d'Origène dans la pratique exégètique d'Erasme: les annotations sur l'epître aux Romains', in *Etudes de l'exégèse au XVIᵉ siècle*, ed. O. Fatio and P. Fraenkel (Geneva, 1978), pp. 17–44.

4   E. Gössmann, *Antiqui und Moderni im Mittelalter: Eine geschichtliche Standortsbestimmung* (Munich/Paderborn, 1974).

3   J. F. G. Goeters, 'Zwinglis Werdegang als Erasmianer', in *Reformation und Humanismus: Robert Stupperich zum 65. Geburtstag*, ed. M. Greschat und J. F. G. Goeters (Witten, 1969), pp. 255–71.

4   M. Grabmann, 'Johannes Capreolus O.P., der "Princeps Thomistarum", und seine Stellung in der Geschichte der Thomistenschule', in *Mittelalterliches Geistesleben III*, ed. L. Ott (Munich, 1956), pp. 370–410.

45 L. Grane, *Contra Gabrielem: Luthers Auseinandersetzung mit Gabriel Biel in der Disputatio contra scholasticam theologiam 1517* (Gyldendal, 1962).

[4] ——, 'Gregor von Rimini und Luthers Leipziger Disputation', *Studia Theologica* 22 (1968), pp. 29–49.

[35] ——, 'Augustins Expositio quarundam propositionum ex epistola ad Romanos in Luthers Römerbriefvorlesung', *ZThK* 69 (1972), pp.304–30.

[35] ——, 'Divus Paulus et S. Augustinus, interpres eius fidelissimus: Über Luthers Verhältnis zu Augustin', in *Festschrift für Ernst Fuchs*, ed. G. Ebeling, E. Jüngel and G. Schunack (Tübingen, 1973), pp. 133–46.

——, *Modus loquendi theologicus: Luthers Kampf um die Erneuerung der Theologie (1515-1518)* (Leiden, 1975).

[36] S. S. Gravalle, 'Lorenzo Valla's Comparison of Latin and Greek and the Humanist Background', *Bibliothèque d'Humanisme et Renaissance* 44 (1982), pp. 269–89.

[3] H. H. Gray, 'Renaissance Humanism: The Pursuit of Eloquence', in *Renaissance Essays*, ed. P. O. Kristeller and P. P. Wiener (New York, 1968), pp. 199–216.

[3] M. Greschat, 'Die Anfänge der reformatorischen Theologie Martin Bucers', in *Reformation und Humanismus: Robert Stupperich zum 65. Geburtstag*, ed. M. Greschat and J. F. G. Goeters (Witten, 1969), pp. 124–40.

——, 'Martin Bucers Bücherverzeichnis', *Archiv für Kulturgeschichte* 57 (1975), pp. 162–85.

——, 'Der Ansatz der Theologie Martin Bucers', *Theologische Literaturzeitung* 103 (1978), 81–96.

[2] H. von Greyerz, 'Studien der Kulturgeschichte der Stadt Bern am Ende des Mittelalters', *Archiv des Historischen Vereins des Kantons Bern* 35 (1940), pp. 175–491.

[3] E. Grislis, 'Calvin's Use of Cicero in the Institutes I:1–5 – A Case Study in Theological Method', *Archiv für Reformationsgeschichte* 62 (1971), pp. 5–37.

[23] M. Grossmann, *Humanism in Wittenberg 1485-1517* (Nieuwkoop, 1975).

[3] H. Haf[f]ter, 'Vadian und die Universität Wien', *Wiener Geschichtsblätter* 20 (1965), pp. 385–90.

[6] B. Hägglund, 'Martin Luther über die Sprache', *Neue Zeitschrift für systematische Theologie und Religionsphilosophie* 26 (1984), pp. 1–12.

[8] Basil Hall, 'The Reformation City', *Bulletin of the John Rylands Library* 54 (1971), pp. 103–48.

[5] A. Hamel, *Der junge Luther und Augustin* (2 vols: Gütersloh, 1934–5).

[45] B. Hamm, *Promissio, Pactum, Ordinatio: Freiheit und Selbstbindung Gottes in der scholastischen Gnadenlehre* (Tübingen, 1977).

[2] M. Hannemann, *The Diffusion of the Reformation in Southwestern Germany* (Chicago, 1975).

[6] H. Hargreaves, 'The Wycliffite Versions [of the Bible]', in *Cambridge History of the Bible* (3 vols: Cambridge, 1963–70), vol. 2, pp. 387–415.

[6] ——, 'Popularising Biblical Scholarship: The Role of the Wycliffite *Glossed Gospels*', in *The Bible and Medieval Culture*, ed. W. Lourdaux and D. Verhelst (Louvain, 1979), pp. 171–89.

[3] D. Harmening, 'Faust und die Renaissance-Magie: Zum ältesten Faust-Zeugnis

Faust-Zeugnis (Johannes Trithemius an Johannes Viridung, 1507)', *Archiv für Kulturgeschichte* 55 (1973), pp. 56–79.

12 D. Hay, *The Church in Italy in the Fifteenth Century* (Cambridge, 1977).

12 P. Heath, *English Parish Clergy on the Eve of the Reformation* (London, 1969).

3 H. Heller, 'The Evangelicalism of Lefèvre d'Etaples: 1525', *Studies in the Renaissance* 19 (1972), pp. 42–77.

12 S. H. Hendrix, 'Luther's Impact on the Sixteenth Century', *Sixteenth Century Journal* 16 (1985), pp. 3–14.

12 H. Hermelink, *Die theologische Fakultät in Tübingen vor der Reformation 1477-1534* (Tübingen, 1906).

6 G. Hobbs, 'Martin Bucer on Psalm 22: A Study in the Application of Rabbinical Exegesis by a Christian Hebraist', in *Etudes de l'exégèse au XVI(('e)) siècle*, ed. O. Fatio and P. Fraenkel (Geneva, 1978), pp. 144–63.

6 ——, 'Monitio amica: Pellican à Capito sur le danger des lectures rabbiniques', in *Horizons européens de la Réforme en Alsace*, ed. M. de Kroon and M. Lienhard (Strasbourg, 1980), pp. 81–93.

4 E. Hochstetter, 'Nominalismus?', *FcS* 9 (1949), pp. 370–403.

4 F. Hoffmann, 'Der Satz als Zeichen der theologischen Aussage bei Holcot, Crathorn und Gregor von Rimini', in *Der Begriff der Repräsentatio im Mittelalter* (Berlin, 1971), pp. 296–313.

5 H. H. Holfelder, *Solus Christus: Die Ausbildung von Bugenhagens Rechtfertigungslehre in der Paulusauslegung (1524/25) und ihre Bedeutung* (Tübingen, 1981).

6 K. Holl, 'Luthers Bedeutung für den Fortschritt der Auslegungskunst', in *Gesammelte Aufsätze zur Kirchengeschichte* (3 vols: Tübingen, 7th edn, 1948), vol. 1, pp. 544–82.

6 M. Hurley, '*Scriptura Sola*: Wyclif and His Critics', *Traditio* 16 (1960), pp. 275–352.

23 J. IJsewijn, 'The Coming of Humanism to the Low Countries', in *Itinerarium Italicum: The Profile of the Italian Renaissance in the Mirror of its European Transformations*, ed. H. A. Oberman with T. A. Brady (Leiden, 1975), pp. 193–304.

25 H. Jedin, 'Ein Turmerlebnis des jungen Contarinis', in *Kirche des Glaubens - Kirche der Geschichte: Ausgewählte Aufsätze und Vorträge I* (Freiburg, 1966), pp. 167–90.

3 H. Junghans, 'Der Einfluß des Humanismus auf Luthers Entwicklung bis 1518', *Luther-Jahrbuch* 37 (1970), pp. 37–101.

3 ——, *Der junge Luther und die Humanisten* (Göttingen, 1985).

5 E. Kähler, *Karlstadt und Augustin: Der Kommentar des Andreas Bodenstein von Karlstadt zu Augustins Schrift De Spiritu et Litera* (Halle, 1952).

8 R. M. Kingdon, *Geneva and the Coming of the Wars of Religion in France* (Geneva, 1956).

8 ——, 'Was the Protestant Reformation a Revolution? The Case of Geneva', in *Transition and Revolution: Problems and Issues of European Renaissance and Reformation History*, ed. R. M. Kingdom (Minneapolis, 1974), pp. 53–107.

[3] G. Kisch, *Humanismus und Jurisprudenz: Der Kampf zwischen mos italicus und mos gallicus an der Universität Basel* (Basle, 1955).

[3] ——, 'Forschungen zur Geschichte des Humanismus in Basel', *Archiv für Kulturgeschichte* 40 (1958), pp. 194–221.

[3] J. M. Kittelson, *Wolfgang Capito: From Humanist to Reformer* (Leiden, 1975).

[23] R. Klibansky, *The Continuity of the Platonic Tradition during the Middle Ages* (Munich, 1981).

[3] K. Koch, *Studium Pietatis: Martin Bucer als Ethiker* (Neukirchen, 1962).

[6] W. Köhler, 'Die Randglossen Zwinglis zum Römerbrief in seiner Abschrift der paulinischen Briefe 1516/17', in *Forschungen zur Kirchengeschichte und zur christlichen Kunst: Johannes Ficker als Festgabe zum 70. Geburtstag dargebracht* (Leipzig, 1931), pp. 86–106.

[34] P. O. Kristeller, *La tradizione aristotelica nel Rinascimento* (Padua, 1972).

[34] ——, *Aristotelismo e sincretismo nel pensiero di Pietro Pomponazzi* (Padua, 1983).

[4] M. de Kroon, 'Pseudo-Augustin im Mittelalter: Entwurf eines Forschungberichts', *Augustiniana* 22 (1972), pp. 511–30.

[6] F. Kropatschek, *Das Schriftprinzip der lutherischen Kirche I: Die Vorgeschichte: Das Erbe des Mittelalters* (Leipzig, 1904).

[35] F. Krüger, *Bucer und Erasmus: Eine Untersuchung zum Einfluß des Erasmus auf die Theologie Martin Bucers* (Wiesbaden, 1975).

[6] E. Künzli, 'Quellenproblem und mystischer Schriftsinn in Zwinglis Genesis- und Exoduskommentar', *Zwingliana* 9 (1949–54), pp. 185–207; 253–307.

[2] D. Kurze, 'Der niedere Klerus in der sozialen Welt des späten Mittelalters', in *Beiträge zur Wirtschafts- und Sozialgeschichte des Mittelalters*, ed. K. Schultz (Cologne/Vienna, 1976), pp. 273–305.

[4] A. N. S. Lane, 'Calvin's Use of the Fathers and Medievals', *Calvin Theological Journal* 16 (1981), pp. 149–205.

[4] G. Leff, *Bradwardine and the Pelagians: A Study of His 'De Causa Dei' and Its Opponents* (Cambridge, 1957).

[2] ——, *Heresy in the Later Middle Ages: The Relation of Heterodoxy to Dissent c. 1250-c. 1450* (2 vols: Manchester, 1967).

[4] ——, *William of Ockham: The Metamorphosis of Scholastic Discourse* (Manchester, 1977).

[234] A. H. T. Levi, 'The Breakdown of Scholasticism and the Significance of Evangelical Humanism', in *The Philosophical Assessment of Theology*, ed. G. R. Hughes (Georgetown, 1987), pp. 101–28.

[3] G. W. Locher, 'Zwingli und Erasmus', *Zwingliana* 13 (1969), pp. 37–61.

[78] ——, 'Die theologische und politische Bedeutung des Abendmahlstreites im Licht von Zwinglis Briefen', *Zwingliana* 13 (1971), pp. 281–304.

——, 'Von Bern nach Genf: Die Ursachen der Spannung zwischen zwinglischer und calvinistischer Reformation', in *Wegen en Gestalten in het Gereformeerd Protestantisme*, ed. W. Balke, C. Graafland and H. Harkema (Amsterdam, 1976), pp. 75–87.

[8] ——, 'Zwinglis Politik – Grund und Ziel', *Theologische Zeitschrift* 36 (1980), pp. 84–102.

[3] G. M. Logan, 'Substance and Form in Renaissance Humanism', *Journal of Medieval and Renaissance Studies* 7 (1977), pp. 1–34.

[3] F. Luchsinger, *Der Baslerbuchdruck als Vermittler italienischer Geistes* (Basle, 1953).

[45] A. E. McGrath, "Augustinianism"? A Critical Assessment of the so-called 'Medieval Augustinian Tradition' on Justification', *Augustiniana* 31 (1981), pp. 247–67.

[35] ——, 'Humanist Elements in the Early Reformed Doctrine of Justification', *Archiv für Reformationsgeschichte* 73 (1982), pp. 5–20.

[25] ——, 'Forerunners of the Reformation? A Critical Examination of the Evidence for Precursors of the Reformation Doctrines of Justification', *Harvard Theological Review* 75 (1982), pp. 219–42.

[4] ——, '*Homo assumptus*? A Study in the Christology of the *Via Moderna*, with Particular Reference to William of Ockham', *EThL* 60 (1985), pp. 283–97.

[4] ——, 'John Calvin and Late Medieval Thought: A Study in Late Medieval Influences upon Calvin's Theological Development', *Archiv für Reformationsgeschichte* 77 (1986), pp. 58–78.

[1] ——, 'Reformation to Enlightenment', in Paul Avis (ed.), *The History of Christian Theology I: The Science of Theology* (Grand Rapids, 1986), pp. 105–229.

[12] F. Machilek, 'Die Frömmigkeit und die Krise des 14. und 15. Jahrhunderts', *Medievalia Bohemica* 3 (1970), pp. 209–27.

[5] H. J. McSorley, *Luther - Right or Wrong? An Ecumenical-Theological Study of Luther's Major Work, The Bondage of the Will* (Minneapolis, 1969).

[3] K. Maeder, *Die via media in der schweizerischen Reformation: Studien zum Problem der Kontinuität im Zeitalter der Glaubenspaltung* (Zurich, 1970).

[1] B. Moeller, 'Probleme der Reformationsgeschichtsforschung', *ZKG* 76 (1965), pp. 246–57.

——, 'Zwinglis Disputationen: Studien zu den Anfängen der Kirchenbildung und des Synodalwesens im Protestantismus', *Zeitschrift der Savigny-Stiftung für Rechtsgeschichte*, Kanonische Abteilung, 56 (1970), pp. 275–324; 60 (1974), pp. 213–364.

[26] ——, 'Die Ursprünge der reformierten Kirche', *Theologische Literaturzeitung* 100 (1975), 642–53.

[1238] ——, 'Luther und die Städte', in *Aus der Lutherforschung: Drei Vorträge* (Opladen, 1983), pp. 9–26.

[3] E. Monnerjahn, *Giovanni Pico della Mirandola: Ein Beitrag zur philosophischen Theologie des Humanismus* (Wiesbaden, 1960).

[6] J. Müller, *Martin Bucers Hermeneutik* (Gütersloh, 1965).

[3] W. Näf, *Vadian und seine Stadt St Gallen* (2 vols: St Gallen, 1944–57).

[3] ——, 'Schweizerische Humanismus: Zu Glareans "Helvetiae Descriptio"', *Schweizerische Beiträge zur allgemeinen Geschichte* 5 (1947), pp. 186–98.

[234] C. G. Nauert, 'The Clash of Humanists and Scholastics: An Approach to Pre-Reformation Controversies', *Sixteenth Century Journal* 4 (1973), pp. 1–18.

[5] W. H. Neuser, *Die reformatorische Wende bei Zwingli* (Neukirchen, 1977).

[3] R. Newald, *Probleme und Gestalte des deutschen Humanismus* (Berlin, 1963).

[1] T. Nipperdey, 'Die Reformation als Problem der marxistischen Geschichts-

wissenschaft', in *Reformation, Revolution, Utopie: Studien zum 16. Jahrhundert* (Göttingen, 1975), pp. 9–34.

[4] H. A. Oberman, *Archbishop Thomas Bradwardine; A Fourteenth Century Augustinian: A Study of His Theology in Its Historical Context* (Utrecht, 1957).

[2] ——, 'Tuus sum, salvum me fac: Augustinréveil zwischen Renaissance und Reformation', in *Scientia Augustiniana: Studien über Augustinus, den Augustinismus und den Augustinerorden*, ed. C. P. Mayer and W. Eckermann (Würzburg, 1975), pp. 349–94.

[1] ——, 'Reformation: Epoche oder Episode?', *Archiv für Reformationsgeschichte* 68 (1977), pp. 56–111.

[1] ——, *Die Reformation: Von Wittenberg nach Genf* (Göttingen, 1986).

[2] A. K. Offenberg, 'Untersuchungen zum hebräischen Buchdruck in Neapel um 1490', in *Buch und Text im 15. Jahrhundert*, ed. L. Hellinga and H. Härtel (Hamburg, 1978), pp. 129–41.

[12] W. A. Pantin, *The English Church in the Fourteenth Century* (Cambridge, 1955).

[4] R. Paqué, *Das Pariser Nominalistenstatut: Zur Entstehung des Realitätsbegriffs der neuzeitlichen Naturwissenschaft (Occam, Buridan und Petrus Hispanicus, Nikolaus von Autrecourt und Gregor von Rimini)* (Berlin, 1970).

[36] J. B. Payne, 'Towards the Hermeneutics of Erasmus', in *Scrinium Erasmianum II*, ed. J. Coppens (Leiden, 1970), pp. 13–49.

[3] R. Peter, 'Rhétorique et prédication selon Calvin', *Revue d'histoire et de philosophie religieuses* 55 (1975), pp. 249–72. (Berlin, 1963).

[34] A. Poppi, 'Il problema della filosofia morale nella scuola padovana del Rinascimento: Platonismo e Aristotelismo nella definizione del metodo dell'ethica', in *Platon et Aristote à la Renaissance* (XVIe Colloque Internationale de Tours: Paris, 1976), p. 105–46.

[234] R. R. Post, *The Modern Devotion: Confrontation with Reformation and Humanism* (Leiden, 1968).

[3] S. Prete, 'Leistungen der Humanisten auf dem Gebiete der lateinischen Philologie', *Philologus* 109 (1965), pp. 259–69.

[3] G. Radetti, 'Le origini dell'umanesimo civile fiorentino nel 1400', *Giornale critico della filosofia italiana*, 3rd series, 12 (1959), pp. 98–112.

[36] S. Raeder, *Das Hebräische bei Luther untersucht bis zum Ende'der ersten Psalmenvorlesung* (Tübingen, 1961).

[36] ——, *Die Benutzung des masoretischen Textes bei Luther in der Zeit zwischen der ersten und zweiten Psalmenvorlesung* (Tübingen, 1967).

[36] ——, *Grammatica Theologica: Studien zu Luthers Operationes in Psalmos* (Tübingen, 1977).

[7] J. Raitt. *The Eucharistic Theology of Theodore Beza: Development of the Reformed Doctrine* (Chambersburg, PA, 1972).

[34] J. H. Randall, 'The Development of Scientific Method in the School of Padua', in *Renaissance Essays*, ed. P. O. Kristeller and P. P. Wiener (New York, 1968), pp. 217–51.

[3]   R. Raubenheimer, 'Martin Bucer und seine humanistischen Speyerer Freunde', *Blätter für pfälzische Kirchengeschichte und religiöse Volkskunde* 32 (1965), pp. 1–52.

[12]   A. Renaudet, *Préréforme et humanisme à Paris pendant les premières guerres d'Italie (1494–1517)* (Paris, 2nd edn, 1953).

[4]   K. Reuter, *Das Grundverständnis der Theologie Calvins* (Neukirchen, 1963).

[4]   ——, *Vom Scholaren bis zum jungen Reformator: Studien zum Werdegang Johannes Calvins* (Neukirchen, 1981).

[4]   M. van Rhijn, 'Wessel Gansfort te Heidelberg en de strijd tussen de "via antiqua" en de "via moderna"', in *Studiën over Wessel Gansfort en zijn tijd* (Utrecht, 1933), pp. 23–37.

[3]   E. F. Rice, 'The Humanist Idea of Christian Antiquity: Lefèvre d'Etaples and His Circle', *Studies in the Renaissance* 9 (1962), pp. 126–60.

[3]   A. Rich, *Die Anfänge der Theologie Huldrych Zwinglis* (Zurich, 1949).

[8]   ——, 'Zwingli als sozial-politischen Denker', *Zwingliana* 13 (1969), pp. 67–89.

[7]   Cyril C. Richardson, *Zwingli and Cranmer on the Eucharist* (Evanston, Ill., 1949).

[4]   G. Ritter, *Studien zur Spätscholatik I: Marsilius von Inghen und die okkamistische Schule in Deutschland* (Heidelberg, 1921).

[4]   ——, *Studien zur Spätscholastik II: Via antiqua und via moderna auf den deutschen Universitäten des XV. Jahrhunderts* (Heidelberg, 1922).

[3]   ——, 'Die geschichtliche Bedeutung des deutschen Humanismus', *Historische Zeitschrift* 127 (1922–3), pp. 393–453.

[3]   D. Robey, 'P. P. Vergerio the Elder: Republicanism and Civic Values in the Work of an Early Humanist', *Past and Present* 58 (1973), pp. 3–37.

[38]   J. Rogge, *Zwingli und Erasmus: Die Friedensgedanken des jungen Zwinglis* (Stuttgart, 1962).

[28]   J. G. Rowe (ed.), *Aspects of Late Medieval Government and Society* (Toronto, 1986).

[36]   H. P. Rüger, 'Karlstadt als Hebraist an der Universität Wittenberg', *Archiv für Reformationsgeschichte* 75 (1984), pp. 297–309.

[5]   E. Gordon Rupp, *The Righteousness of God: Luther Studies* (London, 1953).

[1]   P. Saenger, 'Silent Reading: Its Impact on Late Medieval Script', *Viator: Medieval and Renaissance Studies* 13 (1982), pp. 367–414.

[3]   V. Schenker-Frei, *Biblioteca Vadiana: Die Bibliothek des Humanisten Joachim von Watt nach dem Katalog des Josua Kessler von 1553* (Vadian-Studien 9: St Gallen, 1973).

[4]   H. Schepers, 'Holkot contra dicta Crathorn', *Philosophisches Jahrbuch* 77 (1970), pp. 320–54; 79 (1972), pp. 106–36.

[4]   J. Schilling, 'Determinatio secunda almae facultatis theologiae Parisiensis super Apologiam Philippi Melanchthonis pro Luthero scriptam', in *Lutheriana: Zum 500. Geburtstag Martin Luther* (Archiv zur Weimarer Ausgabe 5: Vienna, 1984), pp. 351–75.

[46]   H. Schüssler, *Der Primät der Heiligen Schrift als theologisches und kanonistisches Problem im Spätmittelalter* (Wiesbaden, 1977).

[4]   M. Schulze, '"Via Gregorii" in Forschung und Quellen', in *Gregor von Rimini: Werk und Wirkung bis zur Reformation*, ed. H. A. Oberman (Berlin/New York, 1981), pp. 1–126.

[28] R. W. Scribner, 'Civic Unity and the Reformation in Erfurt', *Past and Present* 66 (1975), pp. 29–60.

[28] ——, 'Why was there no Reformation at Cologne?', *Bulletin of the Institute of Historical Research* 49 (1976), pp. 217–41.

[3] J. E. Seigel, "Civic Humanism" or Ciceronian Rhetoric? The Culture of Petrarch and Bruni', *Past and Present* 34 (1966), pp. 3–48.

[3] M. Sieber, 'Glarean in Basel, 1514–1517 und 1522–1529', *Jahrbuch'des Historischen Vereins des Kantons Glarus* 60 (1963), pp. 53–75.

[1] R. W. Southern, *The Making of the Middle Ages* (New Haven, 1961).

[23] J. von Stackelberg, 'Renaissance: "Wiedergeburt" oder "Wiederwunsch"? Zur Kritik an J. Triers Aufsatz über die Vorgeschichte des Renaissance-Begriffs', *Bibliothèque d'Humanisme et Renaissance* 22 (1960), pp. 406–20.

[45] E. Stakemeier, *Der Kampf um Augustin: Augustinus und die Augustiner auf dem Tridentinum* (Paderborn, 1937).

[45] C. Stange, 'Über Luthers Beziehungen zur Theologie seines Ordens', *Neue kirchliche Zeitschrift* 11 (1900), pp. 574–85.

[4] ——, 'Luther über Gregor von Rimini', *Neue kirchliche Zeitschrift* 13 (1902), pp. 721–7.

[2] R. Stauffer, 'Lefèvre d'Etaples, artisan ou spectateur de la Réforme?', *Bulletin de la societé de l'histoire du protestantisme français* 113 (1967), pp. 405–23.

[3] ——, 'Einfluß und Kritik des Humanismus in Zwinglis "Commentarius de vera et falsa religione"', *Zwingliana* 16 (1983), pp. 97–110.

[3] J. M. Stayer, 'Zwingli before Zürich: Humanist Reformer and Papal Partisan', *Archiv für Reformationsgeschichte* 72 (1981), pp. 55–68.

[1] D. C. Steinmetz, *Reformers in the Wings* (Grand Rapids, 1981).

[67] ——, 'Scripture and the Lord's Supper in Luther's Theology', in *Luther in Context* (Bloomington, Ind., 1986), pp. 72–84.

[8] ——, 'Luther and the Two Kingdoms', in *Luther in Context*, pp. 112–25.

[?] J. N. Stephens, 'Heresy in Medieval and Renaissance Florence', *Past and Present* 54 (1972), pp. 25–60.

[1] L. D. Stokes, *Medieval and Reformation Germany (to 1648): A Select Bibliography* (London, 1972).

[12] G. Strauss, *Manifestations of Discontent in Germany on the Eve of the Reformation* (Bloomington, Ind., 1971).

[23] R. Stupperich, *Das Herforder Fraterhaus und die Devotia Moderna: Studien zur Frömmigkeitsgeschichte Westfalens an der Wende zur Neuzeit* (Münster, 1975).

[3] ——, 'Das Enchiridion Militis Christiani des Erasmus von Rotterdam nach seiner Entstehung, seinem Sinn und Charakter', *Archiv für Reformationsgeschichte* 69 (1978), pp. 5–23.

[6] G. H. Tavard, *Holy Writ or Holy Church: The Crisis of the Protestant Reformation* (London, 1959).

[14] W. D. J. Cargill Thompson, 'Seeing the Reformation in Medieval Perspective', *Journal of Ecclesiastical History* 25 (1974), pp. 297–308.

[8] ——, 'Luther and the Right of Resistance to the Emperor', in *Studies in the Reformation: Luther to Hooker*, ed. C. W. Dugmore (London, 1980), pp. 3–41.

[8] ——, 'The "Two Kingdoms" and the "Two Regiments": Some Problems of Luther's *Zwei-Reiche-Lehre*', in *Studies in the Reformation*, pp. 42–59.

[2] B. Tierney, 'Ockham, the Conciliar Theory, and the Canonists', *Journal of the History of Ideas* 15 (1954), pp. 40–70.

[2] ——, 'Pope and Council: Some New Decretist Texts', *Medieval Studies* 19 (1957), pp. 197–218.

[2] ——, ' "Tria quippe distinguit iudicia. . ." ' A Note on Innocent III's Decretal *Per venerabilem*', *Speculum* 37 (1962), pp. 48–59.

[3] G. Toffanin, *Storia letteraria d'Italia: Il Cinquecento* (Milan, 6th edn, 1960).

[3] ——, *Storia dell'umanesimo II: l'umanesimo italiano* (Bologna, 1964).

[4] T. F. Torrance, 'La philosophie et la théologie de Jean Mair ou Major (1469–1550)', *Archives de philosophie* 32 (1969), pp. 531–47; 33 (1970), pp. 261–94.

[4] ——, 'Intuitive and Abstractive Knowledge from Duns Scotus to John Calvin', in *De doctrina Ioannis Duns Scoti: Acta tertii Congressus Scotistici Internationalis* (Rome, 1972), pp. 291–305.

[4] D. Trapp, 'Augustinian Theology of the Fourteenth Century: Notes on Editions, Marginalia, Opinions and Book-lore', *Augustiniana* 6 (1956), pp. 146–274.

[3] J. Trier, 'Zur Vorgeschichte des Renaissance-Begriff', *Archiv für Kulturgeschichte* 33 (1955), pp. 45–63.

[3] ——, 'Wiederwuchs', *Archiv für Kulturgeschichte* 43 (1961), pp. 177–87.

[3] C. Trinkaus, 'A Humanist's Image of Humanism: The Inaugural Orations of Bartolommeo della Fonte', *Studies in the Renaissance* 7 (1960), pp. 90–147.

[2] K. Trodinger, *Stadt und Kirche im spätmittelalterlichen Würzburg* (Stuttgart, 1978).

[3] H. Trümpy, 'Glarner Studenten im Zeitalter des Humanismus', *Beiträge zur Geschichte des Landes Glarus: Festgabe des Historischen Vereins des Kantons Glarus* (Glarus, 1952), pp. 273–84.

[12] K. H. Ullmann, *Reformatoren vor der Reformation vornehmlich in Deutschland und den Niederlanden* (2 vols: Hamburg, 1841–2).

[4] W. Urban, 'Die "via moderna" an der Universität Erfurt am Vorabend der Reformation', in *Gregor von Rimini: Werk und Wirkung bis zur Reformation*, ed. H. A. Oberman (Berlin/New York, 1981), pp. 311–30.

[8] H. Vahle, 'Calvinismus und Demokratie im Spiegel der Forschung', *Archiv für Reformationsgeschichte* 66 (1982), pp. 181–212.

[4] P. Vignaux, *Justification et prédestination au XIVe siècle: Duns Scot, Pierre d'Auriole, Guillaume d'Occam, Grégoire de Rimini* (Paris, 1934).

[12] B. Vogler, *Le monde germanique et hélvetique à l'époque des Réformes, 1517–1618* (2 vols: Paris, 1981).

[6] P. de Vooght, *Les sources de la doctrine chrétienne d'après les théologiens du XIVe siècle et du début du XVe* (Paris, 1954).

[8] R. C. Walton, *Zwingli's Theocracy* (Toronto, 1967).

[78] ——, 'The Institutionalization of the Reformation at Zurich', *Zwingliana* 13 (1972), pp. 497–515.

³ D. Weinstein, 'In Whose Image and Likeness? Interpretations of Renaissance Humanism', *Journal of the History of Ideas* 33 (1972), pp. 165–76.

³ F. Wendel, *Calvin et l'humanisme* (Paris, 1976).

⁴ V. Wendland, 'Die Wissenschaftlehre Gregors von Rimini in der Diskussion', in *Gregor von Rimini: Werk und Wirkung bis zur Reformation*, ed. H. A. Oberman (Berlin/New York, 1981), pp. 241–300.

⁴ K. Werner, *Die Scholastik des späteren Mittelalters III: Der Augustinismus in der Scholastik des späteren Mittelalters* (Vienna, 1883).

⁴ E. Wolf, *Staupitz und Luther: Ein Beitrag zur Theologie des Johannes von Staupitz und deren Bedeutung für Luthers theologischen Werdegang* (Leipzig, 1927).

Index